Contents at a Glance

Contents

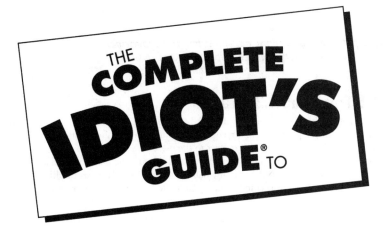

THE COMPLETE IDIOT'S GUIDE® TO

The Federal Reserve

*by Preston Martin
and Lita Epstein*

ALPHA

A Pearson Education Company

To my wife Genevieve Yvonne deVere, a longtime participant in Washington society, for her inspiration and counsel.
—Preston

Copyright © 2003 by Preston Martin and Lita Epstein

International Standard Book Number: 0-02-864323-2
Library of Congress Catalog Card Number: Available upon request.

05   04   03   8   7   6   5   4   3   2   1

Interpretation of the printing code: The rightmost number of the first series of numbers is the year of the book's printing; the rightmost number of the second series of numbers is the number of the book's printing. For example, a printing code of 03-1 shows that the first printing occurred in 2003.

Printed in the United States of America

Note: This publication contains the opinions and ideas of its authors. It is intended to provide helpful and informative material on the subject matter covered. It is sold with the understanding that the authors and publisher are not engaged in rendering professional services in the book. If the reader requires personal assistance or advice, a competent professional should be consulted.

The authors and publisher specifically disclaim any responsibility for any liability, loss, or risk, personal or otherwise, which is incurred as a consequence, directly or indirectly, of the use and application of any of the contents of this book.

For marketing and publicity, please call: 317-581-3722

The publisher offers discounts on this book when ordered in quantity for bulk purchases and special sales.

For sales within the United States, please contact: Corporate and Government Sales, 1-800-382-3419 or corpsales@pearsontechgroup.com

Outside the United States, please contact: International Sales, 317-581-3793 or international@ pearsontechgroup.com

Publisher: *Marie Butler-Knight*
Product Manager: *Phil Kitchel*
Managing Editor: *Jennifer Chisholm*
Acquisitions Editor: *Gary Goldstein*
Development Editor: *Tom Stevens*
Copy Editor: *Drew Patty*
Illustrator: *Chris Eliopoulos*
Cover/Book Designer: *Trina Wurst*
Indexer: *Tonya Heard*
Layout/Proofreading: *Megan Douglass, Becky Harmon*

Foreword

At last—a book has been written on the Federal Reserve System that is interesting, understandable, and authoritative. Previous books on this subject have tended to be too academic, loaded with economic theory, oblique, and filled with jargon. Or they have been authored by journalists who tried to popularize the Fed's activities and saw them from the outside and through interviews with insiders past and present.

As the central bank, the Fed plays a very important role in U.S. and worldwide economics. It influences employment, unemployment, economic growth rates, business opportunities, corporate profits, etc. Although most individuals hear of the Fed's actions to raise or lower interest rates through heavy media coverage, they do not necessarily associate such moves with events in their own business and financial lives, such as layoffs or investment losses.

Co-author Preston Martin realized the need for a presentation on how the Fed really works as seen from the inside by the number-two decision-maker. And he is uniquely qualified to write that story in plain English.

I first met Preston in 1983 when he was vice chairman of the Federal Reserve Board and I was being interviewed for a position on the Federal Home Loan Bank Board, the regulator of S&Ls. Because I had just finished two years as Commissioner of Financial Institutions for the State of Michigan, I was very impressed with his deep knowledge of S&Ls, how they operate, and why so many were failing. Preston also understood why Michigan's antiquated and economically unwise low usury ceilings were weakening commercial banks and worsening our recession/depression. Moreover, he seemed concerned.

I would remind you that the downturn of 1981 and 1982 was the most severe since the Great Depression of 1929 through 1933. Unemployment was painfully high—more than 20 percent in some cities. Businesses were failing, and personal bankruptcies were souring. The unemployed were losing their homes and moving elsewhere. Interest rates were up in the stratosphere—the bank prime rate had topped 21 percent and T-bills passed 16 percent. Yet loans were very difficult to obtain, especially home mortgage and car loans. To complete the miserable situation, inflation was running at double-digit rates.

Later, I learned more about Preston's background that made him arguably the broadest-based, best-equipped person ever appointed to the Fed Board. Although he had earned a Ph.D. in monetary economics, he was not a cloistered academic. He was (and still is) a very successful businessman and entrepreneur who founded PMI Mortgage Insurance Company. He had done significant public service in California as S&L Commissioner and in Washington, D.C., as chair of the Home Loan Bank Board.

When President Reagan appointed me to the Fed Board in 1984, I had the privilege of serving with Preston. In a place of cheap cigars, rumpled suits, bad manners, and arrogance, the vice chair stood out for his charm, sense of humor, class, and dignity. Because he had not spent his whole career within the Fed or Treasury bureaucracy, he had a real understanding of business beyond Wall Street and Washington.

When I think of the many crises the Fed was confronted with during his tenure (1982 through 1986), he was able to tap his experience reservoir and contribute importantly to dealing with them. Besides the gigantic problems of failing S&Ls and banks with the collapse of housing industry, massive third-world debt defaults faced us. The farm economy of the Midwest was in a serious recession with sagging commodity prices while the Oil Patch had its own severe depression.

His greatest contribution came in February 1986, when he headed the "Gang of Four"—demanding that Chairman Volcker bring the requests of the various Fed regional banks for lower rates to the Board for a vote. The economic recovery was stalling in 1985 and 1986, and the Fed banks wanted some policy-easing in the form of cuts in their discount rates. This foursome outvoted the chairman and showed the world that the Fed works better when the full Board gets involved in policy-making rather than having one person rule.

I recommend this book for general reading as well as for courses in banking, financial markets, investments, and macroeconomics. Although aimed at "idiots," I think high-level people at 1600 Pennsylvania Avenue and the U.S. Treasury would benefit greatly from its insights.

Martha R. Seger
Former Governor of the Federal Reserve (1984 through 1991)

Introduction

We are setting the record straight and showing you exactly what the Federal Reserve is, what it does, why it was created, what power it has, and just as important, what powers it doesn't have. We give you an insider's look into the day-to-day workings of the Fed, a look neither you nor America's top journalists have ever before enjoyed. Think of this book as an "all access pass" to the secrets of the Federal Reserve.

No official of the Fed on my level has ever gone public about the inner workings of the Fed to the extent that I do with you in this book. You learn it all. You find out what levers of power the Fed actually controls when it meets behind closed doors. You learn the relationship between the Fed chairman and the president of the United States. And you discover something that most people don't know—that there are serious political and economic limits to the power of the Fed.

This book takes you deep into the politics of money and provides you with an insider's full disclosure of what goes on inside the Federal Reserve and the other financial power centers. You see how they work and how to understand the pressures and forces put on the Federal Reserve by the White House, the Congress, other central bankers, and the financial markets, both domestic and international.

The September 11, 2001, terrorist attacks on New York and Washington make it even more important than ever for us to understand our economy, to plan for our future, and the future of our families. This book shows you how to interpret the news, cut through both the jargon ("Fedspeak") and falsehoods, and make your own determinations about what's really going on in the financial world. We go over the ways to pick up signals from the Federal Reserve, from other squawk boxes in Washington and from the financial markets.

You learn how to read the "tea leaves" from Washington—how to understand that bizarre, arcane language called "Fedspeak," the secret code that Fed chairmen use when addressing the media, Congress, and the nation. You learn what the various pronouncements mean to you, your pocketbook, your family—and the world. And you also learn the other ways in which Washington offers you guidance and special programs, to help you buy a home, educate your kids, live the good life, and plan for your retirement.

If you ignore what's happening in Washington and pursue unchanging family financial planning (or no planning), you can undermine your family's well-being and make retirement a period of dependence and despondency. There is no need to drown in the sea of financial information that assaults our ears and our eyes everywhere. Take the time to learn how to sift through the mutterings of all those media pundits and key in on relevant information from the print media or on the Internet. Your decisions about spending or saving, risky investments or safer ones, and how to both meet your family's current needs and your retirement years will be much easier to make when you know how to read the messages.

How to Use This Book

This book is organized into seven parts:

Part 1, "Creating the Money Machine," shows you why the Fed is important to your every day life. You also find the basics of economics and the history of how the Fed was born.

Part 2, "The Money Machine's Top Dogs," introduces you to the key players at the Fed and the operations of the Federal Open Market Committee.

Part 3, "The Money Machine's Hidden Powers," takes you behind the scenes of the regional banks and staff operations to show you how everything works. We also give you a short course in the language of the Fed—Fedspeak.

Part 4, "The Money Machine's Key Responsibilities," breaks down the Fed's regulatory role, its job as Lender of Last Resort, as well as its new roles in this ever changing economy. We also introduce you to the Fed's numbers game and its role in the stock market.

Part 5, "Sharing Money Power," explores the Fed's relationship with the other powers in Washington as well as the international money power players.

Part 6, "The Money Machine Comes Home," explains the role the Fed plays in being certain there is enough money for community development through its own programs or in cooperation with other federal agencies. We also talk about consumer protection and savings.

Part 7, "The Money Machine's Future," tells you about how you can get involved with the Fed as well as gives you a glimpse of tomorrow's economic world.

We also developed a number of helpers you'll find in boxes throughout the book:

Money Meanings

Help you understand all that economic lingo that might not be part of your everyday conversations.

Fiscal Facts

Interesting information that will add to your knowledge, but not necessary to the basic issues we are discussing.

 **Economic Wisdom**
Useful quotes from economists, Federal Reserve governors, politicians, and others.

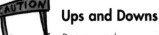 **Ups and Downs**
Point out the warning signs or alerts of critical issues that could impact your daily life.

 **Money Tips**
Send you to interesting websites, let you know about additional reading opportunities, or just give you tips about how you can use what you are learning.

Preston's Points

Personal stories or other key opinions of one of the authors, Preston Martin, a former vice chairman of the Federal Reserve.

Acknowledgments

We would like to thank Kathleen Bennett for her excellent research assistance, Mike Levin for his early writing on e-banking, and Mara Lea Brown for keeping things organized.

Trademarks

All terms mentioned in this book that are known to be or are suspected of being trademarks or service marks have been appropriately capitalized. Alpha Books and Pearson Education, Inc., cannot attest to the accuracy of this information. Use of a term in this book should not be regarded as affecting the validity of any trademark or service mark.

Part 1

Creating the Money Machine

Everyday you read stories about the Federal Reserve and interest rates. You also hear about the ups and downs of the economy, but do you know what all that means? We give you a crash course in how all this works.

We also explore how the money you use each day was created. All your bills are uniform and come from the same source—the Federal Reserve. Things were not always this easy. In this part, we find out how the money machine was created and how it operates today.

Why Care About the Fed?

In This Chapter

- ◆ Your money's role
- ◆ Role of the Federal Reserve
- ◆ The changing world of banks and money
- ◆ Inflation is enemy number one

The media portrays the Federal Reserve (often called the Fed) as the all-powerful, secretive government institution with total control over the economy. A word from the chairman, often depicted as the Wizard of Oz, makes interest rates rise or fall and Wall Street tremble. Whether you can keep your job, get a mortgage, or pay off your credit card is up to him—right?

The simple truth is that the Federal Reserve is extremely powerful, but it doesn't run the U.S. economy. It doesn't control our levels of employment. It doesn't set home mortgage rates. The "talking heads" in the media would have you think the Fed runs the world. Don't believe everything you see on the TV—or your PC screen.

Your Money and the Fed

The decisions made by the Federal Reserve do have enormous implications for the *economy*. If you want to buy a house or a car, the interest rate you'll pay is tied to the decisions made by the Federal Reserve Board (FRB). If you want to pay off your credit card over time, the rate you pay is influenced by their decision as well. The FRB's decisions affect every business and every family in the United States, and because of the economic power of our nation, practically every family and business in the whole world! That's a lot of power!

Money Meanings

An **economy** comprises an entire system of production, distribution, and consumption. An economy's boundaries can be set by a geographic area, such as a nation (the U.S. economy) or group of nations (such as the European economy). Sometimes economies are designated by types, such as an agrarian or industrial economy.

Everybody knows that the Fed has an important role in controlling inflation and setting interest rates, but many people think that's all the Fed does. Not so. The Fed plays many roles in the U.S. economy. Interest rates are only one of the responsibilities the Fed carries.

The duties of the Fed fall into four key categories:

♦ Conducting monetary policy

♦ Supervising and regulating banking institutions and protecting consumers' credit rights

♦ Maintaining a stable financial system

♦ Providing financial services to the U.S. government, the public, and financial institutions both inside and outside the United States

Created by Congress in 1913 (see Chapter 3), the Federal Reserve System is the central bank of the United States. Although it is a federal government agency, it operates with considerably more independence than any other federal entity. Its fight for independence was fought over many years, primarily by very strong chairmen, whose role we'll take a closer look at in Chapter 5.

Before we get into the details, let's take a quick look at how today's Fed is organized and how it carries out its primary duties. We'll be delving more deeply into all its functions as we explore the Fed and its responsibilities throughout this book.

The Fed, Beginning with the Chairman

Some say the Federal Reserve chairman is more powerful than the president. Some say he's more powerful than a speeding locomotive, able to leap tall interest rates with a single bound. Who is the Fed chairman, how does he get that job, and what does he do all day?

The chairman of the Federal Reserve is selected by the president of the United States and must be confirmed by the U.S. Senate. The chairman serves four-year terms. He or she (no, there never has been a woman chairperson—not yet, at least) may be reappointed and reconfirmed.

The chairman is the most public face of the Fed—you see him testifying before Congress, making speeches, announcing board and committee decisions, and publicizing policy. Always remember that he speaks for the Federal Reserve Board (FRB). The chairman didn't make that decision or policy he is talking about by himself. They discuss their positions, he summarizes what he thinks was said, they amend his summary if necessary to reflect their views, and then they vote on their position to give a unified front, or to "dissent" from the majority position. I dissented only seven times in my four years there.

Fiscal Facts

Unlike the presidential office, there is no limit on the number of terms a chairman may serve. Alan Greenspan was appointed in 1987 and has served more than 15 years already. Another long-termer, William McChesney Martin (no relation to one of the authors), has one of the Fed headquarter buildings named after him. (For more on former chairmen, see Chapter 5.)

The Federal Reserve Board

The chairman of the Federal Reserve presides over the seven-member Board of Governors. These are business people, bankers, and bureaucrats drawn from across the United States and a wide variety of governmental and business fields. They, like the chairman, are appointed by the president.

The laws governing the Federal Reserve state that the Board of Governors (BOG) must offer a "fair representation of the financial, agricultural, industrial, and commercial interests and geographical divisions of the country." That means the president is not supposed to appoint governors from the same federal district. (For more about districts, see Chapter 8.)

A Fed governor serves a 14-year term, or the remaining term of his or her predecessor. The BOG usually meets one or more times weekly. The chairman and the vice chairman count among the seven BOG members, with one vote each.

Like the chairman and the vice chairman, the other FRB members meet frequently with high-level government officials and business people from around the world. The political appointees at the Treasury Department attempt to influence the voting on monetary policy at the Fed, and Fed officials try to influence Treasury Department policies—with equal "success."

FRB Responsibilities

The FRB's primary task is to set monetary policy for the country. In other words, they work to control inflation and create an economic climate in the country that favors growth.

Money Meanings

The **discount rate** is the interest rate charged to member institutions by the Fed. Beginning in 2003, the Fed sets a primary discount credit rate for troubled banks. The **Fed funds rate** is the rate member banks charge each other for (largely) overnight deposits with the Fed.

How does the FRB keep an eye on interest rates and on the economic climate in general? By setting and targeting two extremely important rates that affect everyone in the economy, from day laborers to multi-billionaires: the *discount rate*, which the Fed actually sets, and the *Fed funds rate*, which the Fed targets. (For more on the discount and Fed funds rates, see Chapter 4.)

By setting and targeting the two key rates, the Fed is materially able to affect, to a great extent, how much interest governments, banks, businesses, and you and I have to pay when we borrow money in all those financial markets.

How does the Fed go about affecting rates? By looking at a lot of economic statistics. Studying published statistics is like driving a car but only looking in the rear-view mirror; statistics tell you where you've been, not necessarily where you're going. You can talk to all kinds of business people, bankers, and government officials, but how can anyone be sure what nearly 300 million Americans are up to in the near future?

Another key responsibility of the Fed is controlling the *money supply*. By buying and selling *U.S. Treasury securities*, the Fed targets and largely controls the money supply.

Money Meanings

The **money supply** is the currency and deposits held outside the Federal Reserve and the U.S. Treasury. This includes checkable demand deposits, traveler's checks, time deposits, automatic transfer services (ATS), money market mutual funds, as well as OCDs (other checkable deposits).

U.S. Treasury securities come in three types: treasury bills, treasury notes, and treasury bonds. All are issued and backed by the government; the primary difference is their life span or date of maturity. Treasury bills have a one-year life span, treasury notes are for one to seven years, and treasury bonds have a life span of more than seven years.

Working by Committee

Strictly speaking, it's not the FRB that sets rates. It's the Federal Open Market Committee (FOMC), a group of 17 people, with 40 or so staffers. You've already met the first seven members of the FOMC, the seven FRB members. The other members are the 12 presidents of the 12 Federal Reserve banks. Only the president of the New York Fed has a constant vote, because New York is still the financial capital of the country, and perhaps the world. The other 11 Fed bank presidents rotate voting rights yearly, so seven of the Fed bank presidents are not voting. Even if a bank president doesn't currently have voting rights, however, he or she is still an active participant in its discussions.

Spreading Out the Banks

You may already be familiar with the local Federal Reserve banks if you've ever studied the design of an old dollar bill. On the left-front side of a U.S. dollar bill, there's a big black letter indicating which Federal Reserve bank issued it along with their region number (more on the regional banks in Chapter 8):

Boston	A 1
New York	B 2
Philadelphia	C 3
Cleveland	D 4
Richmond	E 5
Atlanta	F 6
Chicago	G 7
St. Louis	H 8
Minneapolis	I 9
Kansas City	J 10
Dallas	K 11
San Francisco	L 12

By the way, the signature below the letter on the bill isn't that of the Federal Reserve bank president, but the then secretary of the treasury.

Each Federal Reserve bank is responsible for determining the adequate money supply for its region, but they must also be sure that there is adequate backing for the Federal notes in circulation. In most cases this backing is in U.S. Treasury securities. Other types of collateral held by the Federal Reserve are gold certificates and certain eligible instruments such as notes, drafts, and bills of exchange.

You can think of the 12 Federal Reserve banks scattered around the country as banks for bankers. These Fed banks provide many of the same kinds of services to banks that commercial and savings banks provide to individuals and businesses. Reserve banks, as they are called, do the following:

♦ Hold the deposit reserves of banks and other member institutions

♦ Make loans to banks and other member institutions

♦ Move currency (bills) and coins into and out of circulation, so your dollar bills look nice and crisp and clean—most of the time, anyway

♦ Provide checking accounts for the U.S. Treasury, so that money can flow from the treasury to banks (and ultimately to you!)

♦ Run FedWire, which handles 60 percent of all transfers by wire (no checks) and payment transfers of government securities

♦ Supervise, regulate, and examine banks to make sure they're running soundly and aiding in community development (and redevelopment)

♦ Maintain staffs of economists who study the local and national economy and contribute to the "Beige Book," a bottom-up regional analysis so the BOG and the FOMC can be better informed when it makes decisions.

Money Meanings

The **Beige Book** is the key document prepared before every FOMC meeting to give committee members a snapshot of current economic conditions in the United States. Each bank reports on its regional economic status. You can find a link to current and archived Beige Books and news reports at www.federalreserve.gov/FOMC.

Money Tips

If you want to get an idea of what goes in to money management, you can take a look at the statistics in the Monthly Monetary Data at the St. Louis Federal Reserve site www.stls.frb.org/fred/data/monetary.html.

Keep the Money Flowing

The United States has a massive payments system. Everyone from a Social Security retiree all the way up to General Motors and Microsoft counts on getting paid. They also expect that the money that's supposed to flow into their bank accounts actually gets there. The Fed banks do that and the FOMC is charged with making sure that happens. The FRB is also ultimately responsible for keeping the whole banking system solid. Those are not two small jobs!

The Fed's New Challenges

I know of no other recent period when the evolution of Federal Reserve policy has been so fundamental—and I served on the Fed Board for four years. Today's monetary policy is implemented differently, as we shall see.

While many banks are closing neighborhood branches and merging for business reasons, we are living through one of the United States's most agonizing times of bank failures and thrift shenanigans. The very financial system we used to take for granted, with all those Jimmy Stewart bankers smiling at us from the teller windows, are gone now. And although there has been a multitude of criminal acts wreaking havoc on our financial institutions, those acts only exacerbated problems already there: poor politics, inadequate banking supervision and regulation, and sheer incompetence of hundreds of management groups in a time of financial change.

> **Economic Wisdom**
>
> "It's not the return *on* my investment I am concerned about, it's the return *of* my investment."
> —Will Rogers, just before the market crash of 1929

We're seeing a similar scenario in the corporate world with scandals surrounding the collapse of Enron and Global Crossing, and others are coming to light. Questions abound about the reliability of the accounting industry and stock market analysts, which add to the mood of crisis and uncertainty. The Fed's new role in the financial markets is still being designed, with new responsibilities for regulating the financial services sector. (We take a closer look at these new roles in Chapter 14.)

> **Fiscal Facts**
>
> Taxpayer costs ranged from $350 billion to $500 billion for the thrift bailouts in the 1980s, the U.S. Congress' General Accounting Office estimated. We'll be taking a much closer look at what happened then and its continuing impact today in Chapter 11.

Even how you communicate with your bank and other financial advisors is changing dramatically. The speed with which you get financial information is changing too. You may even be at the point where you think you are facing financial information overload. Our mail is loaded with offers for new credit cards almost every day. Your telephone may sometimes seem like it's ringing off the hook with new financial offers, and in between those calls, you may actually use the phone—or the Internet—for banking and investment services.

> **CAUTION**
>
> ## Ups and Downs
>
> While most people whose money was tied up in the thrift scandal were protected by Federal insurance, workers at Enron were not so lucky. Enron workers watched as their 401(k) plans dropped from a top value of more than $2 billion to nearly nothing in a matter of a few months. Individual workers nearing retirement reported losing their entire savings of between $500,000 and $900,000, while key executives made millions on the sale of stock options before the major drop in Enron value. What protections will be put in place for workers' retirement funds are still being decided, but change is clearly needed.

No Longer Just Your Community Bank

Banks today can serve you and your business in all sorts of financial ways. They provide all kinds of services, credit cards, cash cards, investment counseling, insurance, and loans for homes or farms. Families and small businesses lacking perfect credit records can even find a way to access these services. Banks trade loans and securities and manage the risk of credit and loans in both old and new ways.

> **Economic Wisdom**
>
> "A bank is a place where they lend you an umbrella in fair weather and ask for it back again when it begins to rain."
>
> —Robert Frost

Managing all that risk has forced financial institutions to invest in computers and software. In a global economy, banks need to be able to track the many currencies utilized by traders in overseas markets and be able to do so in nanoseconds. The enormous trading volumes make for one world tied together financially. You are no longer investing in just one country and its future. Banks and other major U.S. corporations are now global entities more dependent on a stable world environment.

Think about the querulous question, "what's a bank?" You know that banks have to compete with many kinds of financial institutions that are regulated differently, even less rigorously. To survive this ever-evolving financial landscape, bankers are adding affiliates and subsidiaries. Others are forming holding company relationships. Bankers are competing with "nonbank banks." Yes, there are banks on the Internet that have no branches and can operate with much lower costs and less regulation. Does your bank have a branch or two in Europe? In Asia? Don't be surprised!

Job One: Taming Inflation

Even with all this rapid change, however, the number one goal of the Fed is still to avoid *inflation*, Public Enemy Number One in the mind of the Fed. Inflation means that every dollar buys less, which is trouble for the economy. People on fixed incomes suffer when inflation eats away at their income and rates of return on their savings. Wages have to spiral upward so that workers can keep up with the new, higher cost of goods and services. (And as we all know, somehow wages never seem to keep up with inflation!) Businesses have to charge more to pay for higher labor and borrowing costs, making those goods and services even more expensive for consumers.

There's also a powerful psychological effect to inflation. Sure, people who own houses love it, because their investment looks great, but when the value of the dollar weakens, somehow we all feel worse off. And serious inflation (called *hyperinflation*) leads to great social unrest. So keeping inflation in check is important for everybody.

Money Meanings

Inflation is the increase in prices of goods and services. For consumers, the rate of inflation (inflation rate) is measured using the Consumer Price Index, which reflects the change in the cost of a fixed basket of products and services that includes housing, electricity, food, and transportation.

Money Meanings

Hyperinflation means that inflation rates are rising very rapidly. You may think you've experienced inflation in your lifetime, but I can guarantee unless you lived in a country threatened by hyperinflation you don't really know inflation's risks. In the 1980s and early 1990s, Brazil battled inflation rates that were sometimes as high as 20 percent per month. If you delayed making a purchase, the price could increase by 10 percent or more in just two weeks. Wages couldn't possibly keep up, and people were literally getting poorer by the week.

Inflation in America has a powerfully negative effect on the whole world. When we buy products from other countries during an inflationary period, those imports cost less than our own goods and services. When we then sell our goods to other countries, our high prices make it more difficult for them to buy as much—their demand drops. We pay more to them, they pay less to us—meaning our "balance of payments" goes down! In turn, if other countries buy fewer of our goods, we can't afford to buy as much of the rest of the world's goods. Rising inflation in the U.S. economy means the whole world suffers, so taming inflation is Federal Reserve job one!

How does the Fed accomplish the task of taming inflation? By carefully targeting the interest rates on money that banks and businesses borrow and by affecting the growth or decline of the economy's money supply. If it looks as if the economy is becoming inflationary, the Fed clamps down by raising interest rates. This action reduces growth in the quantity of money (known as the M's), making it more expensive for banks and businesses to borrow money, which in turn cuts down on expansion in the economy because banks and businesses cannot expand if they cannot borrow. The less expansion permitted, the less inflation. That is, the smaller the growth of the economy, the less inflation there is. (We'll take a closer look at economic cycles and how all this works in Chapter 2.)

On the other hand, if it looks as if the economy is slowing down, the Fed lowers interest rates, increasing growth in the money supply. This allows borrowers to borrow money more cheaply, which in turn allows them to hire more workers and produce more goods, keeping the economy moving. In the months after the events of September 11, for example, the Fed lowered interest rates 10 times, from 6.5 percent to 1.25 percent for the discount rate, and down to 1.75 percent from 5.5 percent for the Federal funds rate. (See Chapter 15 for an explanation of these rates.)

The only question is this: How do you know when the economy is heating up or cooling down? *That*, my friend, is the multi-billion dollar question! You can rely partly on statistics and on conversations with government officials, bankers, and business people, but it's certainly not an exact science. If it were that simple to figure out what's going on economically with 300 million people, you wouldn't need a Federal Reserve. You could just have some computer genius write a program to move rates up and down, depending on the key economic indicators. (This is precisely what Nobel Prize winner Professor Milton Friedman has suggested, but no one has yet come up with such a machine.)

Before we start looking at how the Fed does it job, we first need to understand a bit of basic economic theory. We'll do that in Chapter 2. Then we'll take a trip down memory lane to see how the Fed got started, before we get into the nuts and bolts of today's Federal Reserve.

The Least You Need to Know

- Despite what you read or see in the media, the Fed isn't all powerful and doesn't control the economy.

- The Federal Reserve System is the central bank of the United States. Although it is a federal government agency, it enjoys much more independence than any other federal entity.

- Financial scandals in the bank and thrift industry, as well as in corporate America, increase the challenges the Fed faces today.

- Taming inflation is the Fed's primary job.

Cycling Through Time

In This Chapter

- ◆ Going for growth
- ◆ Watching the cycles
- ◆ Meeting your demands
- ◆ A mock FOMC meeting

Everyone wishes our economy would remain on a steady upward path of growth without any risk of inflation eating our gains. Unfortunately, our economy experiences ups and downs—periods of inflation and *recession*. We always hope the periods of imbalance will be short, without reaching a state of severe economic shock. We would never want to live through a period of hyperinflation without taking corrective actions to minimize it. Alternatively, certainly no one wants to even consider the possibility of hitting the lows that the United States found itself in during the Great Depression.

Minor economic corrective actions are taken to steady the economy. To understand why corrections are needed, we're going to take a short course in how the business cycle works. Then we'll stop by at a mock meeting of the Federal Open Market Committee (FOMC) to get a glimpse of how the information about the state of the economy is used by the Fed to attempt to maintain equilibrium.

> **Money Meanings**
>
> Not all economists agree on a definition of **recession,** but the most widely accepted is two consecutive quarters of negative growth—that is, two, three-month periods of a decline in the Gross Domestic Product. Most commonly a recession can last six months to two years.
>
> A **depression** is a period of economic crisis in commerce, finance, and industry. It is a time of falling prices, restriction of credit, low output and investment, numerous bankruptcies, and a high level of unemployment. The Great Depression of the 1930s is the most recent one we've seen in the United States.

Why the GDP Matters

Let's take a look at the key measure of how the economy is doing—the *Gross Domestic Product (GDP)*. When all is well the GDP is rising at a slow, but steady pace. If the GDP is growing too rapidly in today's economy, it could be a sign that inflation is just around the corner. When there is negative growth (a classic oxymoron) in the GDP—a declining GDP—it means a recession is on its way, if not already here. The most commonly accepted sign of a recession is two consecutive quarters (which are three-month financial periods) when the GDP decreases.

> **Money Meanings**
>
> **Gross Domestic Product (GDP)** is the market value of all final goods and services produced annually in the United States. These goods can be produced in the United States by a U.S. company or a foreign company. We used the term "final goods" because only goods that are being sold for final use are used in the calculation. Goods that are purchased for the purpose of further processing or manufacture are not included.

The U.S. economy's current GDP is about $10 trillion. If the growth rate of the GDP increases just 1 percent, it means that our growth is about $100 billion output in a year. That's a lot of money that needs to be absorbed. When there is too much growth and not enough buyers to purchase what is produced companies drop prices to get rid of the large inventories that build up. Companies stop or slow the production of new inventory, which usually means job losses as well.

We no longer have an industrial economy where warehouses and lots fill up with products. Companies operate on a "just in time" basis, which means that they order supplies or products just when they are needed. New information technologies allow companies to better manage their inventories so that they can respond to demand as needed, but they don't have to stockpile either inventory or production supplies.

If there is a major surge of new products need, then this new demand leads to a need to rapidly increase production and hire employees to fill the new demand. This leads to lower unemployment, but also a tighter job market. Employers are forced to lure employees away from other companies with promises of higher salaries and better benefits. Ultimately, this will lead to higher prices and, in turn, labor demands for higher wages to pay for more expensive products. All this leads to an upward spiraling and finally inflation.

A History of Recent GDP Ups and Downs

Since 1950, the United States has experienced nine recessions ranging in length from 8 to 16 months. Each time, these periods of recession corrected an imbalance in the business cycle after a period of inflation or high unemployment. Many economists believe recessions are a necessary evil because they give the economy time to rid itself of inefficient or unproductive jobs and businesses and to prepare us for another growth period. Unfortunately, recessions are painful. Many folks lose jobs as the economy contracts. Recessions feed on themselves because people and companies have less money to spend, thus continuing the cycle downward.

1973–1975

The longest and most intense period of recent recession was from 1973 to 1975, when the GDP lost 4.9 percent over a period of 16 months. Inflation, which was 9 percent in 1973 and 12 percent in 1974, was a huge factor in the length and depth of that recession. People's dollars lost value as prices rose, and stocks lost 40 percent of their value.

1981–1982

The economic contraction of 1981–1982 was also a severe one, but it was a little different. This recession included severe agricultural price declines at a time when agriculture in the United States required huge debt levels. Also, during this period factories and jobs left the "costly" United States for overseas low-wage countries around the world. Then the unemployment rate climbed to a post–Great Depression high, reaching 10.8 percent according to William Greider in *Secrets of the Temple*. And 12 million people were out of work and 8 million had become part-timers just after I was sworn in at the Reagan West Wing to my position on the Federal Reserve's Board of Governors. Good timing on my part, right?

1990–1991

Another severe recession hit the U.S. economy from 1990 to 1991. Luckily it was a shorter one of only eight months, and the drop in GDP was less dramatic—1.8 percent. During this period the number of unemployed people increased by 2.5 million (not as bad as the 1970s). The inflation that led into this recession was tamer at 5.4 percent. Nevertheless, in this case it was again the large jump in unemployment that was a critical factor in the start of the recession.

2001–

Fast forward to today. Before the most recent recession was declared on November 26, 2001, the U.S. economy had experienced two key shocks: First, beginning in the spring of 2000, the stock market took a dive (finally) and continued falling. Market weakness continued through at least the first two quarters of 2002. Second, just as there were some signs of recovery in the market in the fall of 2001, the terrorist strike of September 11 destroyed the World Trade Center in New York.

Economic Wisdom

"The American economy has had to absorb some extraordinary shocks over the past year and a half. For the economy to have weathered as well as it has a severe deflation of equity asset values followed by an unprecedented blow from terrorists to the foundations of our market systems is impressive. In my judgment, this performance is testament to the exceptional degree of resilience and flexibility that our economy has gained in recent years, much of which owes to advances not only in information technology, but the globalization and deregulation of our markets as well. The adaptability and resourcefulness of our businesses and workers have been especially important in this trying period."

—Alan Greenspan, January 11, 2002

This recession followed an extremely long period of growth—1991 to 2000. Some folks were even thinking that our traditional business cycles were gone and that the economy could be kept on a continuous growth path. However, those dreams were dashed dramatically with the stock market dive in the spring of 2000 and the downward trend toward recession. To head off a potential round of inflation, the Fed reduced interest rates 10 times to a 40-year low of 1.75 percent before the *National Bureau of Economic Research* officially declared the recession.

Money Meanings

The **National Bureau of Economic Research** (**NBER**), which is the organization that officially declares a recession, is actually a private, nonprofit, nonpartisan, research organization made up of more than 600 university professors around the United States. NBER's primary purpose is to foster a greater understanding of how the economy works. You can learn more about the organization and its research at www.nber.org.

Looking at the Peaks and Troughs

There are actually four episodes to consider when learning about the ups and downs of a business cycle—peak, recession, trough, and recovery. While you might think a peak is a good thing, it's actually a warning of bad things to come. Once the economy reaches its peak, a recession is sure to follow. (Down we go!)

- ◆ **Peak.** The economy is said to be at a peak when business has reached its temporary top. You will most likely see a period of full employment. You will usually also find that the output capacity is near to maxing out and that prices are likely climbing as well.

- ◆ **Recession.** After a peak you are likely to see a period of contraction leading to recession, the time period between a peak and a trough. Output, employment levels, income, and trade all fall. You will see a contraction of business activity in many economic sectors, and if it's very severe this downtrend can lead to a depression.

- ◆ **Trough.** The bottom of a recession is called a trough. Output, employment levels, and trade all "bottom out." Most economists hope the trough will be short-lived, but it can last for months.

- ◆ **Recovery.** When the economy starts pulling itself out of a trough the business cycle is said to be in a recovery, which is a favorite of us all. The recovery is the time period between the trough and the next peak. Everyone hopes the recovery will last for a long time, hopefully years (like the 1980s and 1990s), but eventually the economy reaches a peak and the cycle starts all over again.

You may be wondering what the driving forces are for these phases. The answer is simple: supply and demand. The answer becomes much more complicated, however, when you look at the forces that drive supply and demand.

Weighing In on Supply and Demand

The people or organizations on the supply side of the economy are the ones who produce the products or supply the services for sale. The demand side of the economy is made up of the consumers, companies, or governments that buy the products or services. As a worker you are on the supply side when you produce the goods or services that people want. You are part of the demand side—Mr. or Ms. Consumer—when you buy the goods or services you need or want.

> **CAUTION**
>
> **Ups and Downs**
>
> People who are laid off don't have the money to buy goods. Their participation on the demand side of the economy slows down. This causes companies whose products were normally bought by the people who were laid off to slow their production. Now other companies affected by this slowdown have to cut work hours and lay people off.

To keep your job, you must hope the supply side remains strong. You hope your company will continue to produce its products or services forever so that you don't have to worry about losing your job. Eventually though, in an economic slowdown, your company gets to the point where its products or services are no longer in as high a demand. The inventory starts to build up, and the company needs to slow down or stop the production of its goods. When that happens there will usually be a cutback in work hours or layoffs, not to mention the dismissal of all those "part-timers" that were hired.

You can see how this cycle of slowdown and layoffs, part of what is known as business contraction, can feed on itself and fuel a recession, a drop in the GDP. The economy heads toward the trough phase, where it eventually bottoms out.

When, during the recession, excess inventories are cleaned out to the point that companies need to start producing again, the upward part of the cycle, recovery, begins again. Companies need to increase their production, so they hire more workers. Workers become scarcer, so to keep the workers they have and to hire others away from other businesses, companies increase wages.

At this point in the cycle there are more people and companies demanding goods and services, so the available goods become scarce and prices go up. The competition for the available goods increases. The economy is now on the recovery side of the trough heading toward the next peak.

Predicting the Cycles

Obviously, to minimize their losses, businesses would like to know as early as possible when the country is heading into a recession. The typical span for recovery is 6 to 10 years. Recessions can last six months to two years. The more prepared a business is to weather the storm of a recession, the greater chance it will have to survive.

When recessions start no one can really be sure whether the economy is experiencing a short-term correction that will quickly turn around or whether the business contraction will develop into a full-fledged recession. While no one can actually control the ups and downs of the economy, the Fed does try to minimize any major shocks by raising and lowering the interest rates it controls.

If the Fed fears the country is heading toward recession, it will lower rates to ease credit and make it easier for companies and people to buy things. When the Fed fears that inflation is showing signs of taking hold, it will raise interest rates to slow down the demand for goods. If the Fed overcorrects in either direction, it can speed the start of a recession or fuel inflation. We all make mistakes, don't we? So does our sterling central bank. Its forecasts are "as good as they come" but they are not always correct. I know, I kept tabs on them during my stay there.

One indicator (of many) that has been studied by the Fed as a predictor of recessions is the *yield curve*. The Fed has found this to be a useful tool for predicting a recession two to four quarters before it actually takes hold.

A negative yield curve has preceded all five recessions since 1960. For example, the yield curve spread averaged –2.18 percent in the first quarter of 1981, predicting a recession that occurred four quarters later in 1982. The yield curve is just one of the many useful measurements the Fed considers when deciding whether to raise or lower interest rates. It's an economic theory that appears to have a strong

Money Meanings

The **yield curve** is the spread between the interest rates on the 10-year treasury note and the three-month treasury bill. The Fed looks at the negative steepness of the yield curve as a predictor of U.S. recessions. When short-term rates are higher than long-term rates, the yield curve is negative. A negative yield curve can be one indicator of an impending recession.

correlation. Now that you understand the basics of the business cycle, let's stop by at a mock meeting of the FOMC to see how they use information about the economy to debate and make decisions about interest rates. We'll take a much closer look at the details that go into these decisions in Chapter 10.

How the FOMC Uses Economic Data

When you serve on the Federal Reserve Board (FRB), the chats with fellow board members and the many staff reports from your inbox give you an idea of what you will ask, and perhaps argue for, at the Federal Open Market Committee (FOMC). The Federal Reserve bank presidents who attend will present their region's findings and their leanings toward tightening, loosening, or standing pat on interest rates.

Let's take a quick look at what happens at a meeting and how all the economic theory is used to make decisions. (We'll be taking a deeper look inside the operations of the FOMC in Chapter 4.) First, the committee is advised by business, board, and bank staff members. Reviewing current conditions and projections, the following questions are addressed:

Preston's Points

While serving on the Federal Reserve Board, I was always aided in my preparation for the FOMC meetings and the board's weekly sessions by the two or three staff I had recruited from outside the Board. It is important to develop an independent point of view, and not just to be an intellectual pawn of the Board's own excellent staffers.

Money Meanings

Money supply target is the target for the total amount of money in circulation at a given time. Increased money supply stimulates the economy.

- What are the current conditions?
- More important, what are the future trends?
- What does next year look like, and why?
- How have conditions and trends changed since our last meeting?
- How have the actions taken after the last meeting impacted economic and market performance?
- Did things trend as expected?

A vote will be made to stay the course, tighten, or loosen interest rates depending on the answers to these questions. If the weight of evidence should point to poor performance in the economy, an argument will be made for lower interest rates that will result in a loosening of credit. The *money supply targets* would be increased to stimulate the economy. On the other hand, if inflation is the key concern, a move would be made to raise interest rates and tighten the money supply to slow next year's economy.

Hearing from the Players

After the Fed's staff gives the summary of the state of the economy, each of the "players," maybe all 12 (the 7 board members and 5 of the bank presidents), make his or her observations as to the short-term trends in the economy. Emphasis is on what the future looks like, and opinions are given on what course of action will keep the economy on a straight and steady path. Each is aware that any actions taken to change the discount rate or to the target federal funds rate will usually take at least six months, maybe as long as a year or more to affect the economy.

One might hear reports from a staffer about deep cuts in business investment spending, especially related to lesser outlays for information technology (IT) equipment. Is there an oversupply of some types of products and weakening demand for other products? Also at this FOMC meeting, let's say two of our Federal Reserve bank presidents stress the oversupply of some types of capital equipment and declining demand. How about those uncomfortably high levels of inventories?

Getting the Good and Bad News

Then some of the staff will report good news—it is spelled "consumer." In this mock meeting, sales of new homes (and at times existing homes) continue to set records. In 2001, sales were the highest in history. But have we seen any signs of major house price inflation? No, in 2001, prices rose only a little more than 1.5 percent nationally. That was good news: Demand was high, but inflation was not evident.

Bad news? Let's say the Board's international division director reports the continued slowing in the foreign economies, further reducing the demand for U.S. products and services. The other division directors give us similar negative reports.

Then we see some mixed signals. Mortgage refinancing boomed on. Consumer spending on goods and services popped up whenever big discounts could be had. But on the bad news side we find out that moderate and low-income families were paying bills slowly, and there have been rising defaults.

After hearing all the news, each member contributes individual views of where the domestic and international economies (and the markets) are going. Reports indicate that the various measures of the money supply have continued to grow at an annual 5 to 6 percent rate determined at the previous FOMC meeting.

Time to Take a Stand

Now the arguments begin. Sometimes they can get heated, but they never turn into a shouting match. Board members make pitches on both sides of the issue—tighten or loosen money supply by changing rates. In the mock meeting here, the argument is made that the economy is weaker than many reports have measured because of a time lag. The forward growth indicators are weak and indicate another fallback in the money supply growth numbers, which may over time result in another negative bounce against economic growth. Inflation measures are so low that the "real" (adjusted for inflation) Federal Funds rate is close to zero!

After everyone around that big board table has had a chance to share their analyses and their views, the chairman sums up what has been discussed. He then adds his own view of domestic and international economic trends. He may indicate that with few exceptions the weakening in business activity appears to have become more wide-spread in the six weeks since we last met. Job losses have mounted further and the unemployment rate continues to move higher. The chairman may say that our reports indicate that inflation continues to remain moderate and edging lower. He reminds us that staff projections indicate that inflation expectations "may be well con-tained." The regulatory division chief had already advised that banks had continued to tighten standards and terms on loans.

Economic Wisdom

"Despite a number of encouraging signs of stabilization, it is still premature to con-clude that the forces restraining economic activity here and abroad have abated enough to allow a steady recovery to take hold. For that to happen, sustained growth of final demand must kick in before the positive effects of the swing from inventory liqui-dation to accumulation dissipate."

—Alan Greenspan in a speech in San Francisco on January 11, 2002

It is pretty obvious that the chair is leading us toward another cut in our target fed-eral funds rate. The chairman gives his summary of the economic conditions and trends we have reviewed in our daylong discussion. He moves for a 25 basis point reduction in the Fed funds rate goal or $1/4$ of 1 percent. Motion seconded. Formal dis-sents by FOMC participants are serious actions by committee members and are rarely made. Such dissents and their sources are recorded and published.

Now you've seen how future supply, future demand, and the business cycle fit in to the actions of the Fed. However, before we look closer at how today's Fed operates, let's take a trip back in time to see how we got a Fed in the first place.

The Least You Need to Know

 ◆ While everyone hopes for a steadily growing economy, what goes up must come down.

 ◆ The business cycle has four phases—peak, recession, trough, and recovery.

 ◆ Better tools for predicting a recession help businesses and the country minimize its depth and length.

 ◆ Fed meetings review economic trends predicting the path of the business cycle to determine interest rate decisions.

3

How We Got a Federal Reserve

In This Chapter

- ◆ Early failures
- ◆ Exchanging notes
- ◆ Going into panic
- ◆ Creating the Fed

You can't open a newspaper today without seeing some word about the Fed and the direction interest rates might go. You may think watching rates is almost like a sports game, wondering which side is going to win. Watching interest rates may cause some anxiety, but it's nothing like the crises the United States faced in the nineteenth and early twentieth centuries when financial panics and bank runs were common.

We haven't always had a central bank to control key interest rates. Stories about the Fed's creation weave a pattern of intrigue that include false starts, secret meetings, financial warfare, and political maneuverings that would easily overshadow the headlines of today's interest rate sports game. This chapter takes a short trip back in time to look at the people and politics that helped create the Fed.

Central Bank Failures

You may not be aware that the United States tried to form a central bank three times before the Federal Reserve was created. The first two times massive fraud ended the experiment. The third time the United States toyed with a central bank, politics destroyed the fledgling institution.

The First Central Bank

The first attempt goes all the way back to a plan for a central bank, called the Bank of North America, which was chartered by the Continental Congress in 1781. Colonists were most familiar with the Bank of England and chose that model for their own bank.

The Bank of North America was private but had the right to lend money to the federal government, and it was given the right to issue notes (paper money) that added up to more than it had on deposit. Stories of fraud abounded and soon few trusted the bank notes. The bank's charter was allowed to expire in 1783, and it was converted to a commercial bank serving only the needs of the state of Pennsylvania where it was located.

The Second Central Bank

Central bank advocates didn't want to give up on their pet project, and using a similar design, Congress made a second attempt to create a central bank called the First Bank of the United States. Advocates thought maybe a name change would help. They also got backing from some top private investors including the Rothschilds in Europe. This attempt didn't work either, however. Not much time passed before the fraud that destroyed the first bank again reared its ugly head.

> **Money Meanings**
>
> **Wildcatters** were primarily small frontier banks that issued currency without worrying about whether there was anything to back their notes. When there was no longer a central bank in 1811, these banks took over like wildfire.

Not only was fraud a huge problem, but the creation of money for the government contributed to massive inflation that drained 42 percent of people's resources. The art of managing money to minimize inflation had not yet been honed. In 1811, when it was time to renew the bank's charter, Congress failed to pass the renewal by one vote in each house.

Once the bank was gone, the federal government needed to look to someone to feed'
its coffers. The unpopular War of 1812 required a lot of money, and the government
knew it couldn't turn to the American public for support through taxes. Instead the
government used *wildcatters* as a source of ready cash by encouraging these banks to
purchase war-debt bonds, which the government converted to bank notes that could
be used to finance the war. This move tripled the U.S. money supply in just two years
and sent inflation through the roof at more than 60 percent.

The Third Central Bank

After the War of 1812, the government made a third attempt to handle the crisis
caused by its massive debt. This time, in 1816, only a small name change was made to
the Second Bank of the United States. The design was only slightly different—it had
control of more capital and had more power to regulate state banks. That bank lasted
longer than the first, but it lost favor 20 years later.

This time the central bank's demise was caused by a political power struggle in the
1820s between President Andrew Jackson and bank president Nicholas Biddle.
Jackson thought the bank was a threat to the country because of its economic power.
Sound familiar? State bankers joined the fight because they thought the central bank
hampered their ability to function. Westerners and farmers chimed in to join the
opposition and to voice their objection to control by city folks and overseas interests.
Congress voted to recharter the bank in 1832, but Jackson vetoed the bill and used
the decision as one of the issues that helped him win reelection against pro-bank candidate Henry Clay. The third central bank closed its doors in 1836.

Which Bank Note Should I Use?

You may think it's crazy to ask which note to use, but after the third central bank
closed in 1836, it kicked a 30-year era of free banking. More than 30,000 different
kinds of notes found their way into circulation. Consumers were never sure whether a
store would accept the notes they were carrying. Merchants had to certify currency as
genuine using a registry called the Bank Note Reporters. Estimates are that about one
third of all paper money used during the free banking era was counterfeit.

The notes were certainly colorful. For example, a yellow two-cent note was issued by
the New York druggist Matthew's Bros. And the Hyson Tea Company in New York
issued 25-cent pink notes.

Bank Notes like this one were the currency during the free banking era after the Third Central bank closed in 1836. This three-cent note was issued privately by Peabody Ladies Home Furnishings in Massachusetts from 1862 to 1863. You can view samples of more notes from that era at the San Francisco Federal Reserve website: www.frbsf.org/ currency/expansion/show.html.

Control of these new banking entities shifted to the states, who then created authorities for issuing bank charters. Any private or municipal authority could operate a bank as long as they met the minimal conditions set within their particular state.

There are many stories about how these banks fooled their customers and the regulators. Some tell of attempts to pad a bank's reserves by showing bank inspectors a barrel of nails covered with a layer of gold coins. Wildcat banks in remote areas were known to move the same sack of gold coins from one location to the next to satisfy the rare visit of the bank inspector.

National Banking to the Rescue

Such shenanigans led to a severe money crisis in 1857, and many banks were closed. The outbreak of the Civil War in 1861 compounded the problem, and by 1862, only about 250 banks had notes that were not counterfeited.

Crisis breeds action, and Congress finally stepped in and passed the National Currency Act of 1863, which was then expanded in 1864 to the National Banking Act. National Banks were to be charted and regulated by the comptroller of the currency.

Republicans supported the act and the idea of centralized national banking. Opposition came from the Democrats as well as the mercantile traders and farmers. Republicans in Congress wanted to eliminate state banking completely and replace it with a centralized system of privately owned and operated banks, chartered and regulated by federal law.

State banks balked at the law and decided not to convert to national charters. They liked the less rigid standards set by state authorities and continued to issue their own bank notes. Congress fought back and raised taxes on state notes from 2 percent to 10 percent in 1865, which came close to destroying the state banking systems. Most state banks did convert to national bank charters between 1864 and 1866 and the nation finally had a uniform national currency of national banknotes.

Banking in the South was even more devastated after the Civil War. Many state authorities chose to dissolve the state institutions rather than allow them to convert to national banks.

Fiscal Facts

Bank branching almost disappeared after the National Banking Act. In 1887, the comptroller of the currency recommended that national banks be allowed to establish offices with limited functions as branches. The first survey of state branch banking done by the comptroller of the currency in 1896 found that 13 states did not allow branch banks, 10 states had no law prohibiting them or providing for their establishment, and 20 states did allow them, and some even encouraged their formation. Two states did not respond to the survey.

The banking system in the late nineteenth and early twentieth centuries was largely composed of *unit banks*, geographically specific institutions with no locations in other states—sometimes not even branches in other cities. Inadequate transportation and communications dictated the unit bank as the most practical banking organization to serve communities.

With the economic interdependence of large geographic areas, the expanding growth and mobility of the population, and the growth of big business firms, the emphasis on location and convenience of banks increased. New banks were opened to meet the increasing demand for banking services. As a result, by 1915, unit bank banking gave way to branch banking in many parts of the United States.

Money Meanings

Unit banks are geographically specific institutions with no locations in other states—sometimes not even branches in other cities.

Bank Panic Era Begins

Public trust in the national bank system was short lived when a series of financial panics and bank runs occurred in the late nineteenth and early twentieth centuries. Banks were commonly held by speculators who doubled as bank officials. If the public heard that a speculator was in trouble, they would rush to the speculator's bank and pull out all their funds. If the bank in question couldn't meet depositors' demands, word would quickly spread, and other banks would face a run. If a bank failed, depositors had little chance of seeing their money again. Today we feel more secure with federal deposit insurance, but that safety net didn't exist until 1933.

> **Money Meanings**
>
> **Clearinghouses** were responsible for stabilizing currency fluctuations and processing draft exchanges between banks until the Fed was formed in 1913. The New York Clearing House, still in operation today, was the first one established, and it served 52 banks when it began operating October 11, 1853. You can learn more about the history of clearinghouses at www.nych.org/files/nych_hist.pdf.

Three major bank panics helped to bring about change in our money system and finally gave the impetus to the creation of the Federal Reserve. After the first bank panic in 1873, *clearinghouses* were given expanded powers to help insure liquidity in case of a future run on a bank. Clearinghouses monitored banks to ensure that they were maintaining the proper level of reserves and that they were solvent. Clearinghouses had the right to examine the condition of its member banks.

The second bank panic of 1893 didn't increase support for central banking because both bankers and the public were satisfied that the banks were able to survive the crisis thanks to the clearinghouse systems, especially in New York. There was some criticism that the Chicago banks did not act quickly enough in 1893, but the problem was not considered severe enough to shift support to the idea of a central bank.

Trust Companies Blossom

The entire situation changed after 1896 when the assets of trust companies blossomed, especially in New York. Trust companies initially were conservative institutions that managed trust funds and estates, and they served as a place to park short-term assets. Trusts did not face as much regulation because they were considered less risky, so they had lower capital and cash reserve requirements than national or state banks, especially in New York. The differences were not as great in Chicago.

Speculators soon found they could use the less regulated trusts as a base to make money in much riskier ventures such as the stock market and real estate, whereas national banks were prohibited from these types of investments. Trusts also could offer higher returns to their depositors because they didn't need to maintain the higher reserve levels required of banks, which meant lower reserve taxes. By 1907, the deposits of banks were almost equal to those of trust companies in New York City.

Warburg Enters the Scene

Quietly and behind the scenes, a European banker named Paul Warburg pushed for the establishment of a central bank. Because he was from Europe and there was major objection to setting up a European-style bank in the United States, his bosses at the banking firm of Kuhn, Loeb and Company advised him to keep his ideas quiet. Senior partner Jacob Schiff advised Warburg to show his work on the central banking idea to James Stillman, president of National City Bank of New York. Warburg wrote in his memoir the following brief description of his initial contact with Stillman in 1903:

> "'How is the great international financier?' [Stillman] asked with friendly sarcasm. He then added, 'Warburg, don't you think the City Bank has done pretty well?'
>
> I replied, 'Yes Mr. Stillman, extraordinarily well.'
>
> He then said, 'Why not leave things alone?'
>
> It was not without hesitation that I replied, 'Your bank is so big and so powerful, Mr. Stillman, that when the next panic comes, you will wish your responsibilities were smaller.'
>
> At this, Mr. Stillman told me that I was entirely wrong, that I had the mistaken notion that Europe's banking methods were the most advanced, while as a matter of fact, American methods represented an improvement upon, and an evolution of, the European system, America having already discarded its central bank. He had no doubt that progress would have to be sought, not by copying European methods, but by elaborating on our own."

It wasn't until four years later that Stillman realized how right Warburg was when the Panic of 1907 hit New York. By that time Warburg had built his reputation and made contacts not only with Stillman, but also another key figure, Senator Nelson Aldrich.

Panic That Changed the Banking Landscape

While the panics of 1873 and 1893 were severe, they had not truly threatened the future of banking. However, the popularity of trust companies and their increasing assets between 1896 and 1907 did worry the New York bankers. There is speculation that this fear of competition might have been behind the start of the Panic of 1907.

Fiscal Facts _____

Montana historian Sarah McNelis believes that some players in the banking industry planned to use the fall of a trust company to convince Congress and the public that trust companies were not trustworthy thereby improving the lot of banks. She believes F. Augustus Heinze, a Montana speculator, took the fall to help prove the point. You can learn more about her theories at the Minneapolis Fed's website: minneapolisfed.org/pubs/region/89-08/reg898c.html.

If this was a plan, it certainly went quickly awry. The first story broke on October 14, 1907, that Montana speculator F. Augustus Heinze had lost his fortune trying to corner the stock of the United Copper Company. Heinz was president of Mercantile National Bank, but resigned his post three days after the story broke. The New York Times noted that Heinze was not a banker by training and that he used his post to learn banking by forming relationships with other bankers.

A run started on the Mercantile Bank as well as the Knickerbocker Trust Company, run by a close friend of Heinze's. The National Bank of Commerce announced it would no longer act as Knickerbocker's clearinghouse agent. As a trust company, Knickerbocker was not a member of the clearinghouse and needed an agent to process its checks.

Depositors were so desperate to get their money out of the Knickerbocker Trust that $8 million was withdrawn from the bank on October 22, 1907 in just three hours. The trust closed its doors at noon that day never to reopen. Anyone who did not get funds in that three-hour period lost everything on deposit.

Initially J.P. Morgan & Co. had agreed to help Knickerbocker Trust, but decided instead to help the Trust Company of America because Morgan believed that company was in better shape. Morgan's decision to help Trust Company was announced after he met with U.S. Treasury Secretary George Cortelyou, who traveled to New York to help manage the crisis. After meeting with Morgan, Cortelyou pledged $25 million in U.S. government funds to help New York deal with any future emergencies. John D. Rockefeller pledged to deposit another $10 million in New York financial institutions.

All this money still didn't get people to stop pulling out funds from New York banks and trusts. In fact some people even made as much as $10 a day standing in line for depositors that were waiting to withdraw their funds.

Morgan continued to use his might to get things under control and asked the New York clearinghouse to issue necessary certificates to make up for the scarcity of cash to keep the banks and stock markets open. By October 24, stockbrokers were also having trouble getting the funds they needed and faced the prospect of failure. The panic did not subside until mid-November of 1907.

> **Economic Wisdom** _____
>
> When banks and trusts go crashing down
> From credit's sullied name,
> When Speechifying Greatness adds
> More fuel to the flame,
> When Titan Strength is needed sore
> Black ruin's tide to stem,
> Who is the man who does the job?
> It's J.P.M.
> —McLandburgh Wilson, *The New York Times*, October 27, 1907 in an ode to J.P.
> Morgan

The Panic of 1907 was so severe that it quickly increased public awareness to the problems within the U.S. monetary and banking system. Congress had to act quickly. In May 1908, it passed the Aldrich-Vineland Act to provide for the issuance of emergency currency and to create the bipartisan National Money Commission to study central banking and other alternatives.

Creating the Fed

Senator Nelson Aldrich of Rhode Island, who was chairman of the Senate Finance Committee, was appointed to head the commission. Aldrich split the commission into groups: One group was to study the U.S. banking system and a second to travel to Europe to study the central banking systems of London, Paris, and Berlin.

For Aldrich, the European trip was a life-changing event. Before going he was vehemently opposed to central banking European style, but when he came back he was fully in support of it for the United States.

Aldrich first met Paul Warburg in preparations for the European trip. This relationship was to build over the years and ultimately thrust Warburg into a crucial role as one of the key designers of today's Federal Reserve.

The Federal Reserve was designed at a secret meeting on Jekyll Island, Georgia, in November 1910. The meeting remained secret for many years, but details slowly leaked out. Participants in addition to Aldrich and Warburg were like a who's who of banking in New York during that period:

♦ Frank Vandelip, president of National City Bank

♦ Harry P. Davison, a J.P. Morgan senior partner

- ◆ Benjamin Strong, vice president of Banker's Trust Co.

- ◆ A. Piatt Andrew, former secretary of Aldrich's National Monetary Commission and assistant secretary of the treasury

- ◆ Charles D. Norton, of J.P. Morgan's First National Bank of New York (Whether he was there or not is controversial. Author G. Edward Griffin confirmed his attendance with Tyler Bagwell, historian for the Jekyll Museum.)

Fiscal Facts _____

G. Edward Griffin, author of *The Creature from Jekyll Island*, writes that folks traveled to the secret meeting that started the Fed on Nelson Aldrich's train car:

> "While Aldrich was easily recognized by most of the travelers who saw him stride through the station, the other faces were not familiar. These strangers had been instructed to arrive separately, to avoid reporters, and should they meet inside the station, to pretend they did not know each other. After boarding the train, they had been told to use first names only so as not to reveal each other's identity. As a result of these precautions, not even the private-car porters and servants knew the names of these guests."

When reporters noticed their arrival at the Brunswick station in Georgia, they were told it was not a big deal. The visitors were on a duck-hunting trip.

Warburg wrote in later years about the meeting that Aldrich was "bewildered at all that he had absorbed abroad and he was faced with the difficult task of writing a highly technical bill while being harassed by the daily grind of his parliamentary duties." Some of the key questions to be answered about a central bank included:

- ◆ Who should own the bank, the government, private interests, or jointly?

- ◆ How many institutions should be formed?

- ◆ Should the interest rate be the same for the entire nation or should it vary according to economic conditions in a particular community or region?

Drawing Up the Plans

The bill that came out of this secret meeting became known as the "Aldrich Plan" and recommended the establishment of a central bank in Washington named the National Reserve Association. The crafters planned for 15 branches of the association located in strategic cities across the nation. The association would serve as fiscal agent for the U.S. government and use the reserves of its member banks to become lender of last resort to the American banking system. The idea of lender of last resort became one of the most critical roles for today's Federal Reserve. (For more on the Fed's role as lender of last resort, see Chapter 12.)

Everyone at the meeting contributed ideas, but Frank Vanderlip believed Warburg made significant and important contributions to the final result. Vanderlip said of Warburg, "As a philosophical student of banking, he was first among us at the time."

> **Economic Wisdom**
>
> "The period during which non-political thought held the leadership in the banking reform movement may be considered as having ended with this conference."
>
> —Paul Warburg's take on the meeting at Jekyll Island

The Aldrich Plan was endorsed by Aldrich's National Monetary commission in 1912 in its report to Congress. Warburg went on to head a National Board of Trade, which formed a group called The National Citizens League for the Promotion of Social Banking. The league had the responsibility of educating both businessmen and laymen.

Politics Take Over

When the plan made it to the political arena it was changed. Aldrich was a Republican, and the Democrats won the White House and took control of Congress. The Aldrich Plan was scrapped, but President Woodrow Wilson said it was "60–70 percent correct." The plan was used as the basis for Sen. Robert Latham Owen's bill proposed in May 1913. One of the key changes was a shift from Warburg's reserve and discounting concepts in favor of open market operations. (For more on open market operations, see Chapter 7.)

In 1913, Congress passed the Federal Reserve Act. Its preamble states:

> "An Act to provide for the establishment of federal reserve banks, to furnish an elastic currency, to afford means of rediscounting commercial paper, to establish a more effective supervision of banking in the United States, and for other purposes."

The Fed Is Born

When the Federal Reserve Act passed, Warburg was tapped for the first Federal Reserve Board, but was in the wrong party to be chosen chairman. Benjamin Strong, who became governor of the Federal Reserve Bank of New York, said of Warburg, he is "the real head of the board in Washington, so far as knowledge and ability goes."

The need for more effective bank supervision was urgent when the Federal Reserve Act became law in 1913. The U.S. banking system at the time recognized the sovereignty of both national and state charters and each had responsibilities for auditing banks. National bank examiners, clearinghouse examiners, state examiners, or any combination of the three could audit banks.

While the Fed was only required to supervise state member banks under the 1913 Act, its role has expanded through the years. When the banking crisis hit early in the Great Depression—during which about 10,000 banks failed—the Fed acted to protect member banks, but did not help nonmember state institutions. This was a repeat of what the New York Clearinghouse did in the panic of 1907 when it failed to protect trust companies that weren't members.

The Banking Acts of 1933 and 1935 gave additional supervisory powers to the Fed, in large part to prevent another depression from occurring. The *FDIC* was also established under the Banking Act of 1933, and for the first time, provided governmental insurance on bank deposits up to $20,000.

> **Money Meanings**
>
> The **Federal Deposit Insurance Corporation (FDIC)** is a federal agency that was created in 1933 to insure the deposits of member banks and thrifts. Today deposits are insured up to $100,000 and there are moves to increase that insurance level.

The Fed Grows Up

Over the years, the Fed's supervisory and regulatory growth has mirrored the growth of the financial services industry. As the industry has expanded in the number and type of services it offers, the need to regulate the services and their delivery has expanded. *Bank holding companies* (*BHC*), legal entities that own one or more banks, provided bankers a tool to expand outside their geographic area and into other financial services areas—insurance, securities, etc.

> **Money Meanings**
>
> **Bank holding companies (BHC)** circumvent geographic and business restrictions normally applied to individual banks. They are large, multifaceted institutions that initially faced less regulation than the banks enjoyed. The Bank Holding Company Act of 1956 put the Federal Reserve System in charge of supervising multi-bank holding companies. The BHC Act of 1956 was amended in 1970 to include one-bank holding companies.

The Federal Reserve has also been called upon to regulate bank consumer activities. For example, the Fed is the primary regulator of the Truth in Lending Act of 1968. This act requires that lending institutions properly disclose interest rates and other information on consumer credit.

The International Banking Act of 1978 brought foreign banks within the federal regulatory framework. It required FDIC insurance for branches of foreign banks engaged in retail deposit in the United States. The Financial Institutions Reform, Recovery, and Enforcement Act (FIRREA) of 1989 was enacted to restore the public's confidence in the savings and loan industry. For more on FIRREA, see Chapter 11.

Now that you know how the Fed was born, we'll take a look at what happens inside the Fed today in Chapter 4.

The Least You Need to Know

- Designs for a central bank failed three times before the Fed was born.
- Bank panics were the impetus for putting the muscle behind a workable central bank plan.
- The initial design for today's Fed was crafted at a secret meeting at Jekyll Island, Georgia.
- As banking has changed, the Fed's power has grown to increase its tentacles in today's banking industry.

Part

The Money Machine's Top Dogs

We introduce to the key players that keep the money machine running smoothly. We're sure you've heard of Alan Greenspan, but he has a large army of people that support his decision-making.

We take a peek at how the Federal Open Market Committee operates, meet some Fed Chairmen before Greenspan's reign, as well as other members of the Fed's Board of Governors and key staffers.

Chapter 4

Peek Inside the FOMC

In This Chapter

◆ Who makes the decisions?

◆ Reading the tea leaves

◆ Attending a meeting

◆ Taking a vote

The Fed is probably best known for its role in influencing interest rates, but board members don't actually set interest rates for every type of money instrument available today. The Fed only sets the discount rates, the rates that it charges member banks when they borrow money—primary credit for sound banks and usually a higher secondary credit rate for less financially sound banks. The Fed sets a rate target for the Federal Funds rate, the rate member banks charge each other.

Whenever you borrow money, whether it is a mortgage to buy a house, a loan to buy or car, or the margin rate on your brokerage account, these rates are set by the institution from which you are borrowing the money.

In this chapter, we look at exactly what rate the Board does set and how it is set. We also take a look at how the FOMC targets the Federal funds rate. Then we'll sit in on a Fed meeting to see how the discussions and voting work.

The Members and the Meetings

Every five or six weeks, the media is filled with different prognostications about what the 12 people at the Federal Reserve's Federal Open Market Committee (FOMC) meeting in Washington are going to do about interest rates and commercial bank liquidity. The meeting always starts with an opening statement by the chairman, after which senior staff members present a series of reports from their particular fields and offer projections for the future. These senior staff members include the international finance director, who informs the voting members what's likely to happen around the world economy in the next few months. Next comes the chief staffer of the Division of Monetary Affairs, who speaks about liquidity, the money supply, inflation, and consumer attitudes in the United States. Then the voting members hear from other "directors" (actually staff department heads). Generally, the FOMC members listen respectfully to these reports. The meeting rarely turns into a shouting match or anything like that.

One of the major happenings at each FOMC meeting is to find out what's happening around the country. Each bank president—the individual who runs the Federal Reserve Bank of Cleveland, or Philadelphia, or St. Louis, for example—reports on conditions in his or her multistate district. Then the discussion really gets down to business. I mean *your* business, the costs of credit your company needs and your family has to have.

How They Make Decisions

The result of all these reports and discussions is a decision whether to move interest rates up or down, and by how much, or to leave them alone. There are two key rates that the FOMC can change: The Fed funds rate and the discount rate.

You'll recall from Chapter 1 that the Fed funds rate is the rate one bank charges another if it wants to borrow money overnight. Federal funds (Fed funds) are reserve balances financial institutions hold at Federal Reserve banks to meet their reserve requirements (the percentage of deposits that a bank or other depository institution may not lend out or invest and must hold either as vault cash or on deposit at a Federal Reserve bank). These reserves can be transferred between depository institutions within the same business day.

For example, let's say that on Thursday, Hometown Bank on Main Street needs to borrow $100,000 in order to cover all the checks that their customers wrote that day. They call Friendly Savings over on Elm Street and borrow $100,000. The next morning, Hometown Bank customers deposit their paychecks and Hometown Bank pays off the overnight loan from Friendly Savings. The interest rate that banks charge each other under such conditions is determined by the FOMC—and that's the Fed funds rate.

Now let's turn to the discount rate. This is the rate that the Fed charges when it lends deposits to banks. The more a bank has to pay the Fed bank to borrow deposits, the more it has to charge its customers for the use of that money. So if the FOMC changes the discount rate, chances are that banks will change the rates they charge you for business loans, personal loans, auto loans, lines of credit, credit cards, or mortgages.

Let's say the FOMC has listened to all the arguments, thought things through, and has decided to reduce the Fed funds rate and to cut the discount rate, each by half a percent.

Ups and Downs

Incidentally, the Fed never says "half of 1 percent." Instead, it says, "50 basis points." There are 100 "basis points" in a percent, so cutting a rate by 50 basis points will be reported in the media as a .5 percent rate cut. For example, a cut of 50 basis points means that the rate has gone down by 0.50 percent, from, say, 7 percent down to 6.5 percent. Why does the Fed engage in such confusing terms? Probably because for decades they really didn't want anyone to understand what they were doing!

Now, let's make clear that the Fed has not changed the interest rates you pay on your mortgage, your car loan, or your credit cards. But you can bet your bottom dollar that practically every bank and every thrift in the country will immediately adjust their rates on every financial product they offer, including everything from savings accounts to home equity lines of credit.

The Fed itself doesn't cut the interest rates you pay—it cuts the rates of interest that banks pay, and usually, but not always, the bank passes the savings (or the higher costs) on to you. Why do they react so quickly? They'd lose money if they didn't. Not only that, the information will be in the news immediately—so if your bank doesn't give you the new, better rate, you'll move your account to a bank that will!

Reading the Smoke Signals

Let's take a look at the way this information would be reported in your newspaper. Perhaps there was no decision to raise or lower rates. What would the media report about that kind of situation? You might see a news report that says, "The FOMC gave the Fed chairman authority to change rates in between meetings." Or did the FOMC report a "leaning" toward tightening or loosening credit? (Tightening credit means raising the interest rates so that it's more expensive for people to borrow money. Loosening is the opposite.) These are two important clues that allow you to project what the Fed is going to do over the coming months.

Since the meeting takes place behind closed doors, how does a normal person ever find out what happened? Easy. Watch for the media report on the last FOMC. Note reports in the financial sections of your newspaper quoting comments from that get-together. Check out what they said about the economy, job growth, labor compensation, and inflation, or the lack of it. The only problem is that sometimes the Fed doesn't seem to communicate in English!

The Fed uses a language all its own, which is called Fedspeak (learn more about that in Chapter 10). Historically, the purpose of Fedspeak was to ensure that absolutely no one had any idea what the Fed was doing. Today, things are a little better. Government conducts more of its business in the public eye, and reporters are less cozy with top government officials than in the past. Also, with so many different news shows, cable news channels, and outlets, there are far more reporters than ever chasing stories, which makes it harder for the Fed (or any government entity) to hide.

> **Fiscal Facts**
>
> Even with all this publicity, Fedspeak lingers on. For example, you might see a report in the financial page of your newspaper that described the FOMC this way: They aimed at stimulating growth before it might ultimately lead to a "risk of recessionary imbalances developing in the economy." Or "imbalances exist that are elements that would eventually undermine the long expansion of the economy." Confused? You're supposed to be.
>
> Basically, there is concern expressed in both of these statements that a recession may take hold. You don't have to wait for the minutes—check the "statement" the Fed puts out the day after the FOMC. Keep notes of the changing language.

Let's take a look at the events that followed the terrorist attacks of September 11, 2001. These events unleashed a period of economic uncertainty and almost certainly compounded the recession that the U.S. economy was already entering. So this is a fairly instructive example of how the FOMC works in a crisis.

On November 7, 2001, the FOMC announced the decision to reduce rates—the Fed funds to 2.0 percent and the discount rate to 1.5 percent—their lowest levels since 1961. The FOMC noted in their statement:

> Heightened uncertainty and concerns about a deterioration in business conditions here and abroad are dampening economic activity. For the foreseeable future, then, the Committee continues to believe that, against the background of its long-run goals of price stability and sustainable economic growth and of the information currently available, the risks are weighted mainly toward conditions that may generate economic weakness ....

What a convoluted way to say that we're headed toward more economic trouble.

Reading the Colors

A few days before each FOMC meeting, the 12 Fed bank presidents will have reported on economic conditions in their bank districts in a tome called the Beige Book. (Watch for media discussions of that one.) In addition to the Beige Book, each member of the FOMC also receives a Green Book and a Blue Book. The Green Book contains Federal Reserve Board staff forecasts of the U.S. economy; the Blue Book presents the Board staff's analysis of monetary policy alternatives. Only the Beige Book is available to the public.

Money Tips

You can find the most recent Beige Book online at www.federalreserve.gov/ FOMC/BeigeBook/2002/. Click the most recent month for which a report was issued. This report is published eight times per year. Federal Reserve banks gather information on current economic conditions in each of their districts from bank and branch directors as well as through interviews with key business contacts, economists, market experts, and other sources. The Beige Book summarizes this information by district and sector. Be sure to keep track of the leaning of this report. You may even want to review the leaning of the past two reports to see the direction the Fed believes the economy is moving. You can find Beige Book reports back to 1996 at this site.

I like to review that long media report in the Beige Book to glean the language that each bank president used in writing about his or her section of the country. Do they say labor compensation gains (a long way of saying, salaries) were "moderate"? When they talk about price increases, do they call them "temperate"? Fedspeak, again. But there's enough plain English in the Beige Book for you to make it worth your while to read and note.

Here's an excerpt from the January 2002 Beige Book:

> Reports from the Federal Reserve Districts suggest that economic activity generally remained weak from late November through early January. But while there are still indications of caution, there are also scattered reports of improvement. The Dallas and San Francisco Districts report a continued decline in activity, while the Cleveland District indicates that the regional economy appears to be bottoming out. Economic activity remained slow or weak in the Boston, Chicago, Philadelphia, Kansas City and St. Louis Districts. Activity was mixed according to the Atlanta, Minneapolis and Richmond Districts and showed further signs of rebounding in the New York District.
>
> Many Districts indicate that their contacts believe a recovery will begin by mid-year or earlier, but the timing and strength are uncertain. Several Districts say that uncertainty has led some businesses to budget conservatively for the first quarter.

I know what you're thinking: Maybe the Fed can't control the economy, but they sure can do a great job of curing my insomnia!

Nevertheless, once the Beige Book comes out, all the voting members of the FOMC have a pretty solid idea of how the whole U.S. economy is doing right now. From that you can guess with some accuracy what the Fed is going to do about it. Two weeks after reviewing this information, the FOMC chose to leave rates unchanged. The following is from the FOMC press release on January 30, 2002, explaining their action (or inaction):

> Signs that weakness in demand is abating and economic activity is beginning to firm have become more prevalent. With the forces restraining the economy starting to diminish, and with the long-term prospects for productivity growth remaining favorable and monetary policy accommodative, the outlook for economic recovery has become more promising.

Going to a Meeting

Let's imagine that you are a voting member of the FOMC, and let's walk through a sample FOMC meeting. Play like you will have a vote to loosen or tighten or no change. You vote. Okay, my fellow board member, let's travel to Washington and the Federal Reserve Building, and its palatial board room that FDR and Marriner Eccles designed in the 1930s. This board room is a handsome "palace" of a place. (How do you like that huge marble eagle over the fireplace? I hope you like it. Since you're a taxpayer, you helped pay for it!)

The chairman is the main communicator and leads the meeting. A lot of the arguments and discussions have already taken place the night before, when the Fed Bank presidents dined at the Watergate Hotel (where most of them stay) down the street from the Fed. No, Monica doesn't live there anymore!

All right, now you have reviewed the latest Beige Book, so you have a pretty solid idea of what's happening with the economy. You've read the minutes of the last FOMC, during which the group cut rates. You've had dinner with your Fed colleagues and you have a pretty good sense of whether they want to raise rates, lower them, or keep them where they are. And now the meeting begins.

Rules of Order

The chairman starts us off with brief introductory comments to set the stage. In the chairman's remarks, he reminds us that we have had to reduce interest rates in the last two meetings to maintain low "inflationary expectations." He repeats his public remark about maintaining the market's liquidity around the world. He reminds us of how much he and the Fed had to hustle during the sharp market drop of 1987. The chairman reminds us that when the markets threaten to crash, we, the Federal Reserve, have to step up to the plate and provide tons of cash on the members' bank accounts at the Federal Reserve. These are the *bank reserves*, so the banks can meet unusual demands for cash and deposits. Then he turns the show over to the senior staff people for their reports and forecasts.

Money Meanings

All commercial banks and thrifts in the United States must meet **bank reserve** requirements on their customer checking deposits. The amount of reserves required is based on an average of money held over a 14-day period. These reserve requirements are supposed to ensure that a bank can meet its customer's daily withdrawal habits. Banks don't earn interest on the amount they keep in their reserves, so they always try to keep the reserve amount to its bare minimum. Reserves can include cash in the vault, as well as the money on deposit at the Fed.

The International Staff Director now describes how interest rates have been falling in Britain and Germany (but not in Japan, where they are still struggling with financial problems and "broke banks"). The staffer describes how bond markets around the globe are softening. He argues that our colleagues in those other central banks in the other countries are just too tight with the money supply and the interest rates charged. Every day, every hour, billions of dollars flow around the world through the financial markets. The Fed serves as a kind of risk manager for financial markets. What should the Fed do about what's going on in the rest of the world? Three answers—liquidity, liquidity, liquidity. How? Buying those bonds they have in portfolio.

Treasury securities are bought and sold by the staffers at the Open Market Desk at the New York Fed (more about that in Chapter 7) to reach the targets set for the Federal funds rate. Internationally, the trading values of various currencies are also impacted by the buying and selling of bonds from different countries (we'll talk more about the international markets in Chapter 17).

Federal Reserve staff have a short list of approved bond dealers with whom "they trade." The desk serves the whole Federal Reserve System. The approved dealers in turn serve the commercial banks having reserve deposits at the Fed. When a bank sells bonds to his Fed bank the payment is in "reserve deposits."

The next major report comes from the monetary affairs director who reviews the forward-looking projections of that giant econometric model he uses. Here is what the economy 12 months and 18 months down the road looks like:

- Consumer spending, little change from today.
- International markets for U.S. goods and services? Strongly positive growth.
- U.S. business investment, recovering.
- Governmental spending? Mixed. Defense spending up.
- Other spending, little improvement because of deficit concerns.
- Consumer and housing activity, weak. The mortgage refinancing thrust is history.
- Prices of consumer goods, slightly up.
- Unemployment, rising.

In sum, this staffer warns us that without lower rates and more money supply growth we could be heading for a modest recession.

The international staff director is pretty sure he knows what the committee motion should be. He adds, with a touch of Fedspeak, "Too little money chasing too few assets causes asset-price deflation, then global recession." That's a fancy way of saying, "If we don't lower rates here in the United States, the rest of the world economy is gonna go in the dumper."

So you can see what he wants us to do!

What do all the forecasts mean? Do they all make sense? Just remember what David Stockman, President Reagan's budget director, said as he was leaving Washington: "None of us really understands what is going on with all those Fed numbers." Remember what Harry Truman said, "if you can't convince 'em, confuse 'em." When you're dealing with something as complex as the U.S. (and the world) economies, it's not easy to get a precise handle on things!

Fiscal Facts

What's the easiest way to grasp the role of the Fed for your FOMC vote? Try this: Take your own checking account, the ATM slips you've got lying around a few different drawers, the bank statements you haven't reconciled for the last 12 years, and now multiply all of that by a billion!

Here is where those notes you took are so useful. What did the chairman say at that meeting in Davos, Switzerland? Was the Beige Book recession concerned? Those minutes of a previous FOMC were pretty discouraging, weren't they? You made a note or two when the talking head on the TV financial program told you about the chairman's required report to the Congress, right?

Preparing to Vote

Now it is time to vote. You will want to mentally review what the staff, the bank presidents, and the other members of the Fed Board have been telling us about the economic trends. You'll want to review your:

- FOMC meeting minutes
- Beige Book notes
- Blue Book notes
- Green Book notes
- Staff presentation handouts
- Discussion notes

You might also be considering media reports of comments by the Fed chairman, other board members, and Fed bank presidents. You might glance at all of the statistical charts and graphs hanging on the wall in the board room. (Nobody else does.)

You'll also consider the employment trend picture. Fed Chairman Alan Greenspan is especially interested in something called the *Employment Cost Index*, which indicates whether wages are going up in the future. As salaries increase, so does the risk of inflation. So if this indicator suggests that wages and salaries are rising, it's a cue to the Fed to move rates higher—or risk inflation. (And we all know the Fed just hates inflation.)

Money Meanings

The **Employment Cost Index** tracks the compensation for civilian workers. The index reflects the changes in wages, salaries, and benefits. Another key measurement is how many people are choosing to change jobs.

The *Employment Cost Index* also measures "the quit rate," which is another key to measuring the likelihood of inflation. When the economy is strong and robust, people feel as though they have a lot of options. Don't like your job? Just quit! You'll find another one tomorrow! Don't like your boss? Get a new one at another company down the street … and they'll probably pay you a higher salary just to make the move! Wait a minute! Those thoughts were fine until the September 11 attacks, but they don't work now, do they? Now it's not so easy to find another job with all those layoffs.

When people feel cocky about their employment chances, they quit their jobs more often and get a better deal somewhere else. But if the economy is slow, people get more cautious about quitting. They say to themselves, "Hey, I better not take any chances. I've got a family and a mortgage. If I quit this job, who knows if I'll find another job somewhere else?"

Fiscal Facts

You probably didn't know that a high "quit rate" indicates a booming economy … and the threat of inflation. When the chairman sees that the cost of paying wages and salaries is rising, and people are quitting their jobs in droves, you can be sure he'll want to raise interest rates and reduce the risk of inflation. This is an important figure for you to consider as you decide whether to raise rates, lower them, leave them alone, or give the Fed chairman permission to raise rates between FOMC meetings.

Another factor you'll weigh is how the economy as a whole is going to do next year. Two leading indicators that the Fed relies upon are the National Purchasing Agents' Index and the Economic Cycle Research Institute (ECRI). The first of these two statistics tell you whether the cost of raw materials is going up. Let's say that the price of steel is rising. That will translate down the road into higher car prices. Or let's say the price of sugar is falling. That means that before long, it will be cheaper for food manufacturers to produce, say, ice cream and snack cakes. So the cost of Häagen-Dazs actually plays a role in the setting of interest rates!

The ECRI measures where we are in the economic cycle. Are we in an expansion? Are we heading toward recession? The ECRI will let you know.

Finally, you'll consider the money supply, which means how much money is actually sloshing through the economy at any given time. These "M" numbers used to be much more important a generation ago, before credit cards and payment over the Internet became prevalent. But it's still a key indicator of how the economy is going.

Crunch Time

Okay. Now you know everything a Fed governor knows when voting to raise or lower rates. You know what's happening in the world and across the United States. You know what's happening with the cost of salaries and with the cost of raw materials. You know (roughly) where we are heading in the business cycle—whether the economy as a whole is getting better or worse. And now you've got to crunch that data in your head and come up with a decision. With all that data and all those remarks—spoken and written—it is not so difficult to make up your mind, is it?

All right, are you ready to cast your vote, my friend? Tighten credit? That means you'll vote to raise the rates. You'll also be asked to recommend by how much. Loosen? That means you'll vote to lower rates. If you do vote to lower them, you'll have to decide by how much. Or you can vote to leave rates alone.

Not so easy, is it? As you can see, the notion that the Fed controls the economy just isn't true. The voting members of the Fed do the best they can, sorting through complex and often conflicting information about the U.S. and world economies. Then they just kind of guess about what's going to happen next, and what role they should play. They don't always guess right. If they had a crystal ball that told them exactly what the future held, and what they should do about it, we'd never have any recessions or any inflation. The stock market would never go down. Your investments would be totally risk-free.

But that's not how the world works, of course. There's always risk; and recessions, deflations, and downturns are part of the game. But in just these few pages you've seen that the Fed is not all-powerful. If anything, the Fed reacts to what seems to be going on instead of controlling the situation. Certainly, the ability to set interest rates gives the Fed a great deal of power. But they don't run the show, contrary to everything you hear, see, and read in the news. The Fed is an important part of the Washington Money Machine, but it's not the Wizard of Oz.

What It Means to You

So you've begun to see how the Fed really works. It's clear that the functions the Fed performs have a powerful effect on you, your family's finances, your job, and your future. So it's truly vital to understand exactly what the Fed can do … and what it can't.

Understanding the marvelous money machine is part of the preparation necessary for your family financial planning. Federal Reserve policy is a central piece. I have already admitted that the language used by central bankers is virtually incomprehensible. But it is possible to break that code, and we'll see exactly how to do so. Certain pieces of data measure and, in some cases, anticipate shifts in policy. The factors that go into making up a level of interest rates, high or low, today or tomorrow, leave their mark on all the subjects we'll cover in this book.

In the pages that follow, we're going to deal with financial and money matters. No, not in an abstract way, but rather by going inside and seeing exactly how the powers-that-be move the money machine. We will look at the obstacle courses they steer, and the choices for us that result. This is the backdrop against which we all conduct our financial lives, so let's get going!

The Least You Need to Know

- Two key rates set by the Fed are the Fed funds rate and the discount rate.

- These rates affect the interest rates banks set on home and car loans and on credit cards.

- The Fed looks at the various statistics from the world economy and takes its best guess as to what to do next.

- The Fed tends to hide behind the fuzzy language of "Fedspeak" to keep regular folks from understanding exactly what's going on.

5

Leading Stars of the Fed

In This Chapter

◆ Defining the role

◆ Expanding the power

◆ Seeking independence

◆ Captains of the economic ship

Some say the Federal Reserve chairman is the second most powerful man in America. We don't get to vote on him. We almost never get to ask him questions. The only time he has to talk to the public is during the twice-yearly appearances required by Congress. Just how important is the chairman?

He or she (hasn't been a she yet) does have personal access to the president, the treasury secretary, the congressional leadership, the other central bank presidents around the globe, Wall Street's power brokers, the financial institution chiefs (not just banks), and anyone else who has major economic power in the world. Nice access, right?

As we discussed, the Fed is a "creature of Congress" created in 1913. Congress gave the Fed its power and, at least in theory, has the ability to take some of that power away. But that's not how things work in the real world. Once you give away power, it's awfully hard to take it back!

In fact, Congress doesn't want to take power away. It keeps giving the Fed more to do! The 1999 Bank Reform Act (thanks to Alan Greenspan's leverage with the Congress and the White House) actually widened its powers over the several kinds of financial service providers, not just banks!

Running the Economy

No, the chairman doesn't "run the economy," as some have suggested. No one does, not even the president. The economy is a complex set of powerful economic institutions of which the Fed is the most powerful. But the Fed isn't "all-powerful."

Economic Wisdom

"A central bank in a democratic society is a magnet for many of the tensions that such a society confronts. Any institution that can affect the purchasing power of the currency is perceived as potentially affecting the level and distribution of wealth among the participants of that society, hardly an inconsequential issue."

—Alan Greenspan, December 1996, in a speech titled "The Challenge of Central Banking in a Democratic Society"

Can you really blame the Fed for every single thing that's gone wrong in the U.S. economy over the last 90 years? Of course not. Think a minute of the times when our economy has weakened into recession (or even depression). Was the Fed responsible for all of those contractions?

Sometimes much of the blame can be placed there. For example, in the 1930s after the stock market began to recover from the 1929 crash, the Fed reduced the money supply by about a third, contributing to huge unemployment that persisted for years. The Fed isn't too proud of that one (and probably wishes we didn't bring it up in this book!). On the plus side, the Fed has repeatedly acted as the "lender of last resort" (more on that in Chapter 12) to prevent financial panics and avoid recessions or inflation.

Now, let's turn our focus to the chairman, who leads the Fed.

Getting Down to Politics

Is the chairman's appointment "political"? Of course. There are many talented individuals in the United States capable of fulfilling the responsibilities of the Fed chairman. So talent isn't the only issue.

If you were a newly elected president, wouldn't you want "your" Fed chairman to be someone you worked with extensively. Someone who, you thought, would run monetary policy to meet your economic goals and ultimately strengthen your bid for reelection? Of course! But as we'll show you, once appointed by the president and confirmed by the Senate, the Fed chairman doesn't always dance to the political tune played by the White House. Today the chairman and vice chairman are appointed for four-year terms. Federal Reserve governors are appointed for 14 year terms. To be chairman or vice chairman the nominee must already be a governor or be appointed as a governor at the same time as his or her appointment.

Chairmanship Evolves

First, let's look at how the Federal Reserve Board (FRB) has evolved since being established by the Federal Reserve Act of 1913. Originally the board consisted of seven members: the secretary of the treasury and the comptroller of the currency as members ex-officio, and five members appointed by the president with the "advice and consent of the Senate." Of the five presidential appointees, one was appointed "governor" (the active executive officer) and one "vice governor." The secretary of the treasury was designated as "ex-officio Chairman of the Federal Reserve Board." The board offices were located at the Treasury, with meetings held at the treasury headquarters in Washington near the White House.

Preston's Points

On your next visit to our nation's capital, do go by the palace on Constitution Avenue that President Franklin Roosevelt and Marriner Eccles erected in 1937. The Fed has an art collection you would enjoy, so call in advance and determine if they are having a showing. (Let them know you paid for it! You're a taxpayer, right?) Look for my wife Genevieve's painting of San Francisco's House of Flowers. It's probably still in one of the governor's offices.

In the early days of the Fed, questions arose about how the Fed and Treasury Department would work together. After all, both organizations bear responsibility for the economy. Some Fed board members felt the relationship with the Treasury Department might lead to undue political influence on monetary policymaking. That is, they were afraid that the Treasury would exert too much power over the Fed.

You could say they got something of a political divorce. The conflict was partially resolved when Congress passed the Banking Act of 1935, eliminating the requirement for the secretary of the treasury and comptroller of the currency to serve on the

Board. This act also increased the number of board members to seven and changed the title of governor to chairman and vice governor to vice chairman. The Board moved out of the Treasury Building and into its own headquarters in Washington in 1937. (Cost was no object!)

Establishing Independence

The Banking Act of 1935 stipulates that the president of the United States appoints one of the seven governors to the position of "chairman" for a four-year term. The Senate must confirm this selection. Since 1935, there have been seven different chairmen of the FRB.

Here are the six men who made significant contributions to the identity and independence of the present-day Board:

- ◆ Marriner Eccles
- ◆ Thomas McCabe
- ◆ William McChesney Martin Jr.
- ◆ Arthur Burns
- ◆ Paul Volcker
- ◆ Alan Greenspan

Marriner Eccles (1934–1948)

The first chairman appointed after passage of the Banking act was Marriner Eccles. As the assistant secretary for monetary and credit affairs at the U.S. Treasury, Eccles wrote much of the act and was instrumental in its passage through Congress. Prior to the act, the secretary of the treasury had been ex officio chairman, running the FRB as he saw fit. The secretary at the time was Henry Morgenthau Jr., who had worked with Eccles in the crafting of the act. Morgenthau knew that Eccles agreed the best way to end the Great Depression was to keep interest rates low so that the Treasury could borrow cheaply to finance the various government spending programs that would propel the economy into full-employment mode.

After the depression, of course, came World War II. Eccles was subjected to pressure from Treasury officials to hold rates at substandard levels throughout World War II. However, even before the end of the war, Eccles recognized these expansionary fiscal and monetary policies would likely lead to inflation.

Postwar spending programs included the "G.I. Bill" benefits to all of the servicemen and women who were coming home—benefits that would help them complete their education, buy a house, or start a small business. The Fed had been willing to maintain interest rates within historically low ranges, but the flip side of all those growth-positive programs was rising inflation. The Fed was faced with a dilemma: Should the Eccles Fed cut back on money growth and curb that inflation?

Economic Wisdom

"As long as the Federal Reserve is required to buy government securities at the will of the market for the purpose of defending a fixed pattern of interest rates established by the Treasury, it must stand ready to create new bank reserves in unlimited amounts. This policy makes the entire banking system, through the action of the Federal Reserve System, an engine of inflation."

—Governor Eccles' testimony before the Joint Committee on the Economic Report, U.S. Congress, 1951

Eccles began proposing programs to restrain the developing inflation, programs that incorporated higher taxes and gradually increasing interest rates. These were the sort of things that Treasury officials and politicians inside the Roosevelt and Truman administrations were not interested in, so the Fed simply continued its administration of interest rates and the money supply according to Treasury demands.

Eccles had been a supporter of Roosevelt. However, because of his continued conservative fiscal stance after the war, he was not a favorite of President Truman. Although Truman did not reappoint him when his term expired in 1948, Eccles remained on the board to complete the remainder of his regular 14-year term.

Thomas McCabe (1948–1951)

Truman appointed Fed governor Thomas McCabe to be Eccles's successor. McCabe had been appointed to the Fed in early 1948, when Governor Ronald Ransom died. Before he was appointed to the board, McCabe had served as the liquidation commissioner for the federal government, managing the disposal and sale of excess war materials.

Tensions continued between the Treasury and the Fed. Administration pressure to maintain low interest rates meant that the Fed had to purchase large amounts of treasury securities. By 1950, the Korean War had contributed to the escalation of inflation—17 percent at the wholesale level and 7 percent in the consumer price index. Treasury Secretary John Snyder argued for maintaining low interest rates to optimize governmental borrowing costs.

Fiscal Facts

Thomas McCabe's chairmanship was a casualty of the conflict between him and Treasury Secretary Snyder. Snyder told President Harry Truman he could no longer work with him. McCabe resigned after only three years as chairman. Even though his term was short, he changed the role of the Federal Reserve forever. His removal has been seen as a last ditch effort by the Truman administration to regain control of the Fed. Truman's appointee, then assistant secretary of the Treasury William McChesney Martin Jr. was also a staunch defender of the Fed's independence.

The conflict between the Fed and the Treasury culminated in an unprecedented meeting at the White House between the Federal Open Market Committee and President Truman in January 1951. After the meeting, the White House released a statement to the press stating the Fed would continue market support of low interest rates even though no agreement had been reached. It was left to Eccles, even though he was no longer chairman, to release the confidential minutes of the meeting to the press to refute the White House claims. Shortly after this incident, members of Congress intervened and demanded the Fed and the Treasury iron out their differences.

Fiscal Facts

William McChesney Martin was also the best tennis player on the Board, and he used the two tennis courts outside the headquarters. People used to wonder why the FRB usually adjourned its meetings about 3 P.M. When do you like to play tennis? One of those tennis courts is still there! Take a look on your Washington visit.

William McChesney Martin Jr. (1951–1970)

I'm no relation to this Mr. Martin, although I'd be proud to have him in my family tree. This Martin took the Fed into the postwar world. The 1951 Treasury-Federal Reserve Accord, which he shaped, has been referred to as "the birth of the modern Federal Reserve." As the negotiations between the Fed and the Treasury Department reached their final stage, Treasury Secretary Snyder went into the hospital and the assistant secretary for monetary affairs, William McChesney Martin, became the head negotiator for the Treasury. Martin, a Truman ally, had a thorough understanding of both the Federal Reserve System and financial markets.

Martin's dad had helped create the Federal Reserve in 1913 and he had served as president of the Reserve Bank of St. Louis. Bill worked there for dad, too, as an examiner. (Not a bad starting job if your Yale University degrees were in Latin and English.) At age 31, Martin had already been the youngest president of the New York Stock Exchange, earning the equivalent of today's $500,000. Behind his back, they referred to him as "the wonder boy of Wall Street."

Martin served under five presidents (Truman, Eisenhower, Kennedy, Johnson, and Nixon) for a total of 19 years. Presidents would repeatedly attempt to insert their political needs into his thinking.

But Martin firmly believed in the Fed's independence. Over the 19 years of his chairmanship, he instituted policies that changed the approach the Fed used to establish monetary policy. He didn't believe the Fed could accomplish its goals of low inflation and economic stability by targeting a single economic indicator. He believed many *economic indicators* needed to be considered.

> **Economic Wisdom**
>
> "We have to take away the punchbowl just as the party gets going."
>
> —Fed Chairman Bill Martin summarized the Fed's duties in one remark

Analysts have criticized Martin's Fed for cutting off the long expansion that ended in the middle of the Vietnam War. Yes, it was the inflation that wartime spending had produced which moved the Fed to tighten credit and step up regulatory review of bank assets. Wartime spending escalated, and market interest rates rose significantly as expectations of future federal deficits escalated.

> **Money Meanings**
>
> **Economic indicators** are various types of statistical data used to measure the general trends in the economy. Common examples you'll see regularly in the newspaper include unemployment, housing starts, Consumer Price Index, industrial production, and stock market prices.

In 1968, President Nixon offered Martin the position of the secretary of the treasury so that he could appoint Arthur Burns (a Nixon campaign advisor) to the Fed chairmanship. Martin declined. (Notice that when a chairman has gotten one of those priceless 48-month terms, he hangs in there!) When Martin's term expired in 1970, Nixon appointed Burns chairman.

Arthur Burns (1970–1978)

Arthur Burns had a distinguished governmental and academic career, including stints as president of the National Bureau of Economic Research (NBER) and as

Eisenhower's chairman of the Council of Economic Advisors (CEA). For a time, Burns even met weekly with President Eisenhower!

> **Economic Wisdom**
>
> "Monetary policy can help to establish a financial climate in which prosperity and stable prices are attainable. But it cannot guarantee the desired outcome: The task is much too large."
> —Arthur Burns in testimony before Congress on February 20, 1973 (and revealing of Burns' approach)

Preston's Points

I had the privilege of serving as chairman of the Federal Home Loan Bank Board, FHLBB, during Burns' tenure at the Fed. This institution was the central bank for the 5,000 or so "thrift institutions." You probably don't like getting mail from your bank. Imagine how I felt, getting mail (and phone calls and everything else) from 5,000 "banks"!

Burns was very adept at listening, discussing, and then deciding whether to carry out policy changes suggested by the White House and Treasury officials.

Burns led the research and analysis that produced the "Beige Book," the economic reports published by each Fed district. It was first called "the Red Book," but was changed due to the negative associations with that color.

Paul Volcker (1979–1987)

Paul Volcker was appointed chairman in 1979 by President Carter and reappointed in 1983 by President Reagan. I served as vice chairman for four of his years as chairman (1982–1986). The "second most powerful man in America," and a longtime public servant, Volcker became almost a household name and certainly a celebrity for his FRB's contribution to bringing inflation down.

Volcker was correctly perceived as a master negotiator in domestic and international crises. For this man, the inflation dragon was always right around the corner. His prior experience in government had been throughout the double-digit inflation years, a factor that weighed heavily in every decision he made.

By 1985, the economy was growing weak, and the unemployment rate was high. For our trading partners in the European community, inflation was low and declining—their economic growth was even more modest than our own. The Japanese economy was stronger than that, but there were signs of floundering there, too.

We at the Federal Reserve Board were becoming increasingly concerned about the rising levels of debt by American consumers, governments, and business, which culminated in a total of $7.1 trillion by the end of 1984 (yes, that's "trillion," with a "t"!). The media called it a "borrowing binge."

In November 1985, the Board began to receive requests from Federal banks in various parts of the country to cut the discount rate and the Fed funds target. The board knew that approval could initiate subsequent rate reductions around the country—even in foreign countries. Between November and February, these discount rate requests were regularly brought to the board on Monday morning meetings and routinely turned down. Volcker was dug in on interest rates.

By February 1986, there were three new governors appointed by President Reagan: Governors Martha Seger, Manuel Johnson, and Wayne Angell. Along with myself, we were labeled the "Gang of Four." In fact, we did share a conviction for lower interest rates. We were also pro-growth. Otherwise, we were quite different people, with varying economic backgrounds, from different geographical areas, and with different outlooks.

At the board meeting on February 24, 1986, we voted four to three to cut the rate—a decision that went against Chairman Volcker and Governors Emmett Rice and Henry Wallich. By mid-afternoon, Volcker had pushed all the right verbal buttons to hint to me and to Governor Angell that he would resign if he were outvoted, even occasionally.

Angell and I negotiated a compromise, giving Volcker time to push the Japanese and Germans into similar actions. These were two major sources for imports and exports. I knew that U.S.–German–Japanese rate cuts would be the ideal moves and that Volcker was the only one of us who could successfully bring that about quickly.

We had no intention of embarrassing the chairman or "destroying him," only of getting him "on board." Unemployment in this country, and particularly in Europe, was too high. American exporters desperately needed stronger markets abroad. Lower interest rates would help. We persuaded Volcker to work with central bankers in Germany and Japan. He agreed (reluctantly).

Preston's Points

On March 21, 1986, I announced my planned resignation from the board. I had spoken with James Baker, then the Treasury secretary, about my serving as chairman, but I wasn't exactly invigorated. Jim had three candidates in mind. My background at the time included almost seven years as a regulator of savings and loans—many of which were in trouble or even failing. I declined the possible chairman candidacy and headed back to San Francisco after four years at the Fed. "Enough, already!" This left Volcker to serve out the remainder of his second term before leaving the chairmanship in August 1987.

On March 6, 1986, both the Germans and Japanese cut their key interest rates, and on March 7, the Fed announced its first rate cut in 10 months—a half point. We had strong support from the voting presidents of the Federal Reserve Banks.

This rate cut marked a milestone in the Board's history. Ordinarily, discount rate actions and all the discussion surrounding them are secret. Instead bits and pieces of various meetings and negotiations, including the big news about the chairman having been outvoted earlier on, leaked to the press.

> **Money Meanings**
>
> **Leanings** (or bias) is the way the FOMC announces its perspective on the future state of inflation in the economy. It is a statement that indicates how the Fed is leaning in terms of its next interest rate move.

Until recently, central banks worldwide operated largely in secret. The FOMC published each meeting's minutes but didn't release them until after the next regularly scheduled meeting. Today, we watch closely several days, or even weeks before a meeting, to get some signs of the direction the FOMC might go at the next meeting. The Fed's *leanings* or interest rate changes are announced immediately after the meeting.

Alan Greenspan (1987–)

Alan Greenspan was appointed to his first term of the Federal Reserve Board by President Reagan in 1987. Alan was the quintessential Washingtonian, measured by his contacts, his friendships, and the greatest handshaking skills since the lead in *The Music Man*.

In the 49 months I served as Fed vice chairman, Greenspan was running his New York consulting firm, Townsend-Greenspan & Co. I never attended a single D.C. social where Greenspan wasn't shaking hands and conversing. Greenspan is a good listener, and an excellent inquirer.

> **Preston's Points**
>
> When I was serving as Fed vice chairman, Greenspan observed that my comments, often dissenting from FOMC votes, did not receive much media attention. After his 30 years of Washington interaction he gave me this piece of advice: "Preston, don't be such a nice guy. Say something outrageous!"

Effective crisis management has been the hallmark of the Greenspan chairmanship. The initial challenge was the October 1987 stock market crash. On Monday, October 19, the Dow Jones Industrial Average fell 508 points, a drop of 23 percent. The next day, the market opened by plunging again, to a low of 1450. But Greenspan announced the Federal Reserve would put money into the system to keep it afloat. By the end of the week, stock prices had begun to climb, albeit slowly. It took 15 months for the Dow to return to its pre-crash level of 2247.

The November 1997 stock market crash involved a 554-point drop in the Dow Jones Industrial Average. Greenspan had issued his warning 11 months earlier, referring to the state of the stock market as "irrational exuberance" and predicting that the then bullish market would not be able to sustain itself. He was finally proved right in 2000 and things still look bad through the first half of 2002.

Effective crisis management has been a major contribution of Greenspan to the stability of the financial world. The master of "Fedspeak" has nonetheless led the movement to Fed "transparency." Today you can read the Fed information and opinions shortly after the analysis—even right after the decisions are made. Greenspan contributed to the passage after four decades of debate of the Gramm-Leach-Bliley Act of 1999. That legislative piece brought the different financial services together and crowned the Fed as the "umbrella regulator."

Greenspan deserves—and receives—recognition for how he has worked with Board members, Fed bank presidents, and key staffers to make the Fed more functional. The Fed uses forward-looking data from its monstrous *econometric modeling* and from other sources of data projections. There is less usage of pure theory.

> **Money Meanings**
>
> **Econometric modeling** is a way to apply the use of statistics and mathematical methods to key economic forces such as capital, interest, and labor, to make economic forecasts.

You want your groceries delivered from Safeway? Your boss needs some info about that competitor headquartered in Taipei? What are home prices like in your neighborhood? Greenspan's large staff keeps him up to date on just about any data on any subject he is looking for. What a change from the Arthur Burns days of estimates and guesstimates!

Greenspan runs his Federal Reserve "informational operation" out of a modest-size office where he can often be found hunched over one of the two computers on his desk or gazing intently into his small TV screen. Several research staff members of the FRB's 700 or so are frequently challenged (and somewhat driven mad) by data and possible economic relationships Greenspan comes up with.

As you can see, each Federal Reserve chairman made his mark on the creation of the Fed and its current day powers, but they never worked alone. In the next chapter we'll take a look at the other key players inside the Fed.

The Least You Need to Know

◆ The chairman of the Fed is appointed by the president and serves a four-year term that has no limits on the number of times it can be renewed.

◆ Fed chairmen sought and received independence from the Treasury Department in 1935.

◆ Each Federal Reserve chairman has left his mark on the road to independence.

◆ Presidents appoint the chairman of the Federal Reserve but can never expect to control his or her actions after making the appointment.

Chapter 6

The Other Guys at the Fed

In This Chapter

- ◆ Becoming a governor
- ◆ Playing second fiddle
- ◆ Fixing things
- ◆ Meeting madness

When you read newspaper reports about the Fed, you may get the mistaken impression that Alan Greenspan is a Supermanlike financial guru that runs the U.S. banking system based solely on his ideas. Well that just isn't so.

He has a lot of folks supporting him and, when speaking for the Fed, must represent not only his own viewpoint, but the consensus viewpoint of the Fed's Board of Governors. In addition to the seven members of the Board of Governors, other key players are the 12 presidents of the Federal Reserve banks and the more than 1,700 staff members that support the work of the Federal Reserve Board. This number doesn't include the thousands of staff members that work outside of Washington in the Federal Reserve banks.

Becoming a Fed Governor

A Fed Governor, unlike a state governor, has not been elected by the people. He or she was appointed by the president and confirmed by the U.S. Senate. A Fed Governor is appointed for 14 years or to fill out the term of a governor who has resigned. Each even-numbered year the president gets to appoint one governor. The nominee can either be someone who is already serving and being renominated or can be someone who has never served on the Board. Sometimes appointments back up and a president makes more than one appointment in a year.

There are two governors' spots that have four-year terms, the chairman and vice chairman. If appointed to one of those terms, the chairman or vice chairman either must be a sitting member of the Board or must be dually confirmed by the Senate as a Board member and the chairman or vice chairman at the same time. In the last chapter we discussed the chairman; now we will take a closer look at the roles the other governors play.

Being Number Two

Serving as the "number two" at the Fed Board is both a privilege and a pressure-filled position. I was the twelfth vice chairman. I did the four-year duty for fifty months in the early 1980s, from March 31, 1982, to April 30, 1986. It was a time in which banks and thrifts were failing by the hundreds. A governor's duties as vice chair depend on his or her background and experience. Unfortunately, my previous four years as chairman of the "other central bank," the Federal Home Loan Bank Board, positioned me as "Mr. Workout."

> **Preston's Points**
>
> I resigned my Sears Roebuck holding company CEO position, with its four subsidiaries including my "baby," PMI Mortgage Insurance Company in mid 1982. (I had founded PMI seven years earlier.) The "Reaganauts" wanted me at the Fed, and I couldn't resist.

While serving on the Fed Board, your duties reflect your background and experience. Of course Board meetings and FOMCs are "standard operating procedure," but you know that the Fed has many responsibilities, and the Board members, especially the vice chair, participate in them.

Each governor will take on a different set of responsibilities depending on their expertise, areas of interest and assignments from the chairman. These responsibilities likely will include work in the Fed's key areas including monetary policy, monitoring economic trends, bank supervision and regulation, and financial services. Each Fed governor has a small personal staff, but depends heavily on the work of the general staff. We'll cover staff breakdown in greater detail in Chapter 9.

Governors as Regulators

Let's start with the regulatory duties. When a bank in your region is in real trouble you guide the Fed staff to develop workable recommendations from the risk-focused examination. (We'll talk more about the examination process in Chapter 9.) While a governor doesn't go out to examine banks, he or she does get involved if the field examiners find a problem. The governor, using data collected in the field, must assess whether the institution has adequate reserves to protect itself against potential losses. Enough? No? Then require they add some. Should they do some asset write-offs, which means to take some of those losses now to clean up the balance sheet? Remember Enron and how their hiding of loses brought the company down?

The governors working with their staff make sure the banking institutions are practicing "full disclosure."

Preston's Points

Now, let's review some history. When I was serving as chair of the "Bank Board" in the 1970s, we pressed Congress to deregulate the interest institutions could pay for deposits in that time of rising market interest rates due to the prevailing high inflation. By 1980, Congress found it necessary to enact price and credit controls, all to try to curb inflation. Banks had to cope with wildly gyrating markets, at times having to pay higher rates on their "CDs" (certificates of deposit) than they could earn on their best loans.

Sometimes banks must raise their reserves in order to meet the demands set by the Fed. If present owners cannot meet the demands, then the governor overseeing the situation explores possible merger candidates. These are stronger institutions capable of acquiring and "fixing up" the ailing bank or thrift.

Examining the Banks

Let's take a brief look at how the Fed's staff examines a bank. The Fed's staff examiners must evaluate how bankers use tools to manage all the bank's balance-sheet risk. For example, is a bank we are examining *securitizing loans?* By pooling loans in this way and selling them, the bank can share some of its risks with outside investors.

Another key thing to watch is whether the banks are building up their *"servicing rights"* for added income without the portfolio risk. Are they selling "pieces" of those loan portfolios yet retaining some ownership? If so, the Fed looks at what the risks are of those assets.

When our examiners review a bank's credit-risk management, they also look at those tools (or scoring models) the lending officers use to make better small-business and consumer loans, including home mortgage loans. Examiners check out those scoring models, but keep a watchful eye for any actions that might discriminate against moderate and low-income loan applicants. Of course statistical modeling doesn't apply to all loan officer decisions. Sometimes big, complicated loan applications apply to a group or a "syndicate" of banks that are going to share the credit risks, which limits the credit exposure of the bank currently being examined.

> **Money Meanings**
>
> **Securitizing loans** is the process of pooling a number of loans into one security or bond. These bonds are then sold on the open market.
>
> **Servicing rights** are the rights to continue to manage the payment of the mortgages. The banks are paid a fee to collect the money, keep records of payment, and manage the escrow accounts.

The Fed examiners also need to be certain that small business lending and low-down-payment mortgages made to moderate and low-income families are underwritten properly. If payments aren't being made, the Fed looks at what kind of counseling facilities and staffers have been used to readjust those loans, not just foreclose them.

Now with the data and the analysis in hand, how confident are the Fed's staffers in the capabilities of the top bank management? The Board? The Board's audit committee?

When all the facts are in, the Fed staff meets with the top bank management to discuss the findings. Do they understand how severe the situation is? What do they recommend be done? Do they accept the Fed's analysis of the financial condition of "their" bank? How willing is the management to take the losses recommended by the Fed examiners and respond to demand for more capital? Do the financial markets accept the bank's providing complete financial and performance disclosure, so called "transparency"? Does the bank's board still support the doings of their management, or are they ready to accept a demand by the Fed's Board of Governors to recruit a new chief executive officer (CEO), maybe a new chief financial officer (CFO)? Even a *chief risk officer (CRO)*?

> **Money Meanings**
>
> The **chief risk officer** (CRO) is a senior executive who is charged with independently monitoring risk identification, measurement, mitigation, and controls. They do that risk reporting to the CEO, the board, and to the examiners when they are there.

When the staff finds signs of a serious problem and the bank is not willing to correct, that is when a Fed governor gets more directly involved. Let's take a look at what happens to a failing bank.

Fed as Mr. Fix It

Okay, back to the Fed's action in a major failing bank. Imagine you are the vice chair working with the staff to come up with a proposed "fix-up." ("Staff," of course, refers not just to the Fed Board's immediate staff, it includes those examiners from the Fed bank of the region.) Then you interface with the district's Fed president (he knows the situation better than anyone in Washington). First, the Fed governor will propose a solution that is reviewed with the chair, then with the Board, and finally with the Fed bank president and his staff attending.

Most likely other regulators will be called to the meetings. If this is a state-licensed bank, the state's banking supervisor will be brought in. If there is a problem with the bonds issued by the sick bank, the SEC will invite itself. Others who may be there include the FDIC, and if this is a thrift, the Office of Thrift Supervision. Well, so much for the regulatory responsibility Fed Board members have. We'll take a closer look at these responsibilities in Chapter 11. Let's go on to the other jobs here at the Fed for a governor.

Working with the Staff

During my tenure, working with staffers who participated in producing economic statistics and their policy implications meant information and recommendations from the three "barons" selected by and reporting to the chairman: the director of the division of international affairs, the director of the division of research and statistics, and the director of the division of monetary affairs. When you are serving as a governor or vice chair it behooves you to get info and projections early from the three "barons." Don't wait until they routinely deliver their analysis a few days (or the day before) the FOMC. (We'll take a closer look at their work in the Chapter 9.)

Now that you have a better idea of the role the governor's play in Fed operations, let's turn to the role of the most powerful bank—the New York Fed.

The Least You Need to Know

- ◆ The chairman of the Federal Reserve represents the consensus of the Board of Governors when it represents the Fed.

- ◆ Fed governors do much more than attend meetings to help run the massive central bank operations.

- ◆ Duties of the Federal Reserve governors vary depending on their area of expertise and interests.

- ◆ Governors do get involved as needed in bank examinations and regulatory decision-making, as well as their better known role in monetary-policy setting.

Part 3

The Money Machine's Hidden Powers

Much of what the Fed does is not visible to the public. We take you inside the operations of the Federal Reserve banks and the Washington, D.C., staff.

You can't open up an account at the Federal Reserve but banks and foreign governments can. Some of the topics we explore include open market operations, Discount Window borrowing, and the massive activities of the Fed's payment systems.

The New York Fed: The Power Behind the Throne

In This Chapter

- ◆ Banking center
- ◆ Crisis manager
- ◆ Keeping markets open
- ◆ Looking overseas
- ◆ Serving foreign banks

You may be surprised to learn that the functional central bank of our country is located in New York City in our nation's financial center, not in Washington, D.C. Yes, policies, goals, and targets are made in meetings of the Federal Reserve Board (FRB) and of the Federal Open Market Committee (FOMC) in Washington. However, the New York Fed president is vice chairman of the FOMC. And much of the execution of these policies is done by the New York Fed. The New York Fed also provides services to banks and other financial institutions in this country and around the world.

Let me summarize its principal functions: This Fed bank conducts the open market operations utilizing what is called its Trading Desk, or "the Desk." Yes, the target rates and other performance criteria are set by the FOMC, but they are carried out at the New York Fed.

Secondly, this central bank acts to stabilize the foreign exchange markets of this country and of the planet. The New York Fed provides financial services to foreign central banks around the world. Money transfers by the trillions are conducted there. Investment targets are reached by this bank's activities.

A lesser but still important role is its safekeeping of securities and of currencies and most importantly, most of the world's gold supply. Yes, the American gold supplies are stored in Fort Knox, Kentucky, and elsewhere with only a little of that shiny stuff in the New York Fed. Foreign gold is there in huge quantities though, tens of billions of dollars worth. We'll take a closer look at all these functions in the following section.

Separation of Powers

So it is plain for all these reasons that the New York Fed is literally the "first among equals." Policies are made in Washington, but never exclude the persuasiveness and the data that the New York Fed president and two or more of his staffers can bring to all those meetings in Washington.

Is it possible that the New York Fed president is more important than the president of the United States in terms of the economy? Well, there are moments when that is certainly true, moments of financial crisis, and moments of market volatility. But the president of the United States is able to bring to bear fiscal policy and attitudinal powers that transcend the financial markets at times.

Preston's Points

The working relationship between the president of the New York Fed and the chairman of the Federal Reserve Board is typically a close one. In my four-year service at the Board this was particularly true of the working relationship between New York Fed President Gerry Corrigan and Fed Chairman Paul Volcker. These were old fishing buddies who loved to go out there and get into that boat and run down that river. Then they had that time to talk over the financial matters that they were both concerned with. Volcker brought Corrigan to the New York position from his job as president of the Minneapolis Fed, where Corrigan was serving. Volcker had been the New York Fed president.

In 1998, when the Long-Term Capital Management firm (LTCM) announced that it had lost more than $4 billion in a bizarre six-week financial panic in the summer, the immediate response by New York Fed president William McDonough was to line up commercial bankers and investment bankers who had been financing LTCM. In that paneled meeting room at the Fed of New York, McDonough made sure that they understood after a day or so of negotiating that they were going to have to put up enough capital to refund the giant *hedge fund*, which had lost $4.4 billion.

Money Meanings

A **hedge fund** is a private investment portfolio, usually structured as a limited partnership. The fund is typically open to accredited investors and institutional and wealthy individuals (usually meaning net worth of $1 million or more, and annual income of $200 thousand or more). The funds are managed by a general partner (or partners) with every financial tool imaginable at his disposal. The general partner also invests his own capital and probably pays himself 20 percent (some even 30 percent) of the asset price gains. The funds are not subject to significant government regulation, and disclosures of their finances may be minimal if their management so chooses. There were about 3,000 hedge funds in 1998, with total assets in excess of $200 billion! (And remember that Enron owned a hedge fund!)

Fed to the Financial Rescue After September 11

Crisis management is most often led by the New York Fed. Its post–September 11 performance showed how critical the New York Fed is to the U.S. and world financial markets. Financial markets at home and abroad faced potential breakdowns in security pricing. Would market participants be able to utilize financial instruments to manage risks and finalize financial transactions? If the markets couldn't continue to function, business, government, and consumer decisions would have crashed, too.

One of the first things the New York Fed had to do was take care of itself. After the September 11, 2001, terrorist attacks, the bank had to move across the river to their backup quarters away from "ground zero."

In this information age, a shutdown in New York would have had nanosecond impacts around the United States and then around the world. To calm fears in the financial markets, the Fed needed to issue a public statement that it was open and operating. First, a "secure" telephone talk with Fed Chairman Alan Greenspan, who was in Europe. Second, Vice Chairman Roger Ferguson and New York Fed President Bill

McDonough consulted with the other FOMC members. Next the Fed assured the public that it was open and would provide all needed liquidity. Chairman Greenspan returned from his Basle, Switzerland, central bankers meeting after a day's delay. (Air Force planes were in operation in the days following the terrorist attacks, even though commercial ones remained grounded.)

Fiscal Facts

Now, think of how concerned you were about terrorism, and about your family's financial future when you got up on September 12. Well, the Fed Open Market Desk of the New York Fed got up even earlier that morning, arrived at their desks in the backup buildings across the river, and met all the primary dealers needs that very same day! Not only that, but the reserve banks together used their Discount Windows to extend a world record $46 billion credit and continued to set record levels over the next four days. On Friday, September 14 alone, the desk arranged $81 billion of short-term purchase agreements (more about those in the following sections), another mighty new record.

Rocketing growth in the various measures of the money supply also demonstrated the Fed's liquidity crisis management. Crisis liquidity (or the need to make money available) had to be added to an already expanding money supply. Yes, much of this liquidity will be reduced as the economy moves into more normal rates of growth. This was a panic preventative. Stabilize consumer and business depositor reaction to the recession and to possible liquidity needs coming from the September 11 crisis. Investment bank, commercial bank branches, offices, and infrastructures all shut down in the south side of New York City.

The Fed's regulatory staff at the Board and Fed banks worked with member institutions to serve customers afflicted by the disasters. Thus, even banks whose customers were hardest hit did not have to close, and the "comeback" firms and families were truly served.

Preston's Points

I journeyed to New York shortly after the September 11 attacks to make a presentation to the Habitat organization, the lead agency within the United Nations for coordinating activities in the field of human settlements. The personal and business "renaissance" that was already taking place was most impressive. One couldn't help but recall that old refrain: "New York, New York, it's a wonderful town!" Is there a sequel about the Federal Reserve? Perhaps, "The Fed, the Fed, it's a motherly bank"?

New York Fed's Role in Fed History

The New York Fed has played a leading role in the birth and evolution of the Fed System, starting with its formation in 1913. Up to that time, the J.P. Morgan Investment banking firm had stepped in to support the banking system when runs by depositors and asset valuation crises had occurred.

Benjamin Strong, who served as the first president of the New York Fed, was from the Morgan firm. The Fed's initial roles evolved around providing credit to member banks at "discount rates" set by the Fed Board (with much advice from President Strong).

Almost immediately, staff researchers developed models of the economy and its financial markets. Models with which academicians love to toy today held much less interest to the academic community of those days.

The New York Fed Bank took a leadership role in international financial matters, good and bad, but usually with interface with the Bank of England and other central banks. Just as the first signs were being seen of an upcoming deep recession that ultimately turned into the Great Depression, President Strong passed away in 1927. His successors and officials at the Treasury neither had the Strong vision nor the forward-looking ability Strong possessed. Policies plummeted.

Economic Wisdom

"A key reason for the change in Fed policy in 1928 was the death of Benjamin Strong, president of the Federal Reserve Bank of New York. He was the Alan Greenspan of his day, whose influence over Federal Reserve policy was virtually absolute from the beginning of the Federal Reserve System in 1914 to his death (13 years after). As long as he lived, the system worked tolerably well. But once he was gone, the Fed was virtually leaderless, which contributed to the massive contraction of the money supply by one-third between 1929 and 1933."

—From an October 1999 National Center for Policy Analysis Editorial called "What Caused the '29 Crash and Great Depression?"

The New York Fed remains "the first among equals." Its history and its relationships with the nation's (and the world's) largest banks and investment banks nearby give it leverage. (Remember that old real estate saying, "location, location, location"?)

New York Fed's Power Base

The New York Fed has supervisory jurisdiction over the Second Federal Reserve District, which encompasses New York state, the 12 northern counties of New Jersey, Fairfield County in Connecticut, Puerto Rico, and the Virgin Islands. Although it serves a geographically small area compared with other Federal Reserve banks, the New York Fed is the largest reserve bank in terms of assets and volume of activity.

The New York Reserve Bank has one branch office in Buffalo, New York, which is one of five sites in the country that processes applications for U.S. savings bonds. Additionally, there are two regional offices of the New York Federal Reserve located in Utica, New York and East Rutherford, New Jersey, handling cash and check processing for the district. In 2000, the two centers processed 1.39 billion checks and $320 billion in currency. Busy, aren't they?

Going for the Gold

Since 1916, the New York Fed has stored gold, primarily for foreign governments, central banks, and official international institutions. The gold vault is a fortress resting five stories below street level on Manhattan bedrock. Steel and concrete walls several yards thick encase the vault's interior. No, the September 11 terrorists didn't crack it!

The vault has 122 compartments, each holding the gold of one nation. The main door of the gold vault is a 90-ton steel cylinder that rotates in a 140-ton steel and concrete frame. No one individual knows all the combinations necessary to open the vault, and closed circuit television cameras keep a constant watch.

Fiscal Facts

The New York Fed currently stores approximately $64 billion of monetary gold (valued at $280 per troy ounce). The vault is the largest concentration of monetary gold in the world, constituting one-quarter of the world's official gold supply.

The U.S. government only has a small amount of gold bullion stored in the New York Fed's vaults. The majority of the U.S. gold reserves are held in depositories of the Treasury Department at Fort Knox, Kentucky and West Point, New York. The gold reserves of the United States are valued at the approximate market price of $84 billion.

In addition to the responsibilities the New York Fed shares in common with the other Reserve banks, the New York Fed has some unique responsibilities. These include conducting open market operations and stabilizing foreign exchange markets.

Let's Be Open

Open market operations are one of three basic tools used by the Federal Reserve to reach its monetary policy objectives. The other tools involve changing the terms and conditions for borrowing at the Discount Window and adjusting reserve requirement ratios. (We'll talk more about those tools in Chapter 9.)

The purchase or sale of U.S. *government securities* in the open market (also known as the secondary market) is the most flexible means of carrying out the Fed's objectives. By adjusting the level of *reserves* in the banking system through open market operations, the Fed can offset or support seasonal or cyclical shifts of funds. It thereby affects short-term interest rates and the growth of the money supply. Now you see how they reach "target" interest rates. This is the working principle of supply and demand.

Money Meanings

Government securities are debt obligations of the U.S. government. They can be treasury bonds (mature in seven years or more), treasury notes (have a maturity of one to seven years), or treasury bills (also called "T-bills," having maturities of one year or less). They are sold at public auctions on a regular schedule published by the U.S. Treasury Department.

Reserves are the assets that banks have on deposit at their local FRB and certain liquid assets. This is usually a percentage of their deposits.

The movement of government securities between securities firms, banks, and other investors is what constitutes the open market. The competitive bids at open market auctions determine the interest rate paid on each issue of securities. Primary dealers submit competitive tenders (or bids) at the Treasury auctions. These dealers can hold them, resell them to their clients, or trade them with other securities firms.

Through the purchase and sale of U.S. government securities in the secondary market, the level of reserves in the banking system can be adjusted. By managing the supply of reserves in relation to the demand for them, the Fed can adjust the cost and availability of reserves and induce changes in the Federal funds rate to reach their targets.

Desk Operations

When the Open Market Desk at the New York Fed buys securities, it may add more reserves than member institutions demand, thus causing a decline in the funds rate. Over time, higher reserves and a lower Fed funds rate will stimulate the expansion of money and credit in the economy. Conversely, when demand is higher than reserves, the funds rate rises and the growth of money and credit decline.

The FOMC currently uses the Federal funds rate as the principal guide for evaluating reserve availability. At regularly scheduled meetings, the FOMC is responsible for determining monetary objectives and issuing a policy directive (or set of instructions) as to what the target should be for the Fed funds rate for the current period.

The manager of the system open market account, along with the staff of the Trading Desk at the New York Fed, executes open market operations on behalf of the entire Federal Reserve system. The FOMC policy directive is used as a guide in making decisions about the day-to-day purchase or sale of government securities.

> **Ups and Downs** _____
>
> Remember reserve requirements for banks is the percentage of deposits that a bank may not lend out or invest, holding it either as vault cash or on deposit at a Federal Reserve bank. When an individual bank or financial institution can't meet its reserve shortages it will purchase or borrow reserves from other banks or financial institutions at the Fed funds rate. This does not expand the amount of reserves in the system; it simply redistributes existing reserves.

Getting Directions

The New York Fed gets its directions from FOMC directives. Just to show how that works, here is the FOMC directive for December 2001, as stated in a press release immediately following the meeting. (The directive can also be found on the FOMC website.) Notice the terminology used: "lower its target for the federal funds rate," or in simple language, the goal is to decrease interest rates.

> The Federal Open Market Committee decided today to lower its target for the federal funds rate by 25 basis points to $1^3/_4$ percent. In a related action, the Board of Governors approved a 25 basis point reduction in the discount rate to $1^1/_4$ percent.

Economic activity remains soft, with underlying inflation likely to edge lower from relatively modest levels. To be sure, weakness in demand shows signs of abating, but those signs are preliminary and tentative. The Committee continues to believe that, against the background of its long-run goals of price stability and sustainable economic growth and of the information currently available, the risks are weighted mainly toward conditions that may generate economic weakness in the foreseeable future.

Although the necessary reallocation of resources to enhance security may restrain advances in productivity for a time, the long-term prospects for productivity growth and the economy remain favorable and should become evident once the unusual forces restraining demand abate.

In taking the *discount rate* action, the Federal Reserve Board approved the requests submitted by the Boards of Directors of the Federal Reserve Banks of Boston, New York, Philadelphia, Chicago, and San Francisco.

> **Money Meanings**
>
> Remember the **discount rate** is what Fed banks charge member institutions for borrowing at the discount window. This is short-term (usually overnight or weekend) loans to depository institutions facing unexpected outflows of deposits or insufficient reserves in the money market. The Federal Reserve banks set their rates, but the approval for the change must come from the Federal Reserve Board.

Once the FOMC issues the directive, the Trading Desk at the New York Fed must decipher and implement the policy. How do they accomplish a Federal funds rate of $1^3/_4$ percent without saying the Fed funds rate is $1^3/_4$ percent?

The Trading Desk at the New York Fed manages the Federal Reserve System's portfolio, valued at roughly $520 billion. The Fed adds extra money to the banking system when it buys Treasury securities and drains money when it sells Treasury securities. The laws of supply and demand take over in the reserve markets and the cost of funds for the remaining reserves finds its level at the Federal funds rate, the rate designated in the FOMC directive.

Sounds simple?

This is anything but simple. The staffs at the NY Fed and at the FRB create an objective for each two-week period covered by the FOMC directive. They do this by estimating the amount of reserves needed in the system to meet the FOMC policy objectives. The estimate of nonborrowed reserves is critical because it serves as the basis for judging reserve conditions and conducting day-to-day open market operations. The estimate of reserves determines if there is too much money available (interest rates go down) or not enough money available (interest rates go up).

Like Goldilocks and her oatmeal, it must be just right. And remember, the Fed isn't the only participant in these trading activities—this is an open market.

Reading the T-Leaves

How do they know what the reserves are going to be? The Trading Desk at the New York Fed gathers information about market activities from a number of sources. The Trading Desk deals with "primary dealers," the banks and securities brokerages that trade in U.S. government securities with the Federal Reserve System—the same people who bid on the securities at the Treasury auctions.

As of March 2001, there were 25 primary dealers with trading volumes averaging about $300 billion per day. The Fed traders discuss with the primary dealers what they expect to happen that day. The Fed Traders also talk with the large money center banks about their reserve needs and how they plan to meet them.

Reserve forecasters at the New York Fed and at the FRB in Washington gather and analyze data on bank reserves for the previous day and analyze factors that could affect reserves for the future. The Treasury Department provides information about its balances at the Federal Reserve and accounts at commercial banks. There are also calls to other Federal Reserve bank presidents and staff to find out conditions in their district that might impact the amount of reserves in the system for the upcoming weeks.

Once the reserve forecast is complete, the Trading Desk develops a plan of action for the day. The plan is reviewed with a rotating Reserve bank president who is currently a voting member of the FOMC. This happens by way of a conference call every morning along with a discussion about conditions in the financial markets. A summary of this is sent to all of the members of the FOMC later in the day so that the FOMC can monitor that the Trading Desk is implementing the committee's policy.

The Trading Desk is now ready to enter the market. Depending upon the level of reserves in the banking system, the Trading Desk may take one of several approaches regarding the type of transaction executed. Most often, the transactions the Trading Desk engages in are short-term *repurchase agreements* (*RPs*), which are used in situations that call for temporary additions to bank reserves. With RPs, the Desk buys securities from the dealers, who agree to repurchase them by a specified date at a specified price. When the RPs mature, the added reserves are automatically drained.

However, when there is a temporary need to drain reserves, *matched sale-purchase transactions* (*MSPs*) with dealers are executed. These transactions involve a contract for immediate sale of treasury bills to, and a linked matching contract for subsequent purchase from, each participating dealer.

> **Money Meanings**
>
> **Repurchase agreements** are contracts the New York Fed makes with securities dealers. The New York Fed buys securities from the dealers, who agree to repurchase them by a specified date at a specified price.
>
> **Matched sale-purchase transaction** is a transaction that is immediately followed by the sale of treasury bills by the Trading Desk at the New York Federal Reserve Bank. The New York Fed sells T-bills to the system portfolio to dealers, at the same time it agrees to purchase the same obligations generally in one to seven days.

On occasion, the Desk may engage in outright purchases or sales of securities. In these transactions, dealers are requested to submit offers to sell or bids to buy securities of the type and maturity that the Desk has selected. The lowest prices offered for purchases and the highest prices bid for sales are chosen until the desired size of the transaction is reached. These transactions effectively add or drain reserves on a permanent basis. They address persistent needs to adjust the supply of reserves, as for example those arising from the public's demand for currency.

The Trading Desk initiates trades by sending an electronic message to all primary dealers. The message contains the type of transaction (for example, RP, MSP, outright purchase, outright sale) and the term of operation, but not the size (that is announced later). Dealers submit propositions and receive results electronically. The propositions are evaluated on a competitive best-price basis. Dealers are notified of the results, usually within five minutes after the bids or offers were due. The Open Market Desk uses software programs to facilitate the selection process for the transactions. Once the selection is complete, the total volume of transactions is reported back to the dealers.

In addition to the daily conference call, the Open Market Trading Desk communicates with the FOMC in a number of ways:

 - Two daily reports
 - A weekly report on financial market developments
 - A biweekly report on open market operations for each maintenance period

- An inter-meeting period report on operations and financial market developments prepared for each FOMC meeting

- The manager's report at the regular FOMC meeting

- An annual report on monetary policy operations

Operating Abroad

The New York Fed doesn't only control the U.S. Open Market Operations, it also has responsibility for the foreign exchange (FX) market. In the FX market, individuals, businesses, banks, and governments buy and sell the currencies of different countries to finance international trade, invest, or speculate on currency price changes.

Approximately $1.5 trillion in different currencies is traded daily in the FX market around the world. A change in the value of a foreign currency in the FX market affects the international purchasing power of the dollar. Movements in exchange rates can occur for a variety of reasons, and traders in the FX market react quickly to protect their positions or to make a speculative profit.

There are two primary types of transactions in the FX market:

- A spot transaction, which is an agreement to buy or sell currency at the current exchange rate. These transactions are typically settled two days later.

- A forward transaction is the purchase or sale of currency at a predetermined exchange rate with a settlement three days or more after the transaction. This type of transaction is a hedge against exchange rate risk.

Time for an Intervention

The United States uses foreign exchange intervention to slow rapid exchange rate moves and to signal to the markets that the United States believes that the exchange rate does not reflect fundamental economic conditions.

The U.S. Treasury is responsible for setting foreign exchange rates. The Treasury consults with the Fed in deciding the timing and nature of a foreign exchange intervention and the FX Trading Desk at the New York Fed executes the intervention by buying or selling currency in the spot exchange. The foreign currencies used to intervene usually come from Federal Reserve holdings and the Exchange Stabilization Fund of the Treasury. Currently these holdings consist of euros and Japanese yen.

Fiscal Facts _____

U.S. foreign exchange interventions have become much less frequent since the mid-1990s. The United States intervened in the foreign exchange market on eight different days in 1995, but only twice from mid-August 1995 through January 2002. This was mainly due to the stability of the foreign exchange markets. There was a minimum of volatility in the exchanges between pound sterling, Japanese yen, and other major currency vis à vis the dollar.

Not all New York Fed Trading Desk activities in the FX market are directed by the Treasury Department or Federal Reserve. Often the New York Fed will act as an agent on behalf of other central banks and international organizations. These purchases and sales are not considered to be U.S. FX intervention, and are not intended to reflect any policy initiative of the U.S. monetary authorities.

A foreign central bank can instruct the New York Fed either to conduct an open intervention operation, in which the New York Fed deals directly with inter-bank dealers in the FX market, or to conduct a discreet operation, in which the Fed enters into the brokers' market through a selected inter-bank dealer under a confidential agreement.

In an open intervention, the Fed confirms that it is acting on behalf of the foreign central bank while the operation is conducted. In a discreet intervention, the foreign central bank most often leaves the FX market with the perception of increased natural demand or supply in the currencies involved. In both cases, the Fed avoids signaling an official U.S. intervention.

The Federal Reserve routinely "sterilizes" intervention in the FX market, which prevents the intervention from changing the amount of bank reserves from levels consistent with established monetary policy goals. For instance, if the Fed sells dollars to buy a foreign currency, the sale adds reserves to the banking system.

To sterilize the transaction, the Fed, in its domestic open market transactions, may remove reserves through the sale of government securities. When the Federal Reserve buys and sells currencies on behalf of foreign central banks, the aggregate level of bank reserves does not change, and sterilization is not needed.

The New York Fed—at Your Service

On behalf of the Federal Reserve System, the Federal Reserve Bank of New York offers banking and financial services to over 200 foreign central banks. In addition to providing the foreign exchange services we discussed above, the New York FRB also offers services in demand deposit transactions, investments, and custodial and safekeeping.

In 2001, the New York Fed handled about $8.5 trillion in funds transfers for foreign accounts via *Fedwire*. Foreign account holders also can send U.S. currency to the bank for deposit in their accounts. Remember, these aren't accounts with individuals or businesses—they are accounts for central banks of other countries and international official institutions.

> **Money Meanings**
>
> **Fedwire** is an electronic transfer system that enables financial institutions to transfer funds and securities nationwide. In addition to serving the needs of the Fed banks, the U.S. Treasury and other government agencies, Fedwire connects more than 9,000 online and offline depository institutions. Most large-dollar international funds transfers are handled through Fedwire, or a private sector funds transfer network called CHIPS.

The New York Fed also invests funds for foreign central banks. Investments may be in overnight repurchase agreements, federal funds, or U.S. Treasury and other securities. In 2001, the New York Fed invested about $9.5 trillion on behalf of foreign official institutions.

Many of the assets held by foreign official accounts at the bank are held in the form of marketable U.S. government and agency securities, most of which are deposited in electronic (book-entry) form at the New York Fed. At year-end 2001, foreign official and international accounts held more than $750 billion in U.S. dollar-denominated assets.

Safekeeping services include presenting the securities to the paying agency for coupon-interest payments and for redemption at maturity. The bank provides facilities for the clearing and settlement of a customer's own investment trades. In 2001, these securities settlement transactions amounted to about $9 trillion.

Getting to Be the Leader

How does one get to be the head of the New York Federal Reserve Board? Well, it helped several of them to have been at the top or near the top of Wall Street investment banking houses. It certainly helped a couple of them to have been presidents of the smaller Federal Reserve banks. And of course the friendships and the working relationships you have with the power center persons, the Paul Volckers of your day, may be the most important factor, together with your outstanding record.

The New York Fed's president has a number of international roles not just dealing with foreign bankers with their big branch headquarters in New York. A primary example is Bill McDonough, who has served several years as head of the Basle Committee, which includes representatives of the 10 countries who coordinate supervisory policy for internationally active banks.

McDonough was an outstanding commercial banker based in Chicago developing financial institutions of various kinds, as he was chief executive of one of Chicago's largest banks. His contacts in the international field were such that he first served in Basle on the international banking council and they insisted that he become its chairman.

McDonough has been the chairman of that international committee for several years and he has been a genuine contributor in their work to standardize the capital requirements and measurements for commercial banks around the world. Have they finally reached a final conclusion? Probably not, but they have made real impact on the thinking of the supervisors in most of those countries and how to evaluate the adequacy of capital relative to the risk-taking for the commercial banks and other financial institutions and countries.

Now you know why the New York Federal Reserve Bank is the most powerful of the Fed's banks. You can also understand why it is critical for the president of the New York Fed to be a standing member of the FOMC (remember that membership rotates). He has the most knowledge of day-to-day details of Open Market operations as well as foreign exchange operations. The other reserve banks have crucial roles as well. We'll take a closer look at their responsibilities in the next chapter.

The Least You Need to Know

- ◆ Crisis management is most often led by the New York Fed.
- ◆ The New York Fed is the largest reserve bank in terms of assets and volume of activity.
- ◆ Government securities trading is managed by the New York Fed through its Open Market operations desk.
- ◆ The New York Fed often acts as an agent on behalf of foreign central banks and international organizations.

Chapter **8**

Your Bank's Bank

In This Chapter

- ◆ Picking the locations
- ◆ Where your bank goes for money
- ◆ Membership has its privileges
- ◆ Checks, checks, and more checks

Billions and billions and more billions. We're not talking Carl Sagan and the universe. We're talking about billions of dollars, right in your neighborhood.

Most people don't realize that there are 12 Federal Reserve banks in moderate-to-large-size American cities. These banks don't have drive through windows or ATMs, and you don't get a toaster when you open a new account. But they're just about the most important banks in, well, the universe.

Those 12 Federal Reserve banks, with those billions in assets and all those examiners checking out the commercial banks in your multi-state "district," aren't very well known. The media only pays attention to the Federal banks when there is some failing institution or a "run" by panicky bank depositors. Yet here they sit in 12 prominent cities, with 1,220 (St. Louis) to 3,826 (New York) employees and expense budgets ranging from $109.9 million (Minneapolis) to $263.1 million (San Francisco)—and that was for 1998!

These banks have branches in which much of the check clearing, and some of the wire transferring, is done. Visit your Fed bank or its branch and avail yourself of their public tours. Look at all that money! All those Federal Reserve notes stacked up in there! Nice, huh? Too bad they don't give green souvenirs with pictures of dead presidents at the end of the tours!

Why So Many Banks?

Why did the 1913 Congress establish so many banks and branches? They had a motto back then: "No bank should be more than an overnight's train ride from its Reserve bank."

Preston's Points
I have mixed feelings about this new Fed HQ in Washington, mainly due to my own experience when I was chairman of the other central bank, the Federal Home Loan Bank Board, in the 1970s. At that time, there were enough political repercussions over tearing down a local YMCA to erect our headquarters. We did it! I can only imagine what my successors will have to undergo should they choose to tear down the building I erected!

Today, these regional banking centers are important not only for the services they offer to the banks, but also for their research on the health of the economy within their regions. Today, the system is growing so rapidly that the FRB is already adding its third headquarter edifice in downtown Washington, D.C.

Unlike regular banks, Federal Reserve banks do not offer features such as check cashing or mortgage loans. So, if Federal Reserve banks don't provide "traditional" banking services, what do they do?

Reserve banks hold the deposit and cash reserves of depository institutions (commercial banks and *thrift institution* members) and make loans to their member institutions. They move currency and coin into and out of circulation, collect and process millions of checks each day, provide checking accounts for the U.S. Treasury, issue and redeem government securities, and act as fiscal agents for the U.S. government.

In short, the Federal Reserve banks provide banking services for "bankers" and the U.S. government. As if that weren't enough, they also regulate and supervise the banks in their district to make sure that your money stays safe. We will discuss this in more detail later in this chapter.

Money Meanings _____

A **thrift institution** is an association or bank that was started primarily for the purpose of savings and home mortgage loans. They include savings and loan associations and mutual savings banks. Traditionally these were different from commercial banks because thrifts were not allowed to have demand accounts (checking accounts). Deposits were savings accounts, and those dollars were typically used for home mortgage loans (like the building and loan bank in *It's a Wonderful Life*). In recent years, legislation has been enacted permitting thrifts to offer the same consumer services offered by commercial banks.

Auspicious Beginnings

How did the whole system come about? The Federal Reserve Act of 1913 required the designation of not less than eight or more than 12 cities as "Federal Reserve cities," and that only one Fed bank be located in each of the 12 designated districts.

The task of selecting the central bank location cities was the responsibility of the Reserve Bank Organization Committee. The committee consisted of the Secretary of the Treasury, William McAdoo; the Secretary of Agriculture, David F. Houston; and the Comptroller of the Currency, John Skelton Williams. The trio traveled across the country, visiting 18 cities and taking testimony on the location of district cities and district boundaries. (Records of the expense account for their trip don't survive!)

Money Tips _____

Federal Reserve banks process all of the checks consumers and businesses write each day. For example, you write a check to pay your electric bill. The check is drawn from your account at Bank of America. You mail your check to the electric company, who deposits it in their account at Wells Fargo. Wells Fargo sends the check to the local Federal Reserve bank for clearing. Because all national banks (both Wells Fargo and Bank of America are national banks) are members of the Federal Reserve, the Fed branch bank processes the check, credits Wells Fargo's reserve account for the money, and debits Bank of America, who will then debit your account for the amount of the check. This isn't the only way that checks can clear. Banks may clear checks directly with other banks through clearinghouse associations or other services. The Federal Reserve bank system clears about one-third of the checks processed annually.

At the same time, the Treasury Department sent ballots to more than 7,400 nationally chartered banks to determine their preference for their district headquarters. The committee chose 12 cities as Reserve bank locations (shown in the following figure) in part because of their importance as banking and commerce centers in 1913.

Another critical factor in the decision was transportation, which played an essential role in business growth in the early 1900s and was important in the selection process. A transportation center usually had banking and business interests that supported a region. Furthermore, the amount of capital in a district was critical. The region had to be financially capable of supporting the Fed. And, of course, there were political pressures from members of Congress and business and banking interests nationwide who wanted the prestige endowed on a particular city of their choosing.

Here you see the 12 Federal Reserve bank city locations and their respective regions.

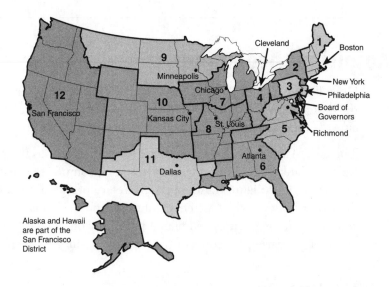

It came as no surprise that not everyone agreed with the committee's decision as to where to locate the 12 Federal Reserve banks. In total, there were eight petitions for review filed with the Federal Reserve Board—the only group with the power to change the original plan. While the Board redrew some district boundaries, all of the original 12 selected cities survived.

Finding Your Local Reserve Bank

The districts set out by the 1913 committee still exist today, having undergone little change since the original district lines were drawn. Do you know which district you are in? (See the preceding map.) Let's take a closer look at each of these banks and their branches.

District 1: Federal Reserve Bank of Boston

600 Atlantic Avenue
Boston, MA 02106
www.bos.frb.org

The Boston Fed serves the states of Connecticut (excluding Fairfield County), Massachusetts, Maine, New Hampshire, Rhode Island, and Vermont. The Federal Reserve bank of Boston is one of only two Federal Reserve banks that doesn't have a branch located elsewhere in its district.

District 2: Federal Reserve Bank of New York

33 Liberty Street
New York, NY 10045
www.ny.frb.org

The New York Fed serves the state of New York, the 12 northern counties of New Jersey, Fairfield County in Connecticut, Puerto Rico, and the Virgin Islands. The New York Fed has a branch office in Buffalo and two regional check processing centers in Utica, New York and East Rutherford, New Jersey. Even though the New York Fed serves a very small geographic area, it is the largest Federal Reserve bank in size of assets and volume of activity. As we discussed in the Chapter 7, the New York Fed conducts open market operations, intervenes in foreign exchange markets and stores gold for foreign banks, governments, and international agencies.

District 3: Federal Reserve Bank of Philadelphia

10 Independence Mall
Philadelphia, PA 19106-1521
www.phil.frb.org

The Philadelphia Fed serves eastern Pennsylvania, southern New Jersey, and the entire state of Delaware. The Federal Reserve bank of Philadelphia is the other (besides Boston) Federal Reserve bank not to have a branch elsewhere in its district.

District 4: Federal Reserve Bank of Cleveland

1455 East Sixth Street
Cleveland, OH 44114
www.clev.frb.org

The Cleveland Fed serves the Fourth Federal Reserve District, which includes all of Ohio, eastern Kentucky, western Pennsylvania, and the northern panhandle of West Virginia. The bank also has a check-processing center in Columbus, Ohio and Pittsburgh, Pennsylvania.

District 5: Federal Reserve Bank of Richmond

701 East Byrd Street
Richmond, VA 23261
www.rich.frb.org

The Richmond Fed serves the Fifth Federal Reserve District, which includes Maryland, the District of Columbia, Virginia, North Carolina, South Carolina, and most of West Virginia. The District has branch offices in Baltimore, Maryland and Charlotte, North Carolina, and two check-processing centers, one in Charleston and Columbia, South Carolina.

District 6: Federal Reserve Bank of Atlanta

1000 Peachtree Street N.E.
Atlanta, GA 30309-4470
www.frbatlanta.org

The Atlanta Fed serves the sixth Federal Reserve District and includes Alabama, Florida, Georgia, and parts of Louisiana, Mississippi, and Tennessee, with branches located in Birmingham, Alabama; Jacksonville and Miami, Florida; Nashville, Tennessee; and New Orleans, Louisiana.

District 7: Federal Reserve Bank of Chicago

230 South LaSalle Street
Chicago, IL 60604
www.chicagofed.org

The Chicago Fed serves the Seventh Federal Reserve District that includes all of Iowa and most of Illinois, Indiana, Michigan, and Wisconsin. The Chicago Fed has a branch office in Detroit.

Money Tips ————————

The St. Louis Fed maintains the FRED database (www.stls.frb.org/fred/index.html), which provides consumers, students, and select institutions with economic and financial information in an easy-to-use format.

FRED is a number nerd's heaven. Just about every statistic ever published by the Federal Reserve and the Treasury is available here in a downloadable format. From the consumer price index of the 1940s and the monetary aggregates (the M's) of the 1950s, to interest rates on all government issuances from as far back as the 1920s. This is a great resource for students doing research on economic trends, economics teachers, or simply those with a fiscal curiosity—or just a little too much free time.

District 8: Federal Reserve Bank of St. Louis

411 Locust Street
St. Louis, MO 63102
www.stls.frb.org

The St. Louis Fed serves the Eighth Federal Reserve District, which includes eastern Missouri, western Kentucky, northern Mississippi, and all of Arkansas. In addition to the Federal Reserve bank in St. Louis, the Eighth District has branch offices located in Little Rock, Arkansas; Louisville, Kentucky; and Memphis, Tennessee.

District 9: Federal Reserve Bank of Minneapolis

90 Hennepin Avenue
PO Box 291
Minneapolis, MN 55480-0291
minneapolisfed.org

The Minneapolis Fed serves the Ninth Federal Reserve District that includes Minnesota, Montana, North and South Dakota, 26 counties in northwestern Wisconsin, and the Upper Peninsula of Michigan. The Minneapolis Fed has one branch in Helena, Montana.

Fiscal Facts ————————

During the construction of the new Minneapolis Fed headquarters, in June 1997, a time capsule was sealed and placed in the building cornerstone at First Street and Hennepin Avenue in Minneapolis. Items selected for inclusion highlight current bank operations, depict employee life, detail construction of the new building, and include current bank and local news publications. A duplicate set of materials is stored in the bank's archives to be opened at a later date—perhaps its 100th anniversary.

District 10: Federal Reserve Bank of Kansas City

925 Grand Boulevard
Kansas City, MO 64198
www.kc.frb.org

The Tenth Federal Reserve District includes Western Missouri, Kansas, Nebraska, Oklahoma, Wyoming, Colorado, and Northern New Mexico. In addition to the Federal Reserve bank in Kansas City, there are branch offices in Denver, Colorado; Omaha, Nebraska; and Oklahoma City, Oklahoma.

The Money Museum, located in the Federal Reserve bank in Kansas City, is the home to the Truman Coin Collection, which includes over 450 coins dating all the way back to George Washington's presidential administration.

District 11: Federal Reserve Bank of Dallas

2200 North Pearl Street
Dallas, TX 75201
www.dallasfed.org

The Eleventh Federal Reserve District includes Texas, northern Louisiana, and southern New Mexico, with branches in Houston, El Paso, and San Antonio, Texas.

District 12: Federal Reserve Bank of San Francisco

101 Market Street
San Francisco, CA 94105
www.frbsf.org

The Twelfth Federal Reserve District includes Alaska, Arizona, California, Hawaii, Idaho, Nevada, Oregon, Utah, and Washington—plus American Samoa, Guam, and the Northern Mariana Islands. Branch offices are located in Los Angeles, California; Portland, Oregon; Salt Lake City, Utah; and Seattle, Washington.

The Twelfth District is the largest in geographic area, covering 1.3 million square miles, or 35 percent of the nation's area, and ranks first in the size of the U.S. economy.

You may be wondering why one bank has responsibility for so much territory. Remember this was decided in 1913. Arizona was a relatively new state and the states of Alaska and Hawaii were still years away from becoming a state.

Getting to the Branches

Because the size of the districts in some cases was quite large, the Federal Reserve Act provided for branches. In order to serve entire districts it was necessary to have multiple locations. Only the Federal Reserve bank of Boston and the Federal Reserve bank of Philadelphia don't have branches located elsewhere in their district because the geographic size of their districts is fairly small. Here's a chart that shows the branches.

Federal Reserve District	Bank Location	Branch Locations
1	Boston	No branches
2	New York	Buffalo, New York
3	Philadelphia	No branches
4	Cleveland	Cincinnati, Ohio Pittsburgh, Pennsylvania
5	Richmond	Baltimore, Maryland Charlotte, North Carolina
6	Atlanta	Birmingham, Alabama Jacksonville, Florida Miami, Florida Nashville, Tennessee New Orleans, Louisiana
7	Chicago	Detroit, Michigan
8	St. Louis	Little Rock, Arkansas Louisville, Kentucky Memphis, Tennessee
9	Minneapolis	Helena, Montana
10	Kansas City	Denver, Colorado Oklahoma City, Oklahoma Omaha, Nebraska
11	Dallas	El Paso, Texas Houston, Texas San Antonio, Texas
12	San Francisco	Los Angeles, California Salt Lake City, Utah Portland, Oregon Seattle, Washington

Membership Has Its Privileges

All national banks (NA) are required by law to be a member of their regional Federal Reserve bank. At the end of 2000, the Federal Reserve System had 3,164 member banks with 47,722 banking offices. State banks are not required to join the Federal Reserve System, but they may elect to become members if they meet the standards set by the Board of Governors.

Member banks must subscribe to stock in their regional Federal Reserve bank, but Federal Reserve stock is not like publicly traded stock. Reserve bank stock cannot be traded, sold, or pledged as collateral for a loan. It is simply a legal obligation that goes along with membership. Reserve bank stock is not available for purchase by individuals.

A nine–member board of directors supervises each Federal Reserve bank. These individuals are a collection of bankers and businesspeople who are familiar with economic and credit conditions in the district. Member banks in the district elect six of the directors, while the remaining three are appointed by the Board of Governors in Washington. The Board of Governors designates one of the directors as chairman and another as deputy chairman, each for one-year terms. This procedure adds to the independence of the Reserve system because the directors are not chosen by politicians, but by members of the business and banking communities to provide a cross section of interests from each district.

Money Tips

State banks are generally smaller in asset size than national banks and many define themselves as "community banks." There is a perception that with a state charter the community banks have more access to the political structure in the state, allowing them to influence legislation that might be of benefit to them locally. They are also regulated by multiple agencies, the state banking commissioner, and the Fed for state-chartered banks that are members of the Fed system. National banks are supervised by the OCC (Office of the Comptroller of the Currency).

There are three classes of directors:

- ◆ Class A directors elected by member banks to represent them
- ◆ Class B directors elected by member banks to represent the public interest
- ◆ Class C directors elected by the Board of Governors to represent the public interest

Directors cannot be members of Congress, and because a Reserve bank directorship is a form of public service, directors are also expected to avoid participating in partisan political activities.

Although they are part-time, Reserve bank directors have important responsibilities, which are assigned by the Federal Reserve Act. They include contributing to the formulation of monetary policy, commenting on major organizational changes, evaluating management performance, and reviewing officers' salaries. One of the most important responsibilities of the Federal Reserve Board is to appoint the bank's president, who is the chief executive officer, and the first vice president, who is the chief administrative officer. These appointments, subject to FRB approval, are for five-year terms.

Annually, the directors appoint the District's representative to the Federal Advisory Council, the Thrift Institutions Advisory Council, and the Consumer Advisory Council. These groups meet on a regular basis with the Board of Governors to consult and advise the board on all matters within the board's jurisdiction. (Each of these groups are discussed in depth in Chapter 9.)

Supervising Banks

As we have discussed, one of the reasons for the establishment of the Federal Reserve System was to prevent repeats of the liquidity crises and financial panics that occurred in the United States prior to 1913. The Fed is one of several government regulatory agencies sharing the responsibility for supervising and examining depository institutions to ensure the financial strength and stability of the nation's banking system.

Money Tips

Fed banks have substantial contact with the communities they serve. Bank management meets with their "district directors," advisory council members, audit committees (one committee for each branch), the boards from each branch, Fed governors who come out to review policy matters, and sessions at which Fed "alumni," like your author, come to complain (and advise).

Each Federal Reserve bank has a staff that conducts examinations of all member institutions. In 1985, the Board adopted a policy requiring Federal Reserve banks to examine all state member banks and large bank holding companies annually.

Banks are examined for:

- Soundness of the their assets and the effectiveness of internal operations, policies, and management

- Capital, earnings, liquidity, and sensitivity to interest rate risk

- Exposure to off-balance-sheet risks

- Compliance with banking laws and regulations, particularly lending to moderate and low-income households

- Overall safety and soundness

Visiting the Discount Window

I mentioned earlier that you can't open an account at your local Federal Reserve bank. But your bank can! (I still don't think they get toasters when they open new accounts, though.) If your bank gets a little low on money, it can go to the discount window and get some cash. Nice, huh?

The quantity of borrowing at the Discount Window tends to be small because the Fed requires that members exhaust all other alternative sources (Federal funds market, loans from correspondent banks, etc.) before borrowing at the window. The rate charged at the window is called the discount rate. By law the discount rate is set every two weeks by the directors of each Reserve bank, and is subject to approval or disapproval of the Board of Governors.

The discount rate is important because changes are interpreted by the market as indicators of monetary policy. An increase in the discount rate would indicate the Fed's concern over inflationary pressures, while a rate decrease often reflects a concern over weakness in the economy. Remember we talked about how the FOMC set this rate in Chapter 4. We'll take a closer look at what goes into changing this rate and the target rate in the next chapter.

Your Money's Route

The Treasury Department ships new paper money printed at the Treasury Office in Washington and coins to the Federal Reserve banks. The Reserve banks pay it out to commercial banks, savings and loan associations, and other depository institutions. Customers of these institutions withdraw cash as they need it. During periods of heavy cash demand, such as the Christmas season, institutions obtain larger amounts of cash from the Federal Reserve banks or their branches. When public demand for cash is light, institutions deposit excess cash with the Reserve banks for credit to their reserve accounts.

Ever wonder what happens to money when it gets old, torn, and wrinkled? There's no liposuction for money that doesn't age well. In fact, it's disposed of in a rather ignominious manner! As currency wears out or becomes damaged, depository institutions redeposit them at the Reserve banks to be exchanged for new bills. The old bills are ground up and handed out to bank visitors. Sorry, no whole samples even of worn bills.

Fiscal Facts

Federal Reserve banks process currency from member banks. As a part of this process, they routinely remove unfit currency from circulation. The New York Fed shreds unfit currency, mixes the remains up, and compresses it into a briquette weighing about two pounds. Each briquette is made up of about 1,000 notes and is disposed at a landfill. Some Reserve banks sell shredded currency to businesses and other Reserve banks turn the shreds into stationery.

Reserve banks destroy unfit currency and return damaged and worn coins to the U.S. Treasury. The Bureau of Engraving and Printing, a Washington division of the U.S. Treasury Department, produces currency for the Federal Reserve banks to replace the damaged or worn notes. Federal Reserve banks issue currency according to the need in their districts. The district letter and number on the face of a note will identify the issuing Reserve bank. For example, a note with "L12" underneath the serial number on the face of the note was issued by the Federal Reserve bank of San Francisco. You can find a chart of each bank's note number in Chapter 1.

Making Some Money?

The Monetary Control Act of 1980 required the Federal Reserve to set prices for its services in much the same way as any other business. Before 1980, the Federal Reserve offered its services only to member banks. After passage of the act, the Federal Reserve had to offer its services to nonmember institutions (including state banks) and to price the services to include a private sector adjustment factor (PSAF). The PSAF is an allowance for taxes and other imputed costs that the Federal Reserve would have to pay if they were a private business rather than a government agency. You can view the current year fee schedule at the Federal Reserve Financial Services website www. frbservices.org. Some of the fee–based services Federal Reserve banks offer are listed in the following sections, along with a brief description.

Check Clearing

Many of us pay for our purchases with checks. Yes, I know that your kids keep arguing that you should use that PC and pay electronically. But today, American individuals and businesses still write more than 60 billion paper checks a year. Checks are a reliable and convenient form of payment that we are all used to, one that is accepted for most financial transactions. Plus, you probably like using them as receipts for tax purposes.

Federal Reserve banks and branches process about 18 billion of these checks each year. Banks also clear checks directly with each other, either through clearinghouse associations or agreements with other banks.

In 1979, the Fed pushed to accomplish "controlled disbursement," meaning check clearing in real time without geographical delays. What this means is that there would be no more "float" time, or free use of the check amount until your bank account was actually debited (charged).

The Fed's check-processing machinery sorts checks at speeds up to 100,000 checks per hour, transferring funds from the bank of origin to the bank of deposit. The routing numbers printed in magnetic ink on the bottom of each check tell the Fed's computers which banks to debit and credit through the accounts that banks hold with the Federal Reserve. Now you know the purpose of that long string of numbers at the bottom of your check.

Automated Clearinghouse (ACH)

Improvements in computer technology have led to the development of electronic alternatives to the paper-based check system as a means of payment. The Automated Clearinghouse (ACH) provides an electronic means to exchange debit and credit entries between depository institutions and customer accounts for such transactions as automatic payroll deposits and bill payment. Your retired dad receives his monthly social security funding by the transmitting of a record of the amount to his account. The evolution of this payment revolution has taken decades, even with leadership (and funding) by the Fed. It wasn't until 1985 that user volume facilitated full-cost pricing, which is a fancy way of saying that things get cheaper when there's more volume. This is also the way your paycheck gets to your bank account. Don't you love the convenience of not having to run to the bank each payday?

Fedwire

For larger transactions, debits and credits are transferred electronically through Fedwire, a highly sophisticated, computerized communications system that can transfer funds almost instantly from one depository institution to another anywhere in this country or the world.

Fedwire is used by Federal Reserve banks and branches, the Treasury and other government agencies, and over 9,000 depository institutions, most of them with online access that allows them to communicate directly with the Fedwire network. In 2000, over 100 million fund transfers were completed over the Fedwire system with a total value of $380 trillion. Transfers over Fedwire require relatively little bookkeeping.

Doing Your Part

If you are active in community affairs or you are running a successful company, consider serving on your region's Federal Bank's board, or at least on its Consumer Advisory Committee. Do some handshaking and get the Fed president to help you get there. If that doesn't appeal to you, get yourself invited to your Fed bank's Consumer Advisory Committee and then maneuver yourself into a membership role in that group. We'll talk more about how you can get involved in Chapter 24.

Now that you know more about how the Fed, its banks and its branches operate, we're going to take you further inside to visit the Fed Committees and learn more about how everything gets done each day. We'll also look at how monetary policy gets made and what goes into changing the discount rate, the Federal funds target, and the money supply.

The Least You Need to Know

- There are 12 Federal Reserve bank districts.
- All national banks are required to be members of their district's Federal Reserve bank.
- The Fed's services are available to nonmember banks as long as they pay the fees.
- The arduous task of check clearing more than 18 billion checks per year has been expedited thanks to efforts made by the Federal Reserve.

9

Going Behind the Scenes

In This Chapter

- ◆ Staffing structure
- ◆ Supervising the banks
- ◆ Policing payments
- ◆ Getting outside help

Unless you work for a bank that is supervised by the Federal Reserve, you probably don't know the names of any Federal Reserve staff. Very rarely are Fed staff members mentioned or seen publicly. Occasionally division directors do testify before Congress, but if you have run into a Fed staffer it's more likely that you work for a bank or attended an educational program at which Fed staff participated.

You may have seen stories about Fed staffer Donald Kohn when President Bush announced that he was being nominated to the Board of Governors. Kohn is Greenspan's right-hand man and is thought to be the one person who really knows how Greenspan reads the numbers and makes decisions. I worked with Don in my years at the Board.

Staffers don't often get the chance to serve on the FRB. If his nomination is successful (his nomination was still in front of the Senate Committee when this book was written), he will be the third Federal Reserve staffer to be appointed directly to the FRB in the history of the Fed. My outstanding colleague at the Board, Lyle Gramley, had been a staffer.

The Fed staff is critical to the operation of the Fed. While members of the FRB are appointed by the president and confirmed by the Senate, Federal Reserve staff are not regular "government employees." The Federal Reserve System was designed to be both a public and private entity operating independently within the federal government.

We'll take a tour behind the scenes and see how the staff works to keep this money machine humming.

Getting Things Divided

First, we'll look at how the staff is structured. Staff is divided into eight divisions plus the Office of Board Members. The eight divisions are as follows:

- Research and Statistics
- Monetary Affairs
- International Finance
- Banking, Supervision, and Regulation
- Consumer and Community Affairs
- Reserve Bank Operations and Payment Systems
- Information Resources Management
- Legal

You can get a gist of their responsibilities just by reading the staff division names. The Board then groups these divisions based on how they fit within the Federal Reserve's key functions—Monetary Policy, Supervision and Regulation, Payment System Policy and Oversight—to meet its stated goals, which are:

- **Monetary Policy.** To conduct monetary policy that promotes the achievement of maximum sustainable long-term growth; price stability fosters that goal.
- **Supervision and Regulation.** To promote a safe, sound, competitive, and accessible banking system and stable financial markets.
- **Payment System Policy and Oversight.** To provide high-quality professional oversight of Reserve Bank operations and to foster the integrity, efficiency, and accessibility of U.S. payment and settlement systems.

Let's take a closer look at the individual roles each division plays in helping the Fed to meet these goals.

Monetary Policy Function

Three divisions share responsibility for monetary policy function:

- ◆ Research and Statistics
- ◆ Money Affairs
- ◆ International Finance

These are the three divisions that directly support the monetary policy decision-making of the FOMC.

The Division of Research and Statistics is the one that compiles all that economic and financial data the board and the FOMC members need. It also provides needed information to system officials regarding the implementation of board and FOMC decisions.

The Division of Money Affairs, which was headed by Donald Kohn before he became Greenspan's chief aide, supports the Board and the FOMC in developing and implementing monetary policy through open market operations, the Discount Window, and reserve requirements. We took a close look at this role in Chapter 4. We also looked at Open Market operations and the Discount Window when we reviewed the workings of the New York Fed in Chapter 7.

> **Money Tips**
>
> One overriding responsibility for all divisions of Federal Reserve staff is research. If you'd like to explore the research studies done by staff and published by Fed, go to www.federalreserve.gov/rnd.htm.

Also, as you know from our discussions in Chapter 4, the Division of International Finance plays a major role in advising the board, FOMC, and system officials regarding international economic and financial developments. It evaluates what's happening and provides forecasts of major economic and financial developments abroad, developments in foreign exchange, and other international asset markets.

We've talked a lot about how monetary policy is formed in Chapter 4 and bank operations in Chapter 7, so we won't spend much time on this function in this chapter. Instead we'll take a closer look at some of the other key roles Fed staff plays.

> **Economic Wisdom** _____
>
> "An administration official said Mr. Kohn may be able to explain, in a way others can use, the chairman's 'cookbook,' the eclectic combination of data, anecdotes, theory and intuition that have made his economic steering so successful. … Mr. Kohn joined the board in 1975, became the head of the newly created Division of Monetary Affairs in 1987, and last year was bumped up to the new post of adviser to Mr. Greenspan and the board. As head of monetary affairs, Mr. Kohn was responsible for the "Bluebook," a document prepared for each policy meeting outlining possible interest-rate actions Fed officials might take and the likely consequences of each. As such, he has been deeply involved in the nitty-gritty of implementing and communicating monetary policy."
>
> —The Wall Street Journal, reporting the news that Donald Kohn would be nominated to serve as a Federal Reserve governor, May 8, 2002.

Supervision and Regulation Function

The supervision and regulatory function also encompasses three divisions:

- Banking Supervision and Regulation
- Consumer and Community Affairs
- Legal

All three can have a direct impact on you, your bank, your credit, and your protection against fraud.

Supervising the Banks

Let's start with the division that has the largest staff—Banking Supervision and Regulation. These are the folks that go out to your bank with their colleagues from the District Fed bank and make sure it's operating in a "safe, sound, competitive, and accessible" manner. They do get involved in other special issues as well, which we'll discuss below.

You may think the Federal Reserve bank examiners are just like accounting auditors. That's not the case. In the mid-1990s the Federal Reserve thought it could make better use of its examiner resources by focusing on the areas of greatest risk to a particular bank.

Federal examiners start by performing a risk assessment of a bank before it even begins any on-site supervisory activities. These risk assessments include identifying the significant activities of a bank, determining the risks inherent in those activities, and assessing the processes a bank has in place to identify, measure, monitor, and control these risks. If a bank has good risk-management processes in place, the examiners can rely on the bank's internal risk assessments rather than perform their own supervisory tests. Banks pay for these examinations, so anything they can do to minimize examiners' time saves them money.

Federal examiners rate each bank by a system called CAMELS. No we're not talking about bringing any animals into a bank. Wouldn't that create some interesting press coverage! CAMELS is an acronym that stands for:

- **C**apital adequacy—how a bank's capital compares to the capital of other banks.

- **A**sset quality—looks at the quality of existing loan and investment portfolios.

- **M**anagement and administrative ability—rates the capability of the bank's board of directors, its audit committees, and management.

- **E**arnings level and quality—looks at the level and trend of a bank's earnings.

- **L**iquidity level—looks at whether a bank can meet its daily cash obligations.

- **S**ensitivity to market risk—looks at how the banks may be impacted by outside risk such as changes in interest rates, foreign exchange rates, the regional economy, commodity prices, and equity prices that could adversely affect the bank's earnings.

Examiners rate a bank between "1" and "5" on each of these aspects. If a bank receives a "1," it indicates the systems in place are strong and less supervision is needed. A "5" would be the weakest rating and require the highest level of supervision.

Federal laws require that a bank undergo a full-scope, on-site examination at least once every 12 months. This can be extended to 18 months if the bank holds less than $250 million in total assets and it received a composite CAMELS rating of a 1 or 2. The bank also must not be subject to formal enforcement actions. The bank also must not have experienced a change

Money Tips

You can keep track of what the Banking Supervision and Regulation Division is doing via the Internet. Actions and orders are published here: www.federalreserve.gov/infoletters/banks/board/. There is a search facility if you want to check on any Federal Reserve actions related to a specific bank. The link for this facility can be found in the left column.

in control to qualify for the longer period between examinations. Problem banks are examined more frequently, some as much as twice a year. A problem bank may provide an office to examiners who "live there."

The Federal Reserve shares its examination responsibilities with the other regulators at both the state and federal level. All agencies involved in bank examination coordinate their examination schedules to inspect banks at about the same time. In Chapters 11 and 18 we'll take a closer look at the other agencies that get involved in bank examination.

Federal Reserve staff also have responsibility for inspecting *bank holding companies.* While the process is similar for examining assets, earnings, capital and management, there is an additional focus on other key aspects unique to holding companies. The acronym for the added inspection elements of bank holding company examinations is BOPEC (not to be confused with OPEC). This acronym stands for:

- ◆ **B**ank subsidiaries

- ◆ **O**ther (nonbank) subsidiaries

- ◆ **P**arent company

- ◆ **E**arnings consolidated

- ◆ **C**apital adequacy consolidated

The first three elements look at the company's fundamental soundness, while the two consolidated elements look at the role a holding company plays in providing financial strength and support to the entire organization. Management is rated for its role in banking, nonbanking, and parent company operations. Management can receive an "S" for satisfactory, "F" for fair, or a "U" for unsatisfactory. How frequently a holding company is inspected depends on asset size, the amount of public debt, and the level of non-banking activities.

Money Meanings

Bank holding companies are institutions that own two or more banks. They must register with the Fed.

In addition to examinations, the Banking Supervision and Regulation Division also does the following:

- ◆ Reports to the FRB regarding current and prospective developments in bank supervision and structure

- ◆ Processes applications to form or expand bank holding companies or make changes in banking structures

- ◆ Administers related regulations

Fiscal Facts

Many immigrant families do not have bank accounts but frequently must send money to the family back home. Western Union will do it, and there are a number of newcomers to the function. One example, Rapid Money, is based in San Antonio, Texas, and is licensed in Texas, Florida, and Kentucky as a "money transmitter." Rapid issues a card to the user, and when he or she brings good ol' U.S. currency to the Rapid Money office the card is used to print a receipt and move the money to Mexico or wherever. The recipient is telephoned, reminded of the family PIN number, and the money is made available in pesos or whatever. (Want to learn more about the process? www.rapidmoney.com/receive.html.)

This division is heavily involved in the Fed's implementation of the USA Patriot Act passed after the World Trade Center attack to address issues related to money laundering (illegal money transfers) and terrorist financing. The role of combating illicit activity through domestic and foreign banking organizations is not new to the Fed. In 1993, the Fed Board created the Special Investigations Section in this division to fight financial crimes such as money laundering.

Economic Wisdom

"Terrorist financing activities are unlike traditional money laundering in a very significant respect. Money used to finance terrorism does not always originate from criminal sources. Rather, it may be money derived from legitimate sources that is then used to support crimes. Developing programs that will help identify such funds before they can be used for their horrific purposes is a daunting task, but we are trying to meet this responsibility along with our colleagues at the U.S. Departments of Treasury and Justice, the Securities and Exchange Commission and other U.S. and international regulatory and law enforcement agencies."

—Richard Spillenkothen, Director, Division of Banking Supervision and Regulation, testifying before the Committee on Banking, Housing, and Urban Affairs, U.S. Senate, January 29, 2002

This division also works with law enforcement agencies as part of the interagency Suspicious Activity Reporting System. If examiners suspect a problem, they will report illicit activities to law enforcement agencies.

The Federal Reserve staff also provides training regarding banking issues to the U.S. Department of the Treasury's Federal Law Enforcement Training Center and the FBI

Academy. In addition, the staff provides training at the U.S. Secret Service and the U.S. Customs Service.

The Fed's money laundering training is not limited to U.S. shores. Federal Reserve staff have also helped to train law enforcement officials and central bank supervisory personnel in many countries including Russia, Poland, Hungary, Brazil, Argentina, and China, plus countries in the Middle East.

Looking Out for Consumers

The Division of Consumer and Community Affairs provides the board with the support it needs to carry out its federal consumer protection responsibilities. The division also administers and ensures that banks are in compliance with consumer protection laws including Truth in Lending, Truth in Savings, Consumer Leasing, and Electronic Funds Transfer.

The Fed seeks to strike a proper balance between protecting consumers and not placing unnecessary burdens on the banking industry. Some bankers will not agree that they have struck the right balance and many will complain about the paperwork required to show they've met their consumer obligations. Have you closed a loan recently? What did you think of all the papers you had to sign?

In addition to all that paperwork, Federal Reserve staff is also charged with a wide range of consumer protection issues including borrowing and savings disclosures, limits on liability for lost or stolen credit and debit cards, resolving errors in credit and debit transactions, and protections against abusive practices. These rules apply to all institutions serving customers, whether they are banks, finance companies, mortgage brokers, retailers, or others.

Consumer protection is a moving target, changing each time new types of scams and frauds are uncovered. Rules must be updated and interpreted regularly to respond to changing business practices. Fed staff also has responsibility for developing effective consumer education. We'll look more closely at consumer protection issues and education in Chapter 20.

Making Things Legal

We're sure you've realized by now the Fed Board has an incredible amount of legal mumbo jumbo to deal with every day. The Legal Division helps to keep the money machine on the straight and narrow by providing the Board with legal advice and services so it can meet its responsibilities under bank and supervisory statutes, as well as develop and implement regulations.

Setting Payment Policies

The Fed's payment system and policy oversight function falls under the responsibility of the Division of Reserve Bank Operations and Payment Systems. This division is responsible for the efficiency, effectiveness, and adequacy of Reserve bank financial services and fiscal agency services. It also recommends policies and regulations to the Board that will improve the efficiency and integrity of the U.S. payment system. The division works collaboratively with other central banks and international organizations to improve the payment system more broadly.

Economic Wisdom

"… [T]he U.S. payment system continues to evolve slowly, but there have been steady changes and a great deal of experimentation over the past few years. Although we are not likely to see paper payment instruments disappear, electronic payment systems are being used more widely and creatively than in the past. Online banking and other services are giving bank customers new and convenient mechanisms to initiate and receive electronic payments. However, simple ideas such as electronic bill payment by consumers and businesses have turned out to be more of a challenge than we imagined a few years ago. In addition, as the market continues to experiment with new systems, the old themes of reliability, security, privacy, and confidence need to be repeated often."

—Vice Chairman Roger W. Ferguson Jr., speaking at the Federal Reserve Bank of

We explored the payment systems when we discussed the Fed banks in Chapters 7 and 8, so we won't spend any more time on these issues. Instead, we'll take a look at the other responsibilities that fall under the purview of this division including information technology and human resources. In addition, the division has responsibility for financial and cost accounting, operating and capital budgets, facilities management, and internal audit.

Staffing Challenges

The division of Reserve Bank Operations and Payment Systems is helping the Board look at the changing requirements created by new technology and communications, as well as demographics and market forces to factor in future staff planning. It helps the Board collect needed information so it can make well-informed decisions to attract, retain, and train staff to meet the increasingly complex Federal Reserve staffing requirements. The Board is considering new forms of pay and benefits, such as variable pay that is more sensitive to market conditions.

Nearly 75 percent of the Board's expenses are associated with staffing. The human resources folks are always looking for ways to use technology to help improve productivity and reduce the staff needed for lower priority work. This leads into additional challenges for the division to keep up with changing technology.

Managing the Information

Technology changes have helped to enhance the Fed's ability to maintain real-time surveillance, but it requires a continuous investment in equipment, communications capability, and staff training. Remember the Board is not only worrying about the needs of its staff, but also how to integrate technology changes so they are carefully synchronized and coordinated with Reserve banks.

The technology staff is also responsible for oversight of strategic infrastructure projects. These include Reserve bank check modernization, cash distribution, web-based application development, and network modernization.

Economic Wisdom

"Technology has also expanded the ways in which customers can conduct business with financial institutions .... For example, the need for "in-person visits" has diminished as financial service providers have established centralized call centers to facilitate telephone banking, developed web sites to allow Internet banking and software to permit PC banking, and promoted the use of direct deposits and pre-authorized debits. ... As the need for in-person visits declines, we might expect customers to broaden the geographic area within which they search for providers of financial services, leading to increased competition. Clearly, mortgages and credit cards already fall into this category of financial products."

—Vice Chairman Roger W. Ferguson Jr., at a symposium sponsored by the Federal Reserve Bank of Kansas City, Jackson Hole, Wyoming, August 31, 2001

In addition to planning for the technology needs of the Federal Reserve and its staff, Fed governors have to keep a close eye on the technology needs of the industry. Banking is changing dramatically with the influx of Internet banking and other technology-driven services.

Getting Advice and Council

The Federal Reserve Board and staff do not work in a vacuum. In additional to regular contact with the business community, academia, and the general public, the Board also has three active councils to gain additional insight into regional and private sector activities. The three councils are as follows:

- Federal Advisory Council, which has one member from each Reserve District, usually a commercial banker. The council meets four times a year with the BOG to discuss economic and banking matters.

- Consumer Advisory Council, whose members include legal specialists in consumer matters, academics, and members representing the interests of consumers and the financial industry. The council meets with the Board three times a year on matters concerning consumers and consumer protection laws.

- Thrift Institutions Advisory Council, whose members include representatives of savings and loan associations, savings banks, and credit unions. The council meets with the board three times a year to provide information and views on the special needs and problems of thrift institutions. I headed this council when I served at the Fed because of my six-plus years of service as a thrift institution "Sup" (Supervisor).

Each Federal Reserve bank also has its own advisory committees that consult on matters such as agriculture, small business, and consumer affairs. This enables them to gain feedback at a grassroots level and provide additional input to help the Reserve bank as well the Federal Reserve Board with monetary policy decisions.

You probably knew the Federal Reserve staff had responsibility for examining banks and developing research for monetary policy decisions. Now you have a better idea of all the other things the staff does to keep the money machine operating smoothly. In the next chapter we'll take a closer look at the special language of the Fed.

The Least You Need to Know

- The Federal Reserve has eight divisions that are organized under its three functional goals—monetary policy, banking supervision and regulation, and payment system policy and oversight.

- Bank supervision concentrates on the risks banks face and how well the banks have managed those risks.

◆ Federal Reserve is not only responsible for bank examination but is a key force in finding ways to expose off-balance-sheet commitments, money laundering schemes, and other illicit activities.

◆ The Federal Reserve staff also looks internally to help the Board make decisions on staff recruitment and training, as well as the most effective ways to meet the new technology changes in banking.

Fedspeak: The Secret Language of Money

In This Chapter

- ◆ Cracking the secret code
- ◆ Learning the sources
- ◆ Understanding money measures
- ◆ Making your notes

Ever had the feeling that someone was talking to you but didn't want you to understand a single word? Ever thought you were crazy because what they were saying sounded kind of intelligent but you just couldn't figure out the meaning? Well, if that's how you feel when the government talks about the economy, guess what—that's how they want you to feel!

The more you understand, the more you'll feel connected to what's going on. And in many ways, the last thing the government wants is for you to know what's really going on and what they did wrong!

Learning Fedspeak

There's even a special language created by the Fed to deliberately keep you—and the rest of America—in the dark about our economy. That language, as we've mentioned earlier, is called Fedspeak. If it sounds like something George Orwell invented, we understand how you feel. It's a deliberately confusing language meant to give people a sense that there's no possible way they could ever understand economics and finance.

And if regular folks can't understand it, then the pros at the Fed and elsewhere in the government will have much less interference, and they can run the economy (or try to run it, anyway!) however they want to.

Ah, but that was before this book came out!

The Fed operates behind closed doors to increase or decrease the money supply (i.e., the currency, deposits, and other financial instruments that you, your company, and your government use on a daily basis). In decades past, the Fed believed that monetary policy was most effective when it was the least transparent. Slowly, over the last decade, the Federal Reserve has moved to become more open and transparent in monetary policy decisions and the implementation of those decisions. But it can still be hard to read those tea leaves. That's why we're here!

> **Economic Wisdom**
>
> "The historical record indicates that the increased transparency of the Federal Reserve has helped improve the functioning of markets and enhanced our credibility. But, to repeat, openness is more than just useful in shaping better economic performance. Openness is an obligation of a central bank in a free and democratic society. The U.S. elected leaders chose to vest the responsibility for setting monetary policy in an independent entity, the Federal Reserve. Transparency of our activities is the means by which we make ourselves accountable to our fellow citizens to aid them in judging whether we are worthy of that task."
>
> —Chairman Alan Greenspan, speaking via videoconference at the Federal Reserve Bank of St. Louis, Economic Policy Conference, St. Louis, Missouri, October 11, 2001

This chapter is a guide to the language of the financial world and how through information you can avoid the pitfalls that sickened your grandparents and maybe your parents. With a bit of work, you will get to the point where you can catch the significant utterances of the Fed, the Treasury, and even messages from the global gyrations of the financial markets. The messages are there—just learn enough Fedspeak and market signals to make better, safer financial decisions. If you don't shape up your financial thinking now, "retirement" will become a four-letter word.

It is possible to break that Fedspeak code. But just how does a normal person ever find out what has happened and get adept enough to predict what might happen in the future?

Finding the Code Words

As we have already discussed, there are several key Fed activities that give clues to what actions they have taken or might be taking in the future (and you can find them all online):

- **Monetary Policy Report to the Congress** (formerly the Humphrey Hawkins Report): www.federalreserve.gov/boarddocs/hh/

- **Beige Book:** www.federalreserve.gov/fomc/beigebook/

- **FOMC announcement:** www.federalreserve.gov/fomc/#calendars

- **Speeches by Federal Reserve officials:** www.federalreserve.gov/boarddocs/speeches/

Monetary Policy Report to the Congress

Twice a year the Fed must report to Congress. This report was mandated by the Full Employment and Balanced Growth Act of 1978, is called the Humphrey Hawkins Report, and is given twice yearly (July and February) by the Fed chairman to the House and Senate Banking Committees, in which he focuses on the economy and Fed policy.

Today, Congress members relish the chance to ask what their staffs assure them are "hard, penetrating questions." At the hearings, the Fed chairman and sometimes other members of the FOMC respond with the balanced Fedspeak that used to drive President Truman crazy. Remember his lament that he needed a "one-handed economist"? (One who couldn't say, "On the one hand ...")

When Humphrey Hawkins became law, Fed officials resisted testifying before Congress. There was a general feeling that the political nature of Congress would have a negative impact on the independence of the Fed's monetary policy making. That's another way of saying that the Fed doesn't want to be bothered by any other part of government as it goes about its business. Hey, Congress was elected by "We, the People!" Who wants the people messing around in anything as important as the economy? What do the people know, anyhow?

Little by little, that attitude began to change. Today, the Fed leaders may not exactly relish the grilling they get practically every time they appear in Congress, but they're becoming increasingly used to the idea of transparency.

To get a better understanding of how Fedspeak works, let's take a look at two recent examples, which followed the terrorist attacks of September 11, 2001.

On February 27, 2002, Alan Greenspan testified to the House Banking Committee, and on March 7, 2002, he testified to the Senate Banking Committee. Historically, the substance of the testimony to these two committees is close to identical, but in this instance there were some significant differences, made more striking by the short time between them.

> February 27—"Despite the disruptions engendered by the terrorist attacks of September 11, the typical dynamics of the business cycle have re-emerged and are prompting a firming in economic activity. An array of influences unique to this business cycle, however, seems likely to moderate the speed of the anticipated recovery."

> March 7—"Despite the disruptions engendered by the terrorist attacks of September 11, the typical dynamics of the business cycle have re-emerged and are prompting a firming in economic activity. **The recent evidence increasingly suggests that an economic expansion is already well under way,** although an array of influences unique to this business cycle seems likely to moderate its speed."

Note: The portion in bold face indicates how swiftly the Fed shifted in belief that economic expansion was already on the way.

> February 27—"One key consideration in the assessment that the economy is close to a turning point is the behavior of inventories."

> March 7—"One key consideration in the assessment that the **economy is moving through a turning point is** the behavior of inventories."

Note: On March 7, Greenspan said the economy was already moving through a turning point while on February 27, he had said only that the economy was close.

> February 27—"But that impetus to the growth of activity will be short-lived unless sustained increases in final demand kick in before the positive effects of the swing from inventory liquidation dissipate."

> March 7—"But that impetus to the growth of activity will be short-lived unless sustained increases in final demand kick in before the positive effects of the swing from inventory liquidation dissipate. **We have seen encouraging signs**

in recent days that underlying trends in final demand are strengthening, although the dimensions of the pickup remain uncertain."

Note: Here again on March 7, the Fed added words to indicate the economy was strengthening.

> February 27—"Even a subdued recovery **beginning soon** would constitute a truly remarkable performance for the American economy."

> March 7—"Even a subdued recovery would constitute a truly remarkable performance for the American economy."

Note: In this case it is the words that were left out that indicate the Fed believed recovery had started.

You can see that sometimes just a few added or subtracted words can give you some clues about the Fed's thinking. Using these clues you'll know whether there is a risk of inflation or a weakening economy. As we discussed numerous times, if the Fed sees signs of inflation they are more likely to move toward an interest-rate increase. If the economy is weakening the Fed may help to lower rates.

Money Tips

Each Federal Reserve bank gathers anecdotal information on current economic conditions in its district through reports from bank and branch directors and interviews with key business contacts, economists, market experts, and other sources. You can read the summary or simply check out the report from your own Federal Reserve bank.

The Beige Book

One good place to find clues is the Beige Book, which is published two weeks prior to each regularly scheduled FOMC meeting. Watch for media discussions of these reports. Do they say labor compensation gains were "moderate"? When they talk about price increases, do they call them "temperate"?

Regional statistical reports are produced with a lag, sometimes as long as two years. This makes the Beige Book a critical roadmap for Fed policymakers to get information about the current state of the regional economies.

Each Reserve bank is responsible for reporting on economic conditions within its own district. The staff economists in each district provide analytical support for the Reserve bank's responsibilities related to monetary policy, banking supervision, payments systems, and financial market issues. In addition to contributing to the formulation and execution of policy in these areas, economists conduct independent research on a wide range of topics.

Economists in each district contact businesses within the district to obtain information on current conditions. To get a clear picture, the Fed gathers a minimum of three responses covering each industry sector. The industry sectors include retail sales, agriculture, finance, telecommunications, manufacturing, and any specific industry sectors that seriously impact the region's economy. A staff economist at the Federal Reserve district bank writes a detailed sectoral description (an analysis of each industry sector) and then writes a regional economic summary. In addition to the reports from each Fed district, the Beige Book begins with a national summary. The responsibility for compiling the national summary rotates among the Reserve banks.

The summary begins with commentary about general economic conditions in all districts. For example, the January 16, 2002, release included the following:

> Reports from the Federal Reserve Districts suggest that economic activity **generally remained weak** from late November through early January. But while there are still indications of caution, there are also **scattered reports of improvement.** The Dallas and San Francisco Districts report a continued decline in activity, while the Cleveland District indicates that the regional economy appears to be in the process of bottoming out. Economic activity remained slow or weak in the Boston, Chicago, Philadelphia, Kansas City, and St. Louis Districts. Activity was mixed according to the Atlanta, Minneapolis, and Richmond Districts and showed further signs of rebounding in the New York District.

> Many Districts indicate that their contacts believe a **recovery will begin by mid-year or earlier, but the timing and strength are uncertain.** Several Districts say that uncertainty has led some businesses to budget conservatively for the first quarter.

I've highlighted some of the crucial phrases in bold. No definitive good or bad news here. The report indicates that the current economic state is "mixed" or "uncertain." Note that at the FOMC meeting held after this report, there was no change to short-term interest rates. The "mixed" or "uncertain" conditions didn't provide a compelling reason to either raise or lower interest rates.

FOMC Announcements

Watch for the media report on the FOMC actions. Note reports in the financial sections of your newspaper that quote comments from the meeting. You can also download the announcement from the Federal Reserve website. The January 30, 2002, announcement:

The Federal Open Market Committee decided today to keep its target for the federal funds rate unchanged at 1¼ percent.

Signs that weakness in demand is abating and economic activity is beginning to firm have become more prevalent. With the forces restraining the economy starting to diminish, and with the long-term prospects for productivity growth remaining favorable and monetary policy accommodative, the **outlook for economic recovery has become more promising.**

The degree of any strength in business capital and household spending, however, is still uncertain. Hence, the Committee continues to believe that, against the background of its long-run goals of price stability and sustainable economic growth and of the information currently available, the **risks are weighted mainly toward conditions that may generate economic weakness in the foreseeable future.**

As you can see from this announcement there are signs of economic recovery, but the FOMC still believes economic conditions are weak. There was no recommendation to adjust interest rates.

There might also be a reference in the announcement to an intention to either raise or lower interest rates before the next regularly scheduled FOMC meeting. You can also download the minutes of previous FOMC meetings from the Federal Reserve website. You can check out what was said about the economy, job growth, total labor compensation, inflation (or the lack of it), and a detail of the discussions from previous meetings.

Speeches by Federal Reserve Officials

Each year, the Fed chairman, vice chairman, and governors make speeches at banking conferences (domestic and international), universities, and a variety of associations and not-for-profit conferences. They speak on a wide range of topics from economic policy to housing to regulatory concerns. Watch media reports on comments made during these speeches. As with the Beige Book and FOMC announcements, you can also download any of the prepared remarks from the Federal Reserve website.

Federal Reserve bank presidents also make speeches to community groups and organizations and banking events inside and outside their districts. Watch the newspapers for reports of a local speech and attend one yourself.

Uncovering the Monetary Aggregates

What about those "Ms" the media often talk about? The term "Monetary Aggregates" (the "Ms") refers to the several techniques of measuring the nation's means of payments. When the dollar volume of transactions increase, there is usually a need for a similar increase in "Ms," the various measures of quantity of money. One group of economists (the "Milton Friedmanites") argues very forcibly that over long periods of time, the growth of a nation's money supply determines the country's future growth and future inflation. They believe in controlling the economy through *monetarism*.

> **Money Meanings** _____
>
> **Monetarism** is the process of managing the economy by controlling the flow of money. This means changing the "Ms" to impact inflation, deflation, and economic growth. The old Friedman theory says that the faster the money supply is increased, the more economic growth is stimulated and the more danger there is of inflation "going up."
>
> Monetarists watch several key money measures:
>
> **M1**—Currency, traveler's checks, demand deposits, other checkable deposits
>
> **M2**—M-1 plus savings deposits under $100,000, money market funds, and certain overnight bank deposits
>
> **M3**—M-2 plus large savings deposits and all other deposits of financial institutions
>
> **L**—M-3 plus nonbank holdings of U.S. savings bonds and short-term treasury securities, commercial paper, and bankers' acceptances

In the 1980s, U.S. Treasury people had been known for many years as some of the strongest advocates of monetarism. Monetarism is the theory of the close relationship between money and the economy from studies that made Stanford's Milton famous and gained him the Nobel Prize in Economic Science in 1976, when he was an economics professor at the University of Chicago.

What really upsets a monetarist is to witness the Fed participating in different rates of growth of the money supply. This is because to them stable growth in the money supply means stable growth in the economy. "Don't change it!" the monetarists yell.

Preston's Points

I can't help but think of the many times during my vice chairmanship when I met with top presidential officials at the Fed Board dining room or the Treasury in Washington. Beryl Sprinkle, the Undersecretary for Monetary Affairs, was my "weekly" (well almost weekly) luncheon guest. One of those men or women would hastily pull out a couple of charts, kept excruciatingly up to date, to point out to me what he or she detected between growth in the money supply (currency and bank deposits) a few months ago and what was occurring in the economy at the moment.

Since 1982, the behavior of money has been, to say the least, erratic, and the Fed has relegated it to just one of several indicators of where the economy may be going. Thus, when you read in the Friday edition of your newspaper's financial page that the money supply has increased by $100 billion more than the monetarists had predicted, it isn't necessary to become very alarmed. My, how the mighty have fallen! There was a time when such a report would have sent the stock market and the bond market escalating or crashing, depending upon the direction the surprise had taken.

Fiscal Facts

From 1979 to mid-1982, the Fed ran its operations with a close eye on money supply growth and found this relationship reasonably useful then. This meant the shift of attention away from interest rates in an effort to curb inflation. Although inflation did indeed come down, it took very high interest rates to do it. By mid-1982, when I joined the board, the United States had had two recessions almost back-to-back. The less-developed country debt situation looked as though it might implode. It therefore became necessary for us at the Fed to pay less attention to the money supply and more attention to the balance of supply and demand of goods and services. That is how policy is made today.

Don't let that induce you to jump on the easy money bandwagon, however. Given enough time in the central bank, the Fed tends to create more money than the economy really needs. The inevitable result is re-inflation. In a period of falling interest rates and lower inflation, it's true that people, companies, and governments may tend to hold more liquid assets and more money, but there's a limit to how much you and I and our organization will hold onto them—and too much money will start chasing too few goods and up go the prices again.

Economic Wisdom

The dean of the monetarists Professor Friedman, has been quoted as saying, "As far as monetarist policy is concerned, there has not been a monetarist policy." What he is referring to is that despite Volcker's pronouncements on the subject, the Fed was never willing to adopt the Friedmanesque policy of keeping the growth of money constant at some fixed percentage.

Monetarists look back with some degree of nostalgia to the 1979–1982 period when Volcker had declared that the Federal Reserve would pay less attention to interest rates and more to the money supply in an effort to bring down inflation.

My four years' experience on the Fed say to me that the monetarists were wrong and that the pragmatic approach to policy I've described is largely correct. The de-emphasis of the narrow money supply and more attention to interest rates has been a positive shift for both the economy and the debt situation. I think lower interest rates stimulated the strong, long, economic recovery that became apparent by the spring of 1991.

Keeping Notes

When you are making those notes regarding various Fed officials' comments (maybe on your daily calendar), pay close attention to their words about the future, about tomorrow's likely inflation—data that point to anticipations by consumers and businesses. Policymakers know that whatever they do today will have its optimum effects six months or even 18 months from now. They call the use of their 300-plus equations econometric model "rational expectations modeling." They accept the theory that people are likely to change their expectations, and then their spending, saving, and investing when Fed policy or fiscal policy is changed.

A lot of work has also been done on behavioral timing. The consumer and business "delayed responses" stem from memories of past interactions between the Fed funds rate, the cyclical state of the economy, and the rate of inflation. Past investor behavior and yesterday's market effects are likewise built into all that mathematical modeling.

My point is that you will understand Fedspeak better if you underline all hints about the Fed's looks into tomorrow when you are reading that newspaper or listening to the comments from those talking heads on TV.

I hope your curiosity has been whetted a bit about the operations of the Federal Reserve and the statements that come from the FOMC meetings. It will benefit you to pay close attention to the language quoted on the talk shows, and in so many of the financial pages and business magazines, for each word is sculpted when that committee convenes.

Now we'll move onto the real nitty-gritty—how the Fed carries out its key responsibilities.

The Least You Need to Know

◆ Fedspeak is the secret language of money.

◆ The best way to learn Fedspeak is to read published reports from the Federal Reserve Board.

◆ The words of Fedspeak are carefully crafted to give hints of Fed thinking to those who watch closely.

◆ Keep careful notes of Fed announcements to see the trends in Fedspeak.

Part

The Money Machine's Key Responsibilities

You know when Alan Greenspan speaks the stock market moves. We take a look at the Fed's key responsibilities that make this happen. You'll learn about all the federal regulations that the Fed controls, how its lender of last resort role actually works, and how the Fed uses all the economic data it collects.

We take a look at the new roles the Fed will be taking on now that the financial services industry has been modernized.

11

Getting Down to Regulations

In This Chapter

- ◆ Identifying the regulators
- ◆ Exploring the regulation maze
- ◆ The bail out craze
- ◆ Learning lessons

When the Fed was first established, there was great opposition even to the thought of a central bank. Today that central bank has spread its wings and now has powers over the entire financial world thanks to Alan Greenspan's successful lobbying for the 1999 Bank Reform Act (Gramm-Leach-Bliley Act). Bank holding companies are now under the scrutiny of Fed staffers, and the Fed's powers have expanded to "overseer for safety and soundness."

No, the Fed is not the only regulator for the banks with responsibility for examining the accounting books and overseeing how loans and investments made by individual banks are doing. The banks holding national charters are examined and supervised by an office of the Treasury through the comptroller of the currency.

Every state and the District of Columbia has a banking "superintendent" poking its nose into the finances and the loan and asset quality of state licensed banks, with quite a bit of "safety and soundness help" from local Federal Reserve bank examiners. We'll take a closer look at the role other regulators play in Chapter 18, but we'll review them briefly here.

Other Regulatory Agencies

The Federal Reserve shares federal supervisory and regulatory responsibilities with the Office of the Comptroller of the Currency (OCC), The Federal Deposit Insurance Corporation (FDIC), and the Office of Thrift Supervision (OTS). They also share responsibilities with state banking agencies of the various states and Washington D.C., with foreign banking authorities for the international operations of U.S. banks, and the operations of foreign banks within the United States.

The Office of the Comptroller of the Currency (OCC)

The OCC is a bureau of the U.S. Department of the Treasury. The OCC's nation-wide staff of examiners conducts on-site reviews of national banks and provides sustained supervision of bank operations. The agency issues rules, legal interpretations, and corporate decisions concerning banking, bank investments, bank community development activities, and other aspects of bank operations. OCC bank examiners supervise domestic and international activities of national banks and perform corporate analyses. Their examiners analyze a bank's loan and investment portfolios, funds management, loss reserves, capital, earnings, liquidity, sensitivity to market risk, and compliance with consumer banking laws, including the Community Reinvestment Act. They review the bank's internal controls, internal and external audits, and compliance with law. They also evaluate bank management's ability to identify and control risk.

The Federal Deposit Insurance Corporation (FDIC)

The FDIC is an independent agency created by Congress. The FDIC provides a federal government guarantee of deposits in financial institutions up to $100,000 per account so that customer funds, within certain limits, are safe and available in the event the institution fails. The FDIC maintains separate insurance funds for banks and savings associations. The FDIC shares supervisory and regulatory responsibility for FDIC-insured institutions with the FRB, the OCC, and the OTS. In addition, the FDIC is the primary federal regulator of federally insured state-chartered banks that are not members of the Federal Reserve System.

The Office of Thrift Supervision (OTS)

The OTS is the primary regulator of all federal and many state-chartered thrift institutions, which include savings banks and savings and loan associations. The OTS was established as an office of the Department of the Treasury on August 9, 1989, and supervises most institutions that would have been regulated by the Federal Home Loan Bank Board previously. Congress created the OTS to take over the supervision from the Bank Board. The board wasn't performing adequately. It wasn't making the S&Ls write down enough bad assets, and it wasn't requiring them to raise enough additional equity capital. Management changes were not pushed, so one after another, institutions failed. OTS has a history of adequate regulation and supervision.

The Federal Financial Institutions Examination Council (FFIEC)

The FFIEC was established in 1978 to facilitate the coordination of regulatory efforts. The council is a formal interagency body empowered to prescribe uniform principles, standards, and report forms for the federal examination of financial institutions by the Board of Governors of the FDIC, the Federal Deposit Insurance Corporation, the National Credit Union Administration, the OCC, and the OTS. The FFIEC makes recommendations to promote uniformity in the supervision of financial institutions.

The Fed, the Fed Banks, the OCC, the OTS, and the FDIC are all at the federal level. Now shift your thinking to the state level. At your state capital there is a banking superintendent, an insurance commissioner, and probably a savings bank (S&L) commissioner. Then there is a regulator of securities transactions and institutions and also a commissioner. Financial regulation is quite an industry, isn't it?

The table below shows the responsibilities by different government regulatory agencies for supervision and regulation for financial institutions.

Type of Institution	Supervisor and Regulator
Bank holding companies	Fed
National banks	OCC
FRB state-bank members	Fed
Non FRB-member state banks	FDIC
Cooperative banks	FDIC/Fed
Section 20 affiliates	SEC/Fed
Thrift holding companies	OTS

continues

continued

Type of Institution	Supervisor and Regulator
Savings banks	OTS/FDIC/Fed
S&L associations	OTS
Edge Act and Agreement Corps	Fed
Foreign banks—branches and agencies	
State licensed	Fed/FDIC
Federally licensed	OCC/Fed/FDIC
Representative offices	Fed

Fed: Federal Reserve
OCC: Office of the Comptroller of the Currency
FDIC: Federal Deposit Insurance Corporation
SEC: Securities and Exchange Commission
OTS: Office of Thrift Supervision

Banks Expanding Financial Role

Banks have made very substantial investments in information technology (IT). You are probably well aware of the way financial information flows around everywhere. You and your family enjoy such gadgets as the home PC, lightweight laptops, cellular phones, pagers, and on and on. Well, your commercial bank has all of those electronic tools and more! All of this was stimulated by deregulation and the offering of more and more financial services from your bank—not just checking deposits, savings deposits, and check-clearing, but a medley of financial services you can use right off that PC of yours.

Banks today perform all sorts of financial services for individuals and businesses. They sell all kinds of services, loans, deposits, credit cards, cash cards, investment counseling, insurance, loans for homes or farms, even loans to families and small businesses lacking perfect credit records. Banks already trade loans, securities, and currencies, and manage risk in both old and new ways.

Managing all that risk has forced financial institutions to invest in computers and software and to hire bright young college grads at salaries unheard of years ago. Yes, in a global economy all those currencies utilized in overseas markets are traded in nanoseconds by traders "everywhere." The enormous trading volumes create one world that is tied together financially and steps up the risks in still another way.

Economic Wisdom

"Twenty years ago, America's largest bank was Citicorp, with assets of around $120 billion. Though Citicorp had a major international banking presence, its domestic banking operation was contained largely in the State of New York. Its major national credit card operation was its most significant departure from traditional banking lines.

"In contrast, today's Citigroup has $1 trillion in assets and is a highly diversified financial services provider operating not only throughout the United States but also internationally. Citigroup's expanded scope is by no means unique. Rather, it is typical of the bank and nonbank consolidation that has taken place. Today, thirteen financial holding companies hold more than $100 billion in assets."

—Federal Reserve Governor Mark W. Olson, Bank Administration Institute, Phoenix, Arizona, April 30, 2002

Think again about the querulous question, "What is a bank?" You know that financial service providers have to compete with many kinds of financial institutions that are regulated differently. *Hedge funds* are not really regulated. So bankers are evolving a brace of affiliates, subsidiaries, and holding company relationships to compete with "nonbank banks." Does your bank have a branch or two in Europe? In Asia? Don't be surprised if it does!

Money Meanings

Hedge funds are specialized institutions providing forward-looking financial contracts which investors use to manage risks. Included in such risks are interest rate changes, financial asset market price changes, and other market risks.

Billions Lost in Bail Outs

You've seen lots of stories about financial institution failures and their taxpayer costs. The lack has been in bringing together the several causes of the massive failures: failures of the politicians, the regulators, Wall Street, and Main Street. One issue not explained is the risk to taxpayers of billions of dollars that may have to be paid to bank and thrift institution investors who raised all that capital to bail out sick institutions. Then the government tore up the bail out contracts and settled the bank or thrift and sold it at big discounts!

When economics gave way to politics, Congress enacted a "punish 'em" statute, the Financial Institutions Reform, Recovery, and Enforcement Act ("FIRREA") of 1989. So many congressmen had been courted and financed by owners of the institutions that the legislators had special guilty feelings. To make up for their bad behavior in the past, they put their shoulders back, they stood up straight, and they wrote legislation to punish the bad guys and the good guys who had bought all those S&Ls.

Preston's Points

In 1986, I partnered with my friend Bill Simon Sr., the former Secretary of the Treasury. We raised the money to buy out four ailing S&Ls, three in California and one in Hawaii. We applied to the Bank Board and their insurance affiliate, the Federal Savings and Loan Insurance Corp., to purchase three S&Ls, not four, but the government made us take on one really sick one to obtain approval. After more than a year of arguing that one, we gave in, and merged the sick one into our most healthy one. What is the task bail-out investors have to perform? Well, you recruit new management, write off the worst of the bad assets, and cut the operating costs, partly by closing branches that are losing money.

The new law replaced the regulators, the FHLBB, and the FSLIC with a new agency—the Office of Thrift Supervision (OTS). The politicians gave their orders to the new regulators (and the old deposit insurer, the FSLIC): Tear up those contracts, and demand much more capital!

The OTS took back the institutions and ended up facing court cases winding their way to the Supreme Court. Many, many lawsuits have been filed by wounded investors like Simon and me. How much will these cost the taxpayers when the court cases are finished?

Economic Wisdom

"Currently pending before the Court of Federal Claims are 120 cases filed by thrifts adversely impacted by FIRREA. ... Depending on the outcome of the individual cases, the government's total liability for breach of contract could be from $10 billion to $30 billion or more."

—Contract Law Division, Office of the Assistant General Council for Finance and Litigation

Cleaning Up the Mistakes

There were a variety of mistakes and poor policy that came together to create hundreds of billions of dollars in damages. Some of the writers have concentrated on the "bad guys," those who failed to discharge their board of directors, oversight of responsibilities, and management who used all those assets for their personal gains. The bad guys misrepresented, lied, and manipulated their regulators, accountants, appraisers, and lawyers.

Bank and S&L regulators were witnesses to a series of regional recessions that drove vacancies up and property values down. The risk-taking thrifts and banks in those regions quickly felt the pinches, first in the "Rust Belt" Midwest, then in Texas and the rest of the Southwest, then in the Pacific states, New England, and so on.

Misunderstanding the regional recessional problem, Congress in 1981 legislated tax breaks to promote commercial real estate development—much of it was financed by the banks and the thrifts. The supply of such properties on the markets in the regional recessionary states skyrocketed. Five years later, when so many commercial properties had been started or completed, Congress pulled the tax plug, which resulted in even more losses.

It is easy to fault Congress for its numerous mistakes, but the greatest of these was the *easy reg* attitude that was communicated to the regulators at the Fed, the Federal Home Loan Bank Board (FHLBB), the FDIC, and the Comptroller of the Currency.

The least acceptance for this relaxed attitude toward bank regulation lay at the Federal Reserve, which was very aware that it would be dragged in as the "lender of last resort" if the Bank Board and the FSLIC could not cope with liquidity demands from failing thrifts and banks. We'll look more closely at the "lender of last resort" role in Chapter 12.

In these changing financial times, it is in the public interest for existing institutions to serve their customer base with new services and products. New products often mean new risks. Governmental examiners, accounting firms, and their Wall Street serving companies share the responsibility that the assets added to those balance sheets from new services accurately and properly reflect their market values.

Money Tips

While theft occurred, fraud, broadly defined, accounted for only 3 to 5 percent of the losses. Competing right across the street from the crooks were managers who simply could not efficiently make the transition from doing mostly fixed-rate, big down payment home mortgages to originating large shopping center and office building loans and investing in securities they didn't understand.

Money Meanings

Easy reg means "let's take it easy on these banker fellers, they're doing the best they can, and if they stick a couple of extra million in their pockets, let's try to look the other way."

Preston's Points

As a 10-year government regulator in three different jobs, my advice was, "Go ahead and make those new loans and acquire those new assets. When you make a mistake, write it down and take those losses immediately in the year or the quarter when they are discovered."

Management has the first responsibility, but it must be repeatedly reinforced by their public accountants, lawyers, and by examiners from the government agency or agencies.

In 1972, my fourth and last year as Bank Board chairman, the data coming in from our examiners clearly pointed toward more risk and more write-downs coming for the S&L industry we supervised, so we raised the *capital requirements.* In the 1980s, capital requirements were softened, then tightened. The regulatory motto should have been, "Too little, too late—then too much, too soon."

Money Meanings

Capital requirements is the amount of money a bank or thrift institution must have on had to meet regulations.

As you can see from the table below, the financial services industry has consolidated in the last 16 years. About 1,600 savings institutions still do business, compared to almost 4,700 in 1970 when I first went to Washington to head the FHLBB. About 5,000 commercial banks are gone, mostly through acquisitions. Congress finally permitted buying the other banks across state lines. Yes, credit unions are plentiful.

Taking It to Court

The thrift institutions/bank litigation goes on in the courts after 10 or 12 lawsuits and countersuits. The "government" (really the U.S. Treasury) is losing, and sometimes paying part of the investor losses.

Number of Depository Institutions in the United States, 1970–1999

Year	Commercial Banks a/	Thrift Institutions b/	Credit Unions Offering Share Drafts c/	Total
1970	13,511	4,694		18,258
1975	14,384	4,407		18,783 d/
1980	14,434	4,319	3,434	23,049
1985	14,417	3,626	5,473	24,528
1990	12,347	2,815	6,111	21,969
1995	9,942	2,030	6,482	19,352
1999	8,581	1,640	6,720	17,134

a/ FDIC—insured commercial banks.
b/ Office of Thrift Supervision, 1999 Fact Book data for savings and loan associations and savings banks.
c/ Credit Union National Association. Data calculated by multiplying total number of credit unions by the reported percentage offering share drafts.
d/ These data do not include the few credit unions offering share drafts between 1974 and 1977. The final regulation on share draft programs was issued on December 8, 1977, with an effective date of March 6, 1978. The Role of the Federal Reserve in the Payments System, *Paul Connolly and Robert W. Eisenmenger, October 5, 2000.*

Litigation went first to various Courts of Appeal, as is the procedure, then to the Supreme Court. The investor litigants sued for the goodwill/net worth taken away and for lost profits that had resulted. Glendale Federal's demand amounted to approximately $1.5 billion. Decisions at most of the appellate courts and at the Supreme Court (in 1996) were in favor of the litigating investors.

Lessons Learned

There are a number of lessons to be learned from the financial institution history of the past three decades. In today's rapidly changing financial world, financial service institutions must be permitted to expand their services offered and their geographical outreach. It may well be that some of the smaller institutions may survive by rendering a limited set of services in a smaller service area. As thousands more institutions are merged or restructured, we will learn the answer to specialization's survivability.

The second lesson is the need for timely regulation and those awful write-downs of the assets that occur. Credit should be given to the Federal Reserve and to the Comptroller of the Currency, who warned as early as July 1998 of the need for stiffer underwriting of credit risks by bank and thrift institution management. Those agencies saw the losses were coming again.

Economic Wisdom

"In its supervisory efforts, the Federal Reserve has for much of the past decade emphasized a risk-focused approach, particularly in the case of large institutions. That approach requires examiners to understand an institution's risk profile and to devote resources to areas presenting the greatest risk. It allows examiners greater flexibility in their oversight activities, focuses attention on an institution's internal processes, and contrasts with the more traditional approach that was based on reviewing and evaluating individual transactions. The sheer volume of bank transactions today and the speed with which individual exposures can change have required us to take that approach. We need to be confident that an institution's internal systems, procedures, and controls are sound and that they will remain effective long after our review.

—Federal Reserve Vice Chairman Roger W. Ferguson Jr. at Washington and Lee University, Lexington, Virginia, March 4, 2002

Agencies struggled with the slowness of action by the Congress, inaction that extended over 8 to 10 years. You may be aware of the succession of "Bank Reform" bills that were introduced, then turned down, by the Congress until 1999. Our senators and representatives reacted to financial trade association objections to the details of each proposed bill. Yes, the "devil is in the details" when regulatory reform is delayed until the next chaos of foreclosures and bad assets takes place.

These regulations and processes have developed gradually since the Federal Reserve was created in 1913.

We've left the biggest regulatory responsibility to be explored in Chapter 12, where we'll take you behind the scenes of three actual cases.

The Least You Need to Know

◆ Federal regulation of banks is a shared responsibility among several federal agencies.

◆ States have separate regulatory bodies that work in conjunction with the federal agencies.

◆ Mistakes made in bank regulation can cost taxpayers billions.

◆ The regulators and Congress must learn from their mistakes and work to update laws as needed, as rapidly as possible, to minimize taxpayer loses.

12

Lender of Last Resort

In This Chapter

- ◆ Saving our banks
- ◆ Protecting a hedge fund
- ◆ Opening the Window
- ◆ Giving a little credit help

Today, we are well informed (maybe too well) about financial setbacks, losses, even indications of probable financial failures. We can't learn enough about Enron!

We live in an "information age," a time when information and statistics (or "sadistics") are around us all the time. Media pundits tend to emphasize the negatives when they talk about financial market developments. The media finds it much more dramatic to report failure than success. That role is nothing new. The media helped to fuel the bank runs in the late 1800s and early 1900s.

Propping Up Our Financial Institutions

Today's Federal Reserve stands behind our financial system and systems around the world with its vital goal of preventing (or cooling off) financial panics. That function is called "the lender of last resort" (LLR).

The global financial system is replete with a long inventory of different kinds of financial instruments useful in managing risk in those volatile markets around the world. Led by the Fed, the many central banks work together (most of the time) to back up those markets when extreme financial stress shows itself—heavy trading volumes, very substantial selling of one kind of security, perhaps heavy buying of another kind.

None of us want to witness a repeat of the 1929–1930s period, when thousands of banks and other service providers were failing. Remember those old black and white movies showing the bankers and the Wall Streeters shutting their doors? There were crowds in the streets pounding on the walls and windows for some money (their deposit money). You remember the "domino theory," if one big institution falls it will hit others, and all will fall! If one big institution can't put up the cash or the credits their customers demand, will their trading partner down the street close its customer's accounts, too?

> **Economic Wisdom**
>
> "We had a bad banking situation. Some of our bankers had shown themselves either incompetent or dishonest in their handling of the people's funds. They had used the money entrusted to them in speculations and unwise loans. This was, of course, not true in the vast majority of our banks, but it was true in enough of them to shock the people of the United States for a time into a sense of insecurity and to put them into a frame of mind where they did not differentiate, but seemed to assume that the acts of a comparative few had tainted them all. And so it became the government's job to straighten out this situation and to do it as quickly as possible. And that job is being performed."
>
> —Franklin D. Roosevelt during his fireside chat on March 12, 1933, discussing his four-day bank holiday

One of Congress' primary goals in creating the Federal Reserve was to address the nation's banking panics. To accomplish this the Fed has been tasked with the responsibility to foster safe, sound, and competitive practices in the nation's banking system.

When No Other Money Is Available

Acting in its capacity of lender of last resort is one of the most important ways that the Fed ensures safety and soundness of the banking system. Historically the Fed has accomplished this through lending at the Discount Window. We talked about how the Discount Window works in Chapter 8.

The Fed used Discount Window lending in the failure of the Franklin National Bank (1974), the Continental Illinois Bank (1984), the Financial Corporation of America (1984), the Texas banks (1987–1989), and the Bank of New England (1990). We'll take a closer look below at two of these situations, the Continental Illinois Bank and the Financial Corporation of America, so you can see how this works.

More recently, Federal Reserve operations classified as LLR interventions appear to be divided between Open Market and Discount Window assistance. The Fed used Open Market Operations in the October 1987 and 1989 stock market upheavals and in 1998 following the Russian debt default and the financial difficulties of Long Term Capital Management, the world's biggest hedge fund.

The way to understand the Fed mission of financial stability is to review its "lender of last resort" performance during periods of extreme financial stress. Let's start with the case of the near failure of Long Term Capital Management (LTCM) in September 1998, and the FRB management of the situation.

Saving Long Term Capital Management

LTCM is a hedge fund established in 1994 by John W. Meriwether. Meriwether had presided over a team of bond traders at Salomon Brothers on Wall Street during the giddy 1980s, where he had been considered a trader with a Midas touch, one whose mathematical models were the vehicles for overwhelming success. His admirers considered his strategies "rocket science." The Meriwether team left Salomon Brothers and set up their own fund, Long Term Capital Management, LP in 1994. Did it work? Early on, yes. For example, Meriwether and his traders reaped some $150 million in trading profits during and after the market "crash" of October 1997, according to an article in *The New York Times* in January 1999 by Michael Lewis.

 Economic Wisdom

"Five traders, mostly one-time Salomon Brothers employees, and a pair of award-winning, market-wise college professors, are seeking $2.5 billion with which to buy low and sell high in almost any market under the sun. The founders of the new fund (who include John W. Meriwether, a former vice chairman of Salomon, and James J. McEntee, the former chairman of Carroll McEntee & McGinley) are putting up the first $100 million.

"The fund is called 'Long-Term Capital, L.P.,' and the hyphenated phrase speaks to the length of the capital lockup: Investors must commit three years. Minimum investment: $10 million. Merrill Lynch, which is raising the money, is said to be working for $35 million."

—*Grant's Interest Rate Observer*, November 1993

Meriwether had attracted three managing partners and 180 "strategists" (not "traders") to LTCM by mid-1998, including a former vice chairman of the Fed, David Mullins, and two Nobel economist laureates, Myron Scholes and Robert Merton. The fund management's early successes brought them vast amounts of equity and borrowed capital. The early years were highly profitable.

No, LTCM was not a bank, nor an investment banker. Thus, the Fed and other regulators, including the SEC, only saw limited financial data measuring LTCM results. Where? The asset values on the balance sheets of the regulated banks that loaned or invested money in the fund. A little indirect, right?

So why did the Fed of New York and the other bureaucrats step in when storm clouds inevitably filled the sky? That has to be the role for the lender of last resort! Stepping up to the plate to avert (or minimize) widespread, maybe international panic.

Fed to the Rescue

Let's review the Fed's actions to minimize the risks threatened by the near failure of Long Term Capital Management (LTCM).

LTCM attracted investments (speculations) in the hundreds of millions, from various investment banks, banks, super-wealthy individuals, and other operators from around the world. When the giant LTCM portfolio "bubble" appeared to be bursting in the 1998 global financial panic, its size and geographical outreach made it necessary for New York Fed president William McDonough to depart his Basle, Switzerland meeting with the planet's other central bankers and fly back to New York. Then he pulled together staffers from the Federal Reserve Board and major banks—initially Goldman Sachs, Merrill Lynch, UBS of Switzerland, and J.P. Morgan.

Ups and Downs

The risk exposure measurement that had figured in the Nobel Prizes for LTCMers proved to be inadequate. Management really could not always forecast the financial world with their technologically turbocharged information technology.

In one of those elegant FRB New York meeting rooms, they met and negotiated. The participants knew that the "trillion-plus" size of the holdings were such that any kind of "firesale" would impair the overall functioning of financial markets. Thus these risks had the potential of extending to many, many nonparticipants in the fund.

Forecasting Failed

Financial markets are vulnerable when major players dump (sell large quantities of stock quickly) their holdings, producing severe widespread losses. That brilliant financial modeling the LTCM gurus performed had worked for more than four years, then it crashed.

Fed teams had been dispatched to LTCM's offices in Greenwich, Connecticut, where they found that the fund could not meet its obligations if its holdings had to be quickly dumped. What is that old cliché—"too much, too soon!"

McDonough reminded the participants, including six other institutions' representatives, that there had been inadequate "stress testing" of risk exposure. Thus it was the New York Fed's president Bill McDonough, who took action backed up by "Greenspan and company."

Minimizing Risks

Minimizing the risks threatened by the near failure of the world's largest hedge fund (LTCM) was vitally necessary. The potential for widespread losses projected by the Fed staffers was ominous.

> **Fiscal Facts**
>
> Warren Buffett offered to rescue the fund, but the group rejected Warren Buffett's offer to purchase LTCM's portfolio. The $250 million offer was just 5 percent of the roughly $4.6 billion equity investment value at the beginning of 1998. Warren Buffett's group buyout plan included another $3.75 billion to run the highly leveraged portfolio, according to a report in *The Wall Street Journal* in September 1998.

How highly leveraged (in debt) was LTCM? If the fund had been forced to sell-off its entire portfolio, its sales could have undermined the market values of financial contracts worth as much as $1.25 trillion (yes, Trillion, with a capital "T") according to *The New York Times* in a story on November 27, 1998.

In a second day of meetings after rejecting an offer to purchase the portfolio by Warren Buffett, McDonough asked the 16 institutions and their regulators, "What now?" "How do we recapitalize this giant entity?"

> **Money Meanings**
>
> **Counterparty exposure** is the risk that a financial institution on the opposite side of a transaction may not be able to fulfill its obligations. In the case of LTCM this involved buyers, sellers, and hedgers on the other side of LTCM transactions. The institutions that helped to rescue LTCM were the counterparties at risk.

First, a "little" analysis. McDonough questioned the adequacy of LTCM's credit analyses of its investments, the effectiveness of their inadequate risk exposure measurement, and the need for "stress testing" of *counterparty exposure.*

After furious deliberations, 14 firms (including three foreign banks) committed $100 million to $350 million each, turning these creditors into owners. The LTCM execs retained, together, a 5 percent equity. The party was over!

How did the Fed act during and after the two-day meetings? Massive purchases of government securities, thus generating significant outpourings of liquidity and extensions of Fed credit to domestic Fed members, overseas central banks, and to foreign banks with affiliates in the United States to prevent international financial panics.

Aiding the Seventh Largest Bank

When the Fed helped rescue LTCM, it primarily used a lot of arm twisting of affected financial institutions backed by its own Open Market Operations. Now we'll turn to the Fed's rescue of the seventh largest bank using its Discount Window.

In 1984, the Continental Illinois National Bank and Trust was the seventh largest bank in the United States, in both assets and deposits. Continental was also the largest commercial and industrial (C&I) lender in the United States between 1976 and 1981, with relatively little retail banking business and small total core deposits. For its massive funding it relied primarily on federal funds and large certificates of deposits purchased in the secondary market.

One of the first indications that Continental was in trouble surfaced in 1982, when Penn Square Bank in Oklahoma City was closed. Continental was the largest "participant" (buyer of pieces) in oil and gas loans at Penn Square. Thus it experienced huge losses on those participations. Additionally, Continental was experiencing problems in its own portfolio, particularly in the energy sector.

Continental's problems continued through 1983 and into 1984.

Electronic Run on the Bank

Another problem—by the end of the first quarter of 1984, Continental's "non-performing" loans (in other words, nonpaying) had increased to $2.3 billion, in large part due to the significant loans Continental had made to less-developed countries. In May 1984, large foreign depositors became nervous after rumors circulated that Continental's failure was imminent. A high-speed massive electronic deposit run on Continental by large institutional depositors ensued. At the same time banks in

Europe and Japan increased rates on their loans to Continental. With news and rumors flooding the financial news waves, Japanese and European money was quickly withdrawn from Continental. By May 19, foreign banks had withdrawn more than $6 billion.

Here's the FDIC's summary about the significance of this case:

> "The Continental open bank assistance transaction is the most significant bank failure resolution in the history of the Federal Deposit Insurance Corporation (FDIC). ... Continental is the single largest bank ever to require financial assistance from the FDIC in the history of the United States; but it was also noteworthy for several other reasons:
>
> ◆ First, the FDIC made a public statement before a final resolution, guaranteeing that all depositors and other general creditors would suffer no loss.
>
> ◆ Second, the FDIC took a significant ownership position in the bank holding company, effectively making Continental a government-owned bank.
>
> ◆ Third, Continental was the first assisted bank in which the assets acquired by the FDIC were serviced by the bank itself under a separate servicing agreement.
>
> ◆ Finally, the Continental open bank assistance transaction affirmed for many the notion that certain banks were simply 'too big to fail.'"

FDIC Steps In

By Friday, May 11, Continental's borrowings at the Federal Reserve Bank of Chicago Discount Window had reached $3.6 billion. The next week the Federal Reserve, the Office of the Comptroller of the Currency (OCC), and the Federal Deposit Insurance Corporation (FDIC) stepped in to formulate a plan for interim financial assistance. It was decided to continue funding Continental at the FRB Discount Window and to try to forestall further runs by the injection of cash in the form of a subordinated note purchase from the FDIC—"open bank assistance" (OBA).

Continental worked with the FDIC, the Fed, and the Comptroller of the Currency to clean up the mess until 1994. The Bank of America bought Continental in 1994 after the problems were worked out.

Backing Up Credit

The Fed has a third mechanism it can use to help out a troubled financial institution called a backup credit extension. We'll look at how the Fed used this tool to help out the Financial Corporation of America.

First let's consider the economic conditions. In the 1980s there was a period of risks, routs, and failures in both banks and nonbank institutions, especially savings and loans (S&Ls). The 1980s were times of deep regional recessions, and very large demands upon the liquidity of the institutions and their sources of liquidity, especially savings and loans.

Arrangements to help financial institutions were offered by the central bank for housing, the Federal Home Loan Bank Board, and the Federal Reserve System. An example? The Fed Board announced in an August 20, 1984, press release that it was establishing a new borrowing rate for "extended credit" to banks and "thrift institutions" under "sustained liquidity pressures."

You don't expect a friendly little interest rate under those conditions, do you? Listen to their explanation, "The new discount rate will be the basic rate of 14 percent and the 4 percent surcharge applies to large, frequent borrowers of short-term adjustment credit."

Problem Child

The largest S&L holding company in 1984 was aptly named "the Financial Corporation of America," FCA. Its main "child" (subsidiary), American Savings, had assets of $35.5 billion, with a sick portfolio of problem loans and foreclosed real estate. American's original assets of $27.5 billion were the result of the merger in August, 1983, of First Charter Corp. with State S&L.

The new CEO, Charlie Knapp, launched a major campaign to bring in "brokered deposits," paying those brokers to support rapid growth in real estate lending, not just in California. Charlie's team ballooned assets by $8.0 billion in just 10 months!

No, that California based lender didn't confine itself to lending in its home state. When the Texas oil industry boomed, American was in there financing those office buildings, shopping centers, and housing, just like they were doing in California and other regions which had been growing rapidly in the 1970s.

Money Meanings

Mortgage backed securities are backed by a pool of mortgages, such as those issued by Fannie Mae and Freddie Mac. (Learn more about these in Part 6.)

Since FCA was a publicly traded company, the SEC was diligent in evaluating the "true value" of large quantities of mortgages which were collateral for FCA *mortgage backed securities* (*MBSs*). As Fed vice chairman, I kept SEC chairman John Shad fully informed. Those were not the only assets on which the SEC required "write-downs."

Preston's Points

As the market values of many of FCA's assets fell in 1984, I was serving as vice chairman of the Fed. My background as a former S&L regulator brought calls from the "other regulators," the SEC, the Federal Home Loan Bank of San Francisco (FHLBk SF), and, of course, the Fed Reserve Bank of San Francisco. All were cooperating in searching for remedies short of closing down such a major institution. None of us could be certain that the closing of the largest S&L would not have financial system-wide impacts.

Losses Spreading

As the news of potential losses spread, American's deposits ran out, and FCA borrowed approximately $500 million from the FHLB of San Francisco in one morning in mid August 1984. We government guys were trying not to unnecessarily require very short-term liquidation of securities positions, which might plunge the financial markets, and trigger savings runs at all those branches, theirs, and their competitors. (American wasn't the only "bad news.")

I had known the then-chairman of the San Francisco FHLB Board, Ed Gray, from his former roles in S&Ls in the San Diego region. Ed warned me that American could have deposit outflows of $8.0 billion, a level which would strain the resources of both the FHLBB and the Fed. Right!

Our staffs then put together lists of S&Ls and banks that could possibly be acquirers of American S&Ls asset groups or acquirers of the entire organization. There were five banks with assets ranging from $21 billion in assets to $44 billion, and six S&Ls with assets ranging from $6.7 billion to $19.7 billion on our lists.

Meetings with our Fed counsel and me at the Fed Board included the Fed Bank of San Francisco, and representatives from the FHLBB, the Office of Thrift Supervision (American's regulator), the $6.3 billion FSLIC (the insurer of deposits up to $100,000), and, of course, the SEC. Other get-togethers involved people from the U.S. Treasury, and yes, the Office of Management and Budget (OMB). (Did we leave out any agency? I don't think so.)

Ousting the Leaders

Meetings had to include the FCA management and what to do to preserve the institution ("prevent failure"). Charlie Knapp, the then CEO, would have to be replaced. FHLB chairman Gray issued a directive on August 22, 1984, directing the removal of members of the board of directors or management of American or FCA. In July, the thrift had lost over $1.4 billion in institutional deposits, even as $800 million-plus in "retail" deposits flowed in.

My candidate to succeed Charlie Knapp as FCA CEO was a former associate during my years as chairman of the FHLB Board, Bill Popejoy. Bill had an outstanding record as the president and co-developer of "Freddie Mac," the Federal Home Loan Mortgage Co. Later when I left the Bank Board to startup a new mortgage insurance company (PMI Mortgage Insurance Co.), my successor, Tom Bomar, made Popejoy "Freddie's" CEO. Bill later held presidential jobs at two major S&Ls. All of us regulators agreed on Popejoy.

Popejoy to the Rescue

Popejoy took only three months to reverse the run on deposits. He replaced the firm's auditors, and sold all those "good things" his management predecessors at FCA had acquired—airplanes, hundreds of cars, and 41 condominiums, according to an article in *Business Week* on December 24, 1984. He found 1,500 layoffs (out of 7,500) were necessary.

Did the Popejoy reorganization work? In three months his team pulled in more than $2 billion in deposits and repaid $743.7 million of FHLB SF advances bringing the borrowings down to $3.24 billion, according to a *Washington Post* report on January 18, 1985.

> ### Economic Wisdom
>
> "Once the public realized that that, if they wished to have their money back we would give it to them, their concern went away."
>
> —Bill Popejoy, *Washington Post*, January 3, 1985

Okay, there was a little bit of luck involved. We at the Fed were lowering our interest rate targets in the face of declining capital demands and a rocky economy.

You can see that the Fed has numerous tools in its lender of last resort magic box to keep things financially sound. Now that we've taken a look at how the Fed impacts banking, we'll turn our sights on Wall Street.

The Least You Need to Know

♦ The Fed is the lender of last resort when a key financial institution is in serious trouble.

♦ Open Market Operations is one of the tools the Fed uses to help financial institutions in trouble.

♦ When a bank has nowhere else to turn to borrow money, the Fed opens its Discount Window.

♦ When banks want the Fed to back up credit, they have to pay extremely high interest rates to get the money.

Chapter 13

Moving the Markets

In This Chapter

- ◆ Focusing on stock
- ◆ Birthing "irrational exuberance"
- ◆ Looking at wealth
- ◆ Tomorrow's roles

When you think about the impact the Federal Reserve has on Wall Street, two words probably come quickly to mind—"irrational exuberance." Federal Reserve chairman Alan Greenspan introduced that phrase into the world of Wall Street watch on December 5, 1996, throwing the world markets into a downward spiral.

In fact, foreign markets were hit harder than the U.S. market on December 6, 1996. The Japanese market started the slide and closed down 3.2 percent, Hong Kong dropped almost 3 percent, Germany's market took the hardest hit with a fall of 4 percent, and London's stock market lost 2 percent. Interestingly, while the Dow Jones dropped 145 points or 2 percent in the first 30 minutes of trading, it lost less than 1 percent by the time the U.S. market closed.

You may wonder how it came to be that a central banker has such a great impact on the stock market, for which the Federal Reserve has no official direct jurisdiction—at least not yet. For 30 years prior to Greenspan's reign, Federal Reserve chairmen treated comments on market thinking as taboo to avoid spooking investors. Many wish Greenspan would honor that taboo and stay away from what they call "jawboning the market." We'll take a look at how Greenspan shifted the role of the Federal Reserve from one of quiet observer to active, at least verbally, participant.

Greenspan's Early Learning Curve

Greenspan's stock market focus actually started long before he took on the role of Federal Reserve chairman. His New York consulting firm advised investment bankers and brokers on how the stock market affected economic conditions. This advice was in addition to the more traditional work of an economist, such as how the economic conditions might affect the stock market. In the early to mid-1980s, just before being appointed chairman of the Federal Reserve, his extensive research for clients centered on the reasons for the Japanese market runup to try to justify the climb.

His early introduction to the Fed as chairman was dramatically impacted by the 1987 crash two months after he took the job. After that crash, his initial statement was, "The Federal Reserve, consistent with its responsibilities as the nation's central bank, affirmed today its readiness to serve as a source of liquidity to support the economic and financial system." This statement served to calm markets so they knew deposits would be available if needed to keep the flow of money going. That is the role of the Fed in the financial markets. The big question many are asking is what function does the Fed have, or should it have, in the stock market?

> **Economic Wisdom** _____
>
> "A central bank in a democratic society is a magnet for many of the tensions that such a society confronts. Any institution that can affect the purchasing power of the currency is perceived as potentially affecting the level and distribution of wealth among the participants of that society, hardly an inconsequential issue."
>
> —Alan Greenspan, December 5, 1996, speaking at the American Enterprise Institute

The Wall Street Journal reported in "Worried About the 'Wealth Effect'" on May 5, 2000, that after this market crash Greenspan ordered a Fed staff member to begin work at 5 A.M. to check on European trading activity and prepare a forecast for him by 7:30 A.M. In 1991, Greenspan asked one of his researchers to "delve into a popular theory that investors' expectations of declining inflation could explain rising stock prices. The ultimate report was dubious." Yet Fed staff continued to be skeptical about the market runup, which is a rapid increase in stock price, in the United States and expected a 20 percent correction.

The Wall Street Journal also reported that when the Fed started raising rates because of perceived inflation in 1994, Greenspan was motivated by the stock market as well. In fact, the *Journal* quoted Greenspan after the Dow dropped 5 percent and the Fed engineered an interest rate raise in February 1994, "We partially broke the back of emerging speculation in equities. We had a desirable effect."

Greenspan watched on the sidelines as the Dow climbed in 1995 by 33 percent, but showed increasing concern. During the FOMC meeting on May 21, 1996, the chairman expressed his growing concern that the stock market runup might be having a negative impact on the economy:

> "The crucial issue at this stage is the evaluation of the real side of the economy. The real side is being bolstered, as best anyone can judge at this stage, by the *wealth effect*. Not that many months ago, everyone was sitting around, here and elsewhere, and wondering what elements in the GDP were going to strengthen and sustain the recovery. We could not find it in residential construction. We could not find it in capital investment. The consumer was dead. The government had gone out of business. And clearly the export side was not doing anything. We are now sitting here and wondering what is going to moderate this expansion. The change has occurred in only a few months and no one can tell me that the world changes that rapidly. What is happening, and one sees it best by looking at the S&P 500, which has been going straight up in the charts, is probably the result of a wealth effect. That effect is lagged sometimes; it is indeterminate. It is very difficult to judge, but one gets the sense that this is where some of the effect is probably stemming from. Obviously, in the capital goods area we are getting some evidence of lower capital costs. We are getting related evidence of increased margins. And it's hard to buy that anything other than the wealth effect is driving the consumer.

> "That gets us down to the question of how long all this will go on. The stock market as best I can judge is high; it's not

Money Meanings

Wealth effect refers to the tendency of people to spend more if they have more assets. This became very evident during the stock market bubble when the value of stocks rose and people felt wealthier and more comfortable about spending.

that there is a bubble in there; I am not sure we would know a bubble if we saw it, at least in advance. But one surely can't argue that the underpinnings of the level of stock prices are all extremely positive. It's hard to believe that if any series of adverse developments were to occur, the market would not come down rather substantially and reverse the wealth effect. That probably would damp economic activity quite substantially."

Interestingly, the discussion among the Federal Reserve governors and bank presidents skirted discussion of this issue at the May meeting.

By November 1996, Greenspan had turned his focus to the rising level of consumer debt and passed on primary responsibility for monitoring the stock market to then Governor Lawrence Lindsey (now Bush's Economic Policy Advisor). Lindsey's report at that meeting is included in the appendix and not available in the transcripts online, but reaction to his report is discussed.

Cathy E. Minehan, President of the Federal Reserve Bank of Boston, sums up the concerns at the November 13, 1996, FOMC meeting:

> **Money Tips**
>
> Transcripts of FOMC meetings are released five years after the year in which the meetings were held. You can read the transcripts of FOMC meetings between 1981 and 1996 at www.federalreserve.gov/fomc/transcripts.

"I want to associate myself to some extent with what Governor Lindsey has said and what Tom Melzer [then President of the Federal Reserve Bank in St. Louis] just said. The financial markets are acting as if interest rates only go in one direction, and with that attitude there are undoubtedly bets being made that are unwise now and will grow to be more unwise as time goes by. We are risking a major asset price bubble unless some sense of caution, some sense of reality is injected into these financial markets at some point, and I think that injection needs to be made relatively soon."

After this meeting a secret conference with Wall Streeters was held on December 3, hosted by Greenspan to look more closely at this issue. Abby Joseph Cohen of Goldman Sachs & Co. gave the optimistic bull market (optimistic that the market will go up) view and the bears (pessimistic that the market will go down) were represented by Yale University's Robert Schiller and Harvard University's John Campbell. What happened next made history.

Birth of "Irrational Exuberance"

When Alan Greenspan gave a speech on December 5, 1996, using the phrase "irrational exuberance" he didn't actually state that this was the case, but instead raised questions about stock market prices and values. How should the Fed evaluate market price impact on the "real economy"? Here's the full set of questions Greenspan raised:

> "[H]ow do we know when irrational exuberance has unduly scalated asset values, which then become subject to unexpected and prolonged contractions as they have in Japan over the past decade? And how do we factor that assessment into monetary policy? We as central bankers need not be concerned if a collapsing financial asset bubble does not threaten to impair the real economy, its production, jobs, and price stability. Indeed, the sharp stock market break of 1987 had few negative consequences for the economy. But we should not underestimate or become complacent about the complexity of the interactions of asset markets and the economy. Thus, evaluating shifts in balance sheets generally, and in asset prices particularly, must be an integral part of the development of monetary policy."

The Fallout

Foreign markets were hit the hardest by Greenspan's remarks, but by the middle of the day in the United States, people realized that Greenspan was asking questions not specifying action. Right! The U.S. market recovered from the initial shock. That night PBS's *Newshour* hosted a discussion with Owen Ullmann, senior news editor in the Washington bureau of *Business Week*, and David Jones, chief economist for securities firm Aubrey Lanston & Company. They attempted to figure out what Greenspan intended with this speech that shook the financial world.

> **Economic Wisdom**
>
> "If we exaggerate the present and future value of the stock market, then as a society we may invest too much in business startups and expansions, and too little in infrastructure, education, and other forms of human capital. If we think the market is worth more than it really is, we may become complacent in funding our pension plans, in maintaining our savings rate, in legislating an improved Social Security system, and in providing other forms of social insurance."
>
> —Robert Shiller in the preface to his book *Irrational Exuberance*

Both guests on the *Newshour* agreed that Greenspan was trying to change the psychology of the market. David Jones said Greenspan did not want to …

> "[C]ause the markets to collapse, but just cool them down a little bit, so that we can keep this expansion going, and if inflation does pick up a bit next year, the chairman still has the option, if he has to, to give us a mid-course correction, which is a tightening move, without causing a crash in markets that were too speculative."

During the show it was also reported that Greenspan and the Fed board had met with outside advisors that included three major brokerage houses on Wall Street. Ullmann said that "among the three major houses, there was disagreement about whether stocks in the United States really are overvalued, but there was complete agreement that if there was a correction, say a 10 percent or more drop, they do not think it would harm the U.S. economy." Both Jones and Ullmann agreed Greenspan was "jawboning" the markets to say "we're keeping an eye on you, we're getting concerned," but we're not ready to raise interest rates yet.

Fiscal Facts

In *The Wall Street Journal's* May 8, 2000, story, it's reported that Greenspan had written the "irrational exuberance" speech before the December 3 meeting with Wall Street and academia. That meeting just confirmed his beliefs. The *Journal* also reported that then Fed vice chairman Alice Rivlin said she "went in to see the chairman and said, 'Do you really want to say that?' He said, 'I think I do.'" The *Journal* reported that Greenspan was "mindful how risky, and difficult, it is for a central bank to pop a bubble." Two examples of failed attempts cited by the *Journal* were the actions by the Fed in 1929 and the actions by the Bank of Japan in 1989.

Greenspan only used the phrase "irrational exuberance" one other time: in a Congressional hearing in February 1997. In a speech on "New Challenges for Monetary Policy" at a symposium sponsored by the Federal Reserve Bank of Kansas City in Jackson Hole on August 27, 1999, Greenspan seemed to abandon the idea of "irrational exuberance" entirely when he said:

> "History tells us that sharp reversals in confidence happen abruptly, most often with little advance notice. These reversals can be self-reinforcing processes that can compress sizable adjustments into a very short time period. Panic market reactions are characterized by dramatic shifts in behavior to minimize short-term losses. Claims on far-distant future values are discounted to insignificance.

What is so intriguing is that this type of behavior has characterized human interaction with little appreciable difference over the generations. Whether Dutch tulip bulbs or Russian equities, the market price patterns remain much the same.

"We can readily describe this process, but, to date, economists have been unable to anticipate sharp reversals in confidence. Collapsing confidence is generally described as a busting bubble, an event incontrovertibly evident only in retrospect. To anticipate a bubble about to burst requires the forecast of a plunge in prices of assets previously set by the judgments of millions of investors, many of whom are highly knowledgeable about the prospects for the specific companies that make up our broad stock price indexes."

One can only wonder if these conclusions would have been different in 1999, if Greenspan knew about the accounting irregularities brought to light in 2002 with Enron, Global Crossing, and many other companies. Also, the scandal regarding the lack of independence of some Wall Street analysts certainly contributed to this stock market runup. Only time will tell how much investors really knew when "irrational exuberance" took over the market.

Who Burst the Bubble?

While Greenspan didn't actually burst the bubble, some folks are giving AOL's Steve Case credit for that task. The online magazine, *The Globalist* (www.theglobalist.com) wrote on January 18, 2000:

"Why could America Online, which owns nothing more than the cables and routers that provide access to the web, be in a position to pay a hefty premium for Time Warner, which owns 'real' things like magazines and film studios? … If Mr. Case decided to bail on the Internet by selling his Internet shares to buy assets in the 'old' economy that, ones that have proven value, perhaps the jig really was up."

We know how badly this merger proved to be when AOL/Time Warner took a $50 billion write-off because the merger was so overvalued. Other similar write-offs were announced throughout 2002 for companies that merged during the stock bubble of the late 1990s and early 2000s.

Even though "irrational exuberance" most likely will no longer be a part of Greenspan's speechmaking, the other key words that became commonplace during this time period, "wealth effect" are certainly still a major part of Fed planning. Let's take a closer look at what this actually means and how the Fed is responding.

Wealth Effect

The only thing that is clear about the wealth effect is that there appears to be a connection between prices in markets and economic growth or decline. More research is certainly needed to understand fully that connection. Federal Reserve Board Governor Edward Gramlich discussed the wealth effect during remarks before the International Bond Congress in London on February 20, 2002. He said the Fed believes,

> "There is little empirical doubt that stock-market wealth and housing wealth influence consumption and the macroeconomy. Nevertheless, our understanding of the empirical relationships and of the theoretical underpinnings of those relationships remain incomplete. Substantial progress has been made, but we should hope that future research will help to untangle the remaining puzzles."

Fiscal Facts

How does the wealth effect show in the numbers? The average ratio of household wealth to disposable income in the United States was about 4.5 between 1970 and 1995. Between 1995 and 2000, that ratio shot up to 6, which was the highest level it had reached during the 50 years that wealth effect data was calculated. Since the stock market bubble burst, there has been a drop in the ratio to 5, which reflects some cutback in spending even though consumption remained strong throughout the 2001 downturn according to Fed statistics.

Currently, the Fed's money modeling (we'll talk more about that in Chapter 15) uses two wealth categories—equity wealth and all other wealth (including housing, noncorporate businesses, and net financial assets). The jury is still out on how the relationship of these models actually works, but several papers developed at the Federal Reserve and by outside economists show evidence that spending patterns change when households experience wealth gains or losses. We know economists don't like to jump to any quick conclusions, right?

Fed Governor Gramlich told his London audience:

> "Between early 1995 and early 2000, the Wilshire 5000 stock-price index (a broad measure of equity prices in the United States) tripled, and nearly $12 trillion was added to the wealth of U.S. households. Over that same period, saving dropped from 6½ percent of disposable income to roughly 1 percent."

Since the drop in the stock market, about half of that wealth was lost, but the savings rate had to yet increase. The Fed at that point was rationalizing the fact that savings hadn't increased.

Economic Wisdom

"Capturing the true complexity of the relationship between stock-market wealth and consumption is extremely difficult with existing data and empirical techniques. As in many areas of empirical economics, we currently must be satisfied by models that capture broad patterns in the data."

—Federal Reserve Governor Edward M. Gramlich before the International Bond Congress in London, February 20, 2002

Looking at the wealth effect in relationship to housing wealth can be even more complicated. Age and housing needs become even greater factors. Some of the numbers are affected by seniors moving to smaller housing and using their assets for other living expenses in retirement. Another factor is the influence of people moving up to larger homes as their income increases. Finally, a third factor is the people taking out money using equity lines or refinances and making their home ownership more liquid.

Fed's Role in Today's Market

The search for more information on the wealth effect goes on. Another huge project facing the Federal Reserve is the new roles it will take in relationship to the stock market. This responsibility was engineered by the Fed. It sought and obtained the powers in the Gramm-Leach-Bliley Act of 1999 (GLB), which was the biggest change in banking in more than 60 years. The act repealed the old post-depression Glass-Steagall Act, which had prohibited banks, securities firms, and insurance companies from affiliating.

Before GLB was actually passed, the Fed gave the green light to Citicorp's 1998 merger with Travelers, which had both securities and insurance businesses under its roof. The Fed gave Citicorp two years to divest Travelers' banned businesses under Glass-Steagall plus (the "Citigroup," as they then were called) the possibility of three one-year Fed waivers after that. "Citi" assumed some form of financial modernization would be passed by Congress long before the assets would have to be divested.

Citigroup planned to cross-sell insurance and investment products through its banking network, so it was not making plans to divest. Soon after passage of the financial

GLB Citigroup gobbled up securities firm Solomon Brothers as well. Rumors flew indicating that Chase and Merrill Lynch would be next to tie the knot. Although that never happened, many smaller banks did gobble up small securities firms. "We are a financial servicer, provider," one of them said.

> **Economic Wisdom**
>
> "To carry out its responsibilities as umbrella supervisor, the Fed has had to work closely with other agencies. We have established formal procedures for sharing information with a number of regulators and have informal arrangements for sharing with many others. We meet periodically with a broad spectrum of agencies to discuss general issues and to coordinate supervision. We continue to work on pilot programs for creating the practical processes of meeting joint responsibilities, especially with the OCC [Office of the Comptroller of the Currency] and the SEC [Securities and Exchange Commission]. Practically, we need to continue to cooperate if we are going to minimize the risks to our banking system that could accompany the new financial structure." Governor Olson wasn't "speechifying"—the system is working.
>
> —Federal Reserve Governor Mark W. Olson before the American Law Institute and American Bar Association in Washington, D.C., on February 8, 2002

Your bank today probably is even dealing in securities and may even be offering opportunities to trade securities online, competing with companies like Charles Schwab who merged with U.S. Trust. Banks were not the only ones doing the gobbling. Metlife gobbled up a few small banks as well, for example.

Now that the walls have come down, the Fed does have a role in securities and insurance firms, if they are owned by a bank holding company. We'll take a closer look at what this actually means for the Fed in the next chapter on "The Fed's New Roles."

The Least You Need to Know

- ◆ The Fed's role as stock market commentator is still controversial, which did not stop Alan Greenspan from introducing the phrase "irrational exuberance."

- ◆ When Greenspan used "irrational exuberance," he was actually asking a question about the state of the market, not stating an absolute fact as was initially misinterpreted.

- ◆ Studying the "wealth effect" and the stock market is still a major part of the Fed's research initiatives.

- ◆ The merger of banks, securities, and insurance companies increases the Fed's role in future stock market regulatory decision-making.

Chapter 14

The Fed's New Roles

In This Chapter

- ◆ Rules for financial services
- ◆ Eyeing insurance companies
- ◆ Watch money managers
- ◆ Too much to do?

We talked a lot about how the Fed got started in Chapter 3 and have been spending a lot of time since talking about how the Fed developed into the massive money machine it is today. As the banking industry has expanded both geographically and in the number and types of services it offers, the need to regulate the services and their delivery has expanded.

The most dramatic change in the Fed's responsibilities came about in 1999, when Congress passed the Gramm-Leach-Bliley Act (GLB). We'll take a closer look at the new roles the Fed is expected to play and how GLB's modernization of the financial industry is expected to impact Fed operations.

Developing the Money Machine

Before getting into the details of the GLB, let's quickly review the key legislation that got us to where we are today.

The Banking Act of 1933

The Banking Act of 1933, or the Glass-Stegall Act (GSA), went through Congress at a time when bank runs and closings had become widespread. President Franklin Delano Roosevelt had to close the whole national banking system, declaring a national "bank holiday," and suspending the gold standard. So GSA called for the separation of commercial and investment banking. It also placed Open Market Operations under the Federal Reserve and required bank holding companies to be examined by the FRB.

The FDIC

The FDIC (Federal Deposit Insurance Corporation) was established in 1934, protecting depositors by "insuring" their deposits up to $2,500—this amount was promptly increased to $5,000. So many banks were failing by then, during the depression, that this legislation was not just "called for," but "screamed for." When a bank failed, your deposits in that institution were promptly restored. Where did the money come from? The banks were taxed via an annual assessment on domestic deposits between 0.04 percent and 0.08 percent per year. No, the FDIC was not just an insurer, it recruited and trained examiners who were known for their prompt (and tough) action on any bank's asset problems. "Write it down!"

One of the Fed's original roles was the use of the Discount Window for banks that needed liquidity to discharge their lending roles in their communities. Importantly, the Discount Window was also a kind of safety net providing money to contain runs on the bank cash window by panicked depositors. Regulation of Fed member banks was aimed at encouraging prudent lending, consumer protection, and later, community reinvestment. Cyclical economic volatility (crash, crash, crash) was significant between the Civil War and World War I.

Economic Wisdom

"Government programs, too, often have unintended business-cycle effects. The safety net, particularly deposit insurance and access to the discount window, clearly has an impact beyond the stability it brings by containing the deposit runs that once led to financial implosion. It induces intermediaries to take on more risk with less capital, creating what is arguably the largest problem facing modern bank supervisors—wide swings in credit quality."

—Chairman Alan Greenspan at the Conference on Bank Structure and Competition, Federal Reserve Bank of Chicago, May 10, 2002

Well, this system has worked so well for more than six decades that deposits now are insured up to $100,000. In May 2002, the House approved legislation to increase the amount of insurance to $130,000 for individual accounts and $260,000 for retirement accounts. The bill still had to be approved by the Senate where it faced opposition from both the Federal Reserve and the Treasury Department.

The Banking Act of 1935

The Banking Act of 1935 called for more changes in the structure of the Fed. It created the Federal Open Market Committee (see Chapter 4 for more information about the FOMC). The FOMC is made up of the seven Fed governors and the twelve Fed bank presidents. The 1935 Act made the FOMC a legal entity. It removed the Treasury Secretary and the Comptroller of the Currency from the Fed's governing Board. (Talk about an "independent central bank!") The Act established Fed governors' terms at 14 years, and the chairman's tenure of four years (per appointment).

Yes, these term appointments have to be ratified (or rejected) by Congress. I survived three of those Senate Finance Committee hearings. You never know about those hearings: Two were tough questioning sessions, one was what my wife Genevieve said was a "love fest."

The Employment Act of 1946

The Employment Act of 1946 mandated the federal government "to promote maximum employment, production, and purchasing power." This act identified the objectives for government in general, but not the Fed specifically. It was generally viewed that the Act applied to the Fed as reporting to the Congress, not the president.

The Bank Holding Company Act of 1956

The Bank Holding Company Act of 1956 designated the Fed as the regulator for bank holding companies owning more than one bank and required Federal Reserve Board approval for the establishment of a bank holding company. The BHC Act of 1956 was amended in 1970 to include FRB regulatory power over holding companies owning only one bank. Now the Fed "had 'em all!"

1977 Amending

In 1977, Congress amended the Federal Reserve Act requiring the FRB and the FOMC to "maintain the growth of monetary and credit aggregates commensurate with the economy's long-run potential to increase production, so as to promote effectively the goals of maximum employment, stable prices, and moderate long-term interest rates." You can see that Congress believed that growth and decline of the "money supply," M1 was closely related to the growth or decline of the economy. That M1 measure consisted of the bank deposits, currency outside the Treasury, and other means of payment such as nonbank travelers checks, those "NOW" accounts that businesses used, and, yes the "other checkable deposits." We have already shared with you the Volcker/Martin negotiations of the 1982 to 1986 period. The "money supply" matters were de-emphasized in FOMC decision making in the 1980s.

Humphrey Hawkins Act

The Humphrey Hawkins Act of 1978 required the Fed chairman to report to Congress twice annually on monetary policy goals and objectives: growth and disinflation. While the Humphrey Hawkins Act itself expired in mid-2000, the semiannual report to Congress continues.

The Truth in Lending Act of 1968

The Federal Reserve has also been called upon to regulate bank consumer activities. For example, the Fed is the primary regulator of the Truth in Lending Act of 1968, requiring lending institutions to properly disclose interest rates and other information on their consumer credit.

The International Banking Act of 1978

The International Banking Act of 1978 brought foreign banks within the Fed's regulatory framework. It required FDIC deposit insurance for branches of foreign banks engaged in retail deposit-taking in the United States.

Modernizing Banking Under GLB

Now let's get down to the business of the Fed's new roles. These roles all center around the Gramm-Leach-Bliley Act (GLB Act) of 1999. This bill is the product of more than 40 plus years of political infighting and outfighting, in the United States and overseas, particularly at the central banking Bank for International Settlements (BIS), meetings in Basel, Switzerland. I attended those for four years in that urban place where all the Swiss train lines converge. (To learn more about Basel, read Chapter 17's discussion of the BIS.)

The GLB Act eliminated legal barriers to affiliations between banks, insurance companies, securities firms, and other financial services companies. The Act permits the creation of new financial holding companies (FHCs) that can offer a full range of financial products through their affiliates including securities underwriting and dealing, insurance agency and underwriting activities, and merchant banking activities. These newly consolidated organizations are now supervised under the principle of "functional regulation."

 Economic Wisdom _____

"Changes in the market and the adoption of Gramm-Leach-Bliley have brought an enhanced role and have expanded the Federal Reserve's role as an umbrella regulator. In that role, the Fed, along with the Treasury, will evaluate requests for new product approval. Also, the Fed will work actively with the other federal and state regulators to ensure that the concept of functional regulation, which is a critical pillar of GLB, works well."

—Fed Governor Mark W. Olson at the 107th Annual Convention of the Maryland Bankers Association, Palm Beach, Florida, May 21, 2002

What does this mean for the Federal Reserve? (Why do you think the Fed is buying its third office building in D.C.?) The original 1913 Fed Act limited it to one office building! Ha! When they had to have a second office building they connected the two with a tunnel under 20th Street.

Specifically, GLB requires that the Federal Reserve serve as an "umbrella" supervisor of all BHCs, including FHCs, and rely on functional regulators to conduct the necessary examinations of each individual organization. Who are these "functional" regulators? (Don't kid yourself, the Fed "sups" and examiners will be looking over their shoulders and their Internet printouts.) Well, the regulation that was being done continues:

◆ The Office of the Comptroller of the Currency continues to regulate and supervise national banks.

◆ The Federal Deposit Insurance Corporation and state banking departments regulate state nonmember banks.

◆ The Federal Reserve and state banking departments regulate state Fed member banks.

◆ The Office of Thrift Supervision regulates thrifts.

For the financial services subsidiary of the new FHC (Federal Holding Company), the functional regulator is the state insurance authority for insurance affiliates and the Securities and Exchange Commission for brokerage and securities affiliates. The functional regulator maintains responsibility over the subsidiary. However, the umbrella supervisor (the Fed) evaluates the strength and activities of the holding company, ensuring the strength and viability of the FHC's financial condition and the viability of subsidiary depository institutions.

Sweep Deposits

So now you can obtain more and more services from your "bank." (Should we now call them "service providers"?) If you are a trust or fiduciary customer of your bank it can buy and sell securities when you tell them to, and it will establish "networking" arrangements with registered broker-dealers to provide you with many other securities services.

> **Money Meanings**
>
> A **sweep deposit** is a deposit in which the cash balance is transferred into an interest-bearing investment, such as a money market fund, or equities, such as stock or mutual funds.

If you want, your bank will *sweep deposit* funds into shares of no-load money market mutual funds. (Well, watch it, those funds aren't exactly high paying!) We could fill up this page with all of these new services, but it will be more pragmatic for you to sit down with the right functionary at your bank and find out more about what your bank has to offer. Yes, I know you like to "bank" on that PC, good old "Internet banking." More about that later.

Have you been seeking counsel from your financial services provider regarding that new financial venture? Well, some of the largest holding companies are funding venture capital. The largest banks earned $7.7 billion in 2000 and lost $4.5 billion in 2001. Now you know what the term "venture" means!

Securitizations

How about "securitization" activities by financial service providers? You know, pooling a number one kind of asset and issuing a "security" backed thereby. I spent years promoting MBSs (home mortgage backed securities) after I founded Freddie Mac (FHLMC).

Some securitizations require the loss risks remain with the bank issuer, some require just part of the risk remain therein. Yes, that holding company or that bank had to have capital resources and full disclosures their examiners might find inadequate. So management must disclose "everything" about the process including the charge-offs and the delinquency statuses.

Today's Financial Services

Today's financial services world reflects the increasing sophistication of financial institution customers and their "servers," not just the old fashioned one office, one state "bank." That bank you deal with is one player on a team including investment banker-counselors, insurance coverage providers, and deposit-and-loan sources, all under the same holding company. You receive all those financial service offers in your e-mail and your mailbox and your telephone and your "personal information manager" gadget, don't you? Is all that tech development positive? No, all those servers have real-time access to your credit info and your public records.

Well, there are still more than 6,000 banking organizations in the United States. They have thousands of competitors that don't have bank charters. The largest financial service provider is Citigroup, with more than $1 trillion in assets. Is it alone up on that financial mountain? No, there are 13 financial holding companies with more than $100 billion in assets, and an international array of customers. Remember those financial gorillas overseas, in addition. Of course they are coming to do financing in the world's largest mega market, the United States.

Is the FRB Overworked?

With all of the added responsibilities, the consolidation of the financial services sector, and the varied new services being offered by financial institutions, how does the Federal Reserve System get the job (all the jobs) done?

One of the biggest challenges that the FRB system faces is that most examination and supervisory duties need to be done in each of the Federal Reserve districts. The individual Fed banks and branches are in daily contact with the banks in their districts and have the most current data available to assist in supervising member banks. Remember, there are 12 districts, each with their own board of directors and executive staff and their own way of doing things. This is one of the great strengths of the FRB system, but it has proven to be an enormous challenge to developing a common consistent approach to supervision and regulation.

In late 2000, the FRB approved a major realignment of supervisory staff to enable the Federal Reserve to fulfill its role as the "umbrella supervisor." The change in the organizational structure was designed to improve coordination and consistency of supervision, particularly in regard to policy development, coordination of system automation projects, and supervision of global financial institutions.

This change was the result of a System Strategic Planning Coordinating Group made up of members of the FRB, Reserve bank presidents, and senior managers appointed by the FRB in 1995. Their mission was to build a framework to enable the Board, the banks, and Fed product and support offices to produce their own more detailed and coordinated plans. Within the framework of this group, strategic planning and resource allocation is done with a system-wide perspective but still allows each Federal Reserve district to address particular regional needs.

Future organizational changes will ensure that the system as a whole is prepared to deal with changes in the industry and the recent changes resulting from the GLB but still stay responsive to the regional needs of each Federal Reserve district.

Economic Wisdom

"Changes in bank activities over the past decade, however, have created new risk-management issues. Increased use of off-balance-sheet activities has allowed banks to reduce risk exposures, and for that reason these sophisticated activities constitute important improvements to risk management. But they can also involve complex transactions that may require expanded risk-management capabilities. They also require tight controls and careful attention to the accounting issues to ensure that their income-recognition and risk-transfer intent is reflected in the institutions' financial reporting. Though the Federal Reserve has not noticed widespread abuse in this area, we have uncovered instances in which the financial reporting has not reflected the substance of the transaction, and we have asked that it be corrected."

—Fed Governor Mark W. Olson at the 107th Annual Convention of the Maryland Bankers Association, Palm Beach, Florida, May 21, 2002

Planning to Meet New Responsibilities

In the Fed's Strategic Planning Document for the years 2001 to 2005, six key issues were identified as part of the Fed's planning to adapt to its new roles:

- ◆ **Human Resources and Board Development.** The new work to be conducted by the Board will require new skill sets for some employees or the hiring of employees with skills not needed before. This could require employee incentives and benefits as well as workplace flexibility to attract the best talent.

◆ **Financial Modernization and Reform.** Multinational and highly complex mergers, creation of large financial conglomerates, the volume and complexity of OTC derivatives, and the growth of hedge funds will stretch the capacity of current supervisory programs. The Fed will work with other regulators in the United States and abroad to develop methods for incorporating all the new complexities.

◆ **Assistance to Support Foreign Governments, Central Banks, and International Organizations.** This area is not only affected by changes from GLB, but also new pressures after September 11, 2001, and the need to control terrorists funds. Fed staff works with various international bank regulators, the World Bank, Agency for International Development, State Department, and Treasury.

◆ **Technology.** All the new responsibilities of the Fed especially related to its umbrella duties requires keeping with technological advances. The Fed not only needs to keep pace with technological innovation, but also must keep an eye on risk management strategies. The volume of data gathered, stored, and analyzed will grow rapidly as the Fed takes on its new responsibilities.

◆ **Communications.** The Internet is playing a larger role in helping to keep the public informed about the Fed's old and new roles.

◆ **Facilities.** All these duties will of course require space to work. Long-term space planning is important to keep the money machine's staff operating in its most efficient and cost effective manner. Security improvements and employee safety is a key issue here as well.

No one can really answer the question of how the Fed will respond to all the challenges the changes that financial modernization will ultimately bring to bear on the money machine. Fed governors and staff have made plans for the changes already identified and must continue their close scrutiny for indicators of activities not yet identified.

One thing you can be sure of is that the Fed's new roles will be in a constant state of flux, requiring its ability to act quickly as needs arise.

The Least You Need to Know

◆ The Gramm-Leach-Bliley Act of 1999 was the most dramatic change to banking in the last 40 years.

◆ The Fed's new responsibilities as "umbrella" regulator have given it regulatory authority over many new and old forms of financial services.

◆ Banking modernization has brought new complexities to the role of the regulators and created the need for new staff as well as technological development.

◆ The Fed is working with regulators both in the United States and abroad to develop mechanisms to ensure safe and sound banking practices as the roles of banks shift in this new financial economy.

15

Playing the Numbers Game

In This Chapter

◆ Modeling money

◆ Charting a path

◆ Numbers growth

◆ New economy numbering

When the Federal Reserve was first established in 1913, the Fed's monetary policy mandate was to "provide an elastic currency." In order words, a monetary system that was flexible enough to avoid the financial panics that frequently plagued the banking community in the late nineteenth and early twentieth centuries.

There were no legislative mandates to "promote maximum employment, production and purchasing power." That came in 1946 with the passing of the Employment Act of 1946. Or no mandate to "promote full employment and production, increased real income, balanced growth, a balanced Federal budget." That was mandated by the Full Employment and Balanced Growth Act of 1978, or Humphrey-Hawkins as it is commonly known.

As the Fed and its responsibilities have evolved since its inception in 1913, so has the process of developing and executing monetary policy. Let's take a look at how the Fed crunches the numbers to meet its mandates.

Econometrics—Money Modeling

Fed economists and researchers develop economic forecasts and plan monetary policy by using a technique called econometrics, which enables them to study the numbers and develop economic theories. Essentially, econometrics is a technique of economic analysis that expresses economic theory in terms of mathematical relationships and then tests that theory through statistical research.

> **Fiscal Facts**
>
> Econometrics is generally attributed to Norwegian economist Ragnar Frisch, a professor of economics at the University of Oslo in Norway. He and economist Jan Tinbergen received the first Nobel Prize in Economics for their work in econometric modeling and measurement. Frisch invented the word "econometrics" to refer to the use of mathematical and statistical techniques to test economic hypotheses, and was also the first to use the words microeconomics and macroeconomics.

Econometrics or money modeling is almost a religion at our central bank. The Fed first used econometric modeling in the 1960s. In the 1970s, the Division of International Finance at the Fed began to develop an international model. The current models used by the FRB were developed in the early 1990s.

The main policy model used at the Fed today is called FRB/WORLD and includes 250 behavioral equations. The high turnover of staff (and Board members) at the Board has added to the use of the FRB/WORLD model, but the Board staff still does an enormous amount of the research in addition to its models to formulate monetary policy.

You have read the chairman's comments on productivity and on both positive and negative aspects of our new economy. Well, partly new, right? Let's take a look at where the numbers were in early 2002.

Give the current FRB credit—they have acted and reacted strongly (and rightly) to stabilize U.S. economic growth and maintain historically low inflation. March 2002 unemployment figures were not encouraging, increasing to 6 percent, which was the highest in 8 years. In 2000, unemployment was only 3.9 percent.

The total Fed monetary base (the Fed supply of permanent reserves) was up $61.4 billion on May 1, 2002. Did you ever think that we would even see a projection of only "about 1.5 percent '*chain-type*' price inflation" from the FOMC? That was their projection in the 2002 Money Report to Congress. The message was that banks had ample "reserves" (deposits with the Fed) and that near term inflation did not appear to be a problem.

Money Meanings

A **chain-type** index is a calculation method that enables the comparison of nonadjacent years. First, a calculation is made to determine the real changes between adjacent years. Annual rates of real changes are then chained (multiplied) together to find the rate of real change between nonadjacent years. Chained dollars are preferred to constant dollars because they capture the effect of changes in the components of the GDP, while constant dollars only reflect overall price inflation. Aren't you glad you don't have to do these calculations?

In that same report, the FOMC told the Congress they were concerned that 2002's "real" GDP's "central tendency" would only range between 2.5 percent and 3 percent. Before we start crunching the numbers, let's quickly review why the number crunching is important.

Inflation—What Is That Anyway?

Inflation is an increase in the general level of prices in the economy. If things cost more, and your income remains the same (or declines) you won't be able to buy as much. Before 2000, the Fed measured inflation using the Consumer Price Index (CPI)—a measure of the change in cost of a representative basket of goods and services such as food, energy, housing, clothing, transportation, medical care, entertainment, and education.

In the February 2000 Humphrey Hawkins report, the Fed began forecasting the rate of inflation based on an inflation measure contained in the GDP (Gross Domestic Product) report. That measure is called the chain-type price index (or deflator) used by the Fed staff when they project future consumer spending. In Fedspeak the staff calls this "the personal consumption expenditures," or PCE. PCE is the amount of money individuals spend on goods and services. It's the single largest component of the GDP, approximately two thirds of the whole thing.

Some more good news. How many econometricians projected the prompt and easy recovery from the good ol' recession of 2001? Consumer spending was watched in the mild recession, watched with awe. Carol Consumer and her husband refinanced their home mortgage and bought that shiny RV with zero rate financing and all that price discounted "information equipment" for the den. There is something about 6 percent (or lower) home mortgage interest rates and the generous sale prices in most markets that give refinancing a boost.

Economic Wisdom

"In past Monetary Policy Reports to the Congress, the FOMC has framed its inflation forecasts in terms of the consumer price index. The chain-type price index for PCE draws extensively on data from the consumer price index but, while not entirely free of measurement problems, has several advantages relative to the CPI. The PCE chain-type index is constructed from a formula that reflects the changing composition of spending and thereby avoids some of the upward bias associated with the fixed-weight nature of the CPI. In addition, the weights are based on a more comprehensive measure of expenditures. Finally, historical data used in the PCE price index can be revised to account for newly available information and for improvements in measurement techniques, including those that affect source data from the CPI; the result is a more con-sistent series over time. This switch in presentation notwithstanding, the FOMC will continue to rely on a variety of aggregate price measures, as well as other information on prices and costs, in assessing the path of inflation."

—February 2000 Humphrey Hawkins Report

Home sales, housing starts, and shipments of nondefense capital goods turned up and modest step-ups in manufacturing were measured. That homebuilder down the street had would-be buyers lined up, 10 to a house! Did you hear that TV head say that "real" interest rates were zero?

Charting Fed Actions

I don't have to remind you that economics is the "dismal science." Think about the May 19, 2002, utterances. No, they did not say "we don't know how to project this period." The FOMC language was: "for the foreseeable future the risks of economic weakness and of heightened inflation pressures are balanced." Good communicating!

That was the first such pronouncement since February 2000, when the Fed committee consented to issue readable statements weighing those risks. How important? Look at the following table, which relates "risk statements" and subsequent rate "target actions."

Monetary Trends—Balance of Risk Statements and Subsequent Rate Target Actions Since February 2000

Risk Statement at Previous Meeting	Target Cut	No Change in Target	Target Increase
Weakness	11	2	0
Inflation	0	5	2

You can see that it will serve you to make a little note of the FOMC statements, anticipating that next action. Start with the 13 times since February 2000 when the committee commented that the risks were weighted toward conditions which might produce economic weakness. You can see in the previous chart that 11 out of 13 "weakness" warnings were followed by easing target actions, 25 basis points ($1/4$ of 1 percent) or 50 ($1/2$ of 1 percent) basis point target Fed funds reductions. Three of these cuts were made between meetings (serious, right?). Only two were action "passes" (no action). How about warnings regarding the possible return of that old inflation dragon? Twice the rate target was raised, but five "passes" occurred. (Aren't you glad you didn't bet on this one?) You can see that the statements of both varieties do give indications of possible, or probable actions in the near future. Useful? Certainly.

> **CAUTION**
>
> **Ups and Downs**
>
> In recent years the FOMC has not signaled (or "leaned") one way in the utterances and reversed itself in the subsequent targeting action. The committee's language was careful as they commented on "... the risks to the outlook as weighted mainly toward economic weakness." Now they call their Fedspeak their "bias."

The committee's economic projections were equally careful. You certainly recall that the Fed had acted very promptly and strongly following the September 11 terrorist attacks, effectively countering their depressing economic impacts, however temporary.

Voting in Public View

One more useful development in Fed language. Beginning with its statement after the March 19, 2002, meeting, the "roll call"—the votes by each FOMC member—has been published. The September 24, 2002, FOMC statement communicated that "The Federal Open Market Committee decided today to keep its target for the federal funds rate unchanged at $1^3/4$ percent." Then came the new Fedspeak: "Voting against the action were Edward M. Gramlich and Robert D. McTeer. Governor Granlich and President McTeer preferred a reduction in the target for the federal funds rate."

No staff member has to remind the FOMC committee in 2002 that the full effects of the Fed's huge money pumping was taking effect 6 to 12 months after the increases in the "Ms" (the various measures of the money supply). Similarly, the committee rightly foresaw the temporary increase in the unemployment level which occurred in 2002, projected to range between 6 and 6.5 percent. Greenspan and other members have commented repeatedly about today's U.S. gains in productivity (the output per hour of workers in nonfarm businesses).

Preston's Points

Believe me, I am so glad that this listing of dissenters was not the custom when I was so often dissenting from Paul Volcker and his majority. I had enough press coverage as a "troublemaker" as I argued and voted for lower rates and more support for economic growth. The Fed's rates at 16 percent and higher were having negative impacts. Ask former Fed governor and state banking supervisor Martha Seger when next you attend one of her presentations. We dissented together several times.

Growing by the Numbers

The Wall Street Journal's May 13, 2002, headline screamed, "Greenspan Expresses Optimism for Growth of U.S. Economy." According to the *Journal*, Greenspan said, "the economy may be able to grow faster than even the impressive productivity figures of the late 1990s indicate, as companies start to reap benefits from the last decade's investment binge."

The Wall Street Journal went on to say that numbers reported by Greenspan showed:

> "… Higher productivity, or output per hour, enables companies to produce more and pay higher wages without raising prices, thereby raising living standards. Its growth accelerated to 2.4 percent from 1995 to 2000, from 1.4 percent in the two preceding decades.

Still quoting "Sir Allen" (he was knighted in 2002, in Britain, you know) …

> "It [productivity] held up surprisingly well during last year's recession …. Because of these 'disruptive effects,' underlying productivity growth in the late 1990s, when investment boomed, 'may have been somewhat underestimated,' Mr. Greenspan said after a speech at a Federal Reserve Bank of Chicago conference. … Sir Allen said one reason for the 7 percent productivity growth in the last two calendar quarters may be 'that contrary to what intuition would suggest,' last year's investment bust enhanced productivity by reducing disruption …. 'We don't have enough evidence' to know if this effect is important, 'but we are obviously struggling to find out.'"

Let's take a quick look at what was behind these statements from Greenspan. The Fed found that one set of quarterly changes in the prior year's inventory cutback appeared to be over, with some restocking oncoming. The Bush administration's higher spending for defense and other needs, together with the tax cuts and the extensions of unemployment benefits which Congress had authorized, both were noted.

Another quantitative measure reviewed by the May 7, 2002, FOMC was the continuing negative balance of payments as the United States continued to import so much more than it could export and market to our trading partners overseas. First, the dollar rose in its market value, trading with the yen and the euro. That rise made U.S. goods and services less competitive (more expensive overseas).

In 2002, as the economy recovered, the dollar fell in the market (you get more bucks for your Euro), but still the investors from overseas kept buying U.S. securities. Fed bank presidents from the districts with formidable farm lobbies warned that Congress would likely step up the trade barriers to many of those foreign food and material imports. Oil prices and other energy costs were likely to rise during an Iraqi war so that the 2001 stimulus to consumer spending from that cheaper power source would be absent, or perhaps reversed in 2002. This meant that the lagged, indirect effects on producer costs still might affect the pace of price increases.

Now that you know "all" the numbers being considered by the FOMC, (only kidding) take a minute to read the May 7, 2002, statement following this FOMC meeting. The FOMC decided to leave interest rates unchanged:

> "The Federal Open Market Committee decided today to keep its target for the federal funds rate unchanged at 1¾ percent.

> "The information that has become available since the last meeting of the committee confirms that economic activity has been receiving considerable upward impetus from a market swing in inventory investment. Nonetheless, the degree of the strengthening in final demand over coming quarters, an essential element in sustained economic expansion, is still uncertain.

> "In these circumstances, although the stance of monetary policy is currently accommodative, the committee believes that, for the foreseeable future, against the background of its long-run goals of price stability and sustainable economic growth and of the information currently available, the risks are balanced with respect to the prospects for both goals."

Note that the FOMC highlights the fact that there is upward impetus from the swing in inventory investment, but other key economic signs are still uncertain. The committee left rates unchanged because the numbers showed a balance of risks between inflation and recession.

My Numbers Can Beat Up Your Numbers

Why is the economy doing so well? Well, the Fed reduced interest rates 11 times following the September 11 terrorist attack on New York and D.C. One commentator joked in a *New York Times* column on September 25, 2001, that lenders are almost giving away money.

Yes, it is difficult historically to find a mild recession with a quick, soft recovery. Economists since the 1960s have believed that if unemployment rates went below 4.5 to 5.0 percent for an extended period of time, the ensuing rising labor costs would translate into higher prices and a wage-price spiral that would be hard to contain. Reversal would require recession, many argued (and projected). In 2002, we had 1.5 to 2.0 percent unemployment, with millions of part timers and contract workers. For many firms the motto is "outsource, outsource, outsource."

Preston's Points

Back when I was vice chair of the Fed, most forecasters would have been highly (and publicly) critical of those of us who had not voted to raise rates and rate targets to slow an economy that was operating at today's low unemployment. (I know, it happened to me.) Back then, even if you couldn't see inflation looming on the horizon there was no doubt that that big old bear was waiting to grab the "Goldilocks Economy."

When you watch those talk shows with their forecasters and pundits, often it sounds as though the dismal science is alive and well, doesn't it? Always keep in mind your own experience and those of your family in the workplace. Part of our economy truly is "new," and information technology driven. Our 2000–2002 experience is truly encouraging. Remember the Clinton campaign motto in his first run for the presidency? "It's the economy, stupid."

I know of no other recent time when the evolution of Fed monetary policy has been so fundamental, and so effective. Did the Burns Fed match this "Greenspan Star Wars" progress in policymaking effectiveness? No. Did the Volcker Fed? No (and I was there). More good news: The four new appointees of the Bush administration are innovative individuals whose forward thinking abilities were shown in the previous positions they held (one a chief staffer at the board—Don Kohn). I remember vividly my colleague who had held such a prominent Board staff position, and how effective a governor he was (Lyle Gramley). New Governor Ben S. Bernanke will lead a discussion on fundamentally reforming FOMC policymaking. Former Princeton professor Bernanke has proposed changing FOMC targeting. He favors policy targeting on the Fed funds rate or its equivalent.

Explaining the New Economy

So how do we explain our second millennium economy? Has there been a fundamental improvement in the structure of the U.S. economy, making it less inflation-prone, or is it being influenced by temporary factors that might return to "normal" and send the economy into an inflationary wage-price spiral? Today's U.S. "new economy" (well, partly new) is such a different economic universe than we have ever experienced before. You would have to look into your crystal ball to answer my question.

Technology skills are now at a premium, but workers may be insecure about the marketability of their skills and their ability to land a new job in our emerging service-based economy. There may also be more aggressive employer resistance to labor cost increases than previously. Business owners and managers appear to have a strong belief that today's business environment is so competitive that if they attempt to pass cost increases on to their customers every time they will lose business to their competitors.

Employers have been able to increase productivity enough to absorb some compensation increases without comparable price increases. Whether employers will be able to sustain this growth remains to be seen, but comments from several Fed officials indicate that for the year 2002–2003 term, economic expansion is expected to continue.

Fighting Over the Models

You are well aware of the many research teams that the Fed board and its 12 Fed bank colleagues utilize. Remember, we took a close look at that in Chapter 9. None of us can escape the media quotations of the St. Louis Fed's econometric model, as only one example.

The London *Economist* weekly is another source, outside the Fed. It argued on November 11, 2000, that one of its concerns was the rising probability of "deflation" (falling prices) in many countries around the world. We have been seeing "the friendly sort," of price cutting (disinflation) when new technology and rapid productivity growth push down costs, as in the computer and telecom industries. This boosts real incomes and spending power. The second (dangerous) variety (deflation) is caused by a slump in demand and huge excess capacity, which can trigger a downward spiral of falling prices, shrinking demand, and financial distress. The friendly type of disinflation has been evident for several years, but now there are signs that the malign sort may be spreading.

You may be utterly confused by the numbers game. We hope you have a better idea of why you've had such difficulty understanding economists when they open their mouths, but now feel better armed to read through the numbers. Now we'll move from the number crunchers to the power brokers who use those numbers to make decisions.

The Least You Need to Know

- For Fed governors and staff, econometrics is like a religion for planning monetary policy.

- You can develop a simple chart of Fed statements and projections to track the likely future moves.

- There are competing money models that frequently give different economic projections.

- Is there a new economic structure? The jury is still out on that one.

Part 5

Sharing Money Power

Sometimes you may think the Fed is all powerful, but it's not. We look at some of the key players in the United States and internationally that share money power with the Fed.

You've certainly seen Alan Greenspan answer to Congress, but that's not the only federal agency with which the Fed must coordinate its policy-making decisions. You meet the agencies here in the United States and abroad.

Chapter 16

Politics as Usual

In This Chapter

- ◆ Who's in charge
- ◆ Grilling the chairman
- ◆ Uneasy allies

Politics in Washington, D.C., is like a game of Chinese Checkers. People take one step forward, one step back, and often jump over opponents to get to where they want to go.

The Federal Reserve, especially under the leadership of Alan Greenspan, is very good at the game. When the parties get into a fight they can't resolve, the courts get to play referee.

Let's take a look at the interplay between the Fed and the other key players—the president, Congress, and the Treasury Department.

The Fed and the President: Who's in Charge?

I'm sure you remember from our discussions in Chapter 5, that the president has the authority to appoint the most powerful monetary policy makers in the land, the secretary of the treasury and the chairman and vice chairman of the Federal Reserve.

The secretary of the treasury is a political appointment, a cabinet position selected by the new sitting president. When the president leaves office the secretary of the treasury leaves with him.

The Fed chairman and vice chairman terms do not end when the administration changes. When the Fed chairman's four-year term is up (currently two years after the presidential election), the new chair is appointed by the president and confirmed by the Senate. Actually there are two confirmations. First as a governor for a 14-year term, then as chairman of the Board of Governors for a 4-year term. The president also appoints (or reappoints) other governors of the Fed Board, as those long terms run out.

Preston's Points

Because I inherited the two year remaining term of my predecessor, Reagan twice appointed me governor (two year remaining term, then full four-year term) and once to the vice chairmanship. Those Senate confirmation hearings can be brutal. Senior senators have many staff members, so they may have information about your academic or business career to use. Yes, the political mistakes you made if you served in state government (I did) can come back to haunt you. One of the senators at my first Fed confirmation hearing didn't like my founding of FHLMC (Freddie Mac) when I was Federal Home Loan Bank chairman. He made me admit to some of the errors made by Freddie, but I tried to demonstrate how it is in the public interest to support such a strong "secondary" (resale) market for home mortgages (no sale to the senator). He took another tack: "You wrote that real estate college textbook glorifying real estate brokers, didn't you?" "Yes, Senator, but the book helped people understand the home-buying process." "Ha," he smirked. (I lost that round, but the committee confirmed me, anyway.)

It may seem difficult to understand how the FRB can remain independent from the other branches of government. If you do your job you "may" be reappointed or you may not.

In recent history FRB Chairman Greenspan was appointed by President Ronald Reagan, and reappointed by Presidents George H. Bush and Bill Clinton. Paul Volcker was first appointed by President Jimmy Carter when Carter couldn't persuade Bank of America president Tom Clauson to move his family to Washington, then later Volcker was reappointed by President Ronald Reagan.

A Personal Look

Let me tell you about some of my personal experiences during eight years of Washington office holding. It certainly taught me the vital importance of independence and will help you to understand the relationship between the White House and the Fed.

Once you are confirmed you change your very working behavior. I appreciated inter-facing with the White House's Ed Meese and Treasury Secretary Jimmy Baker before my appointment (I had known Meese in our state governmental days when I was California Savings and Loan (S&L) commissioner). Once I was confirmed as Fed vice chair, I stopped going over to the Oval Office to chat with my friends. Yes, I periodi-cally briefed the vice president (Papa Bush) about domestic and international eco-nomic trends, but that I saw as my job.

I met about once a week with the undersecretary of the treasury, Beryl Sprinkel, to exchange economic and regulatory views. This was a rather formal exchange, though. I only saw the president and his lieutenants at big formal meetings and at trade asso-ciation get-togethers. I never, I repeat never, told then Vice President Bush nor Sprinkel what I thought the next Fed actions would be, nor anything about the super-visory actions we had or were going to take. Remember, I was serving in the early 1980s (1982–1986) when the Texas economy was going through some hard times. Let me give Bush some credit, too—not once did he plead for lower interest rates (we had them "at the ceiling") nor for less regulatory action by the Fed in the Texas problem banks and thrifts. Not once!

Presidential Briefing

Notice I said "some credit." Years later, right after George H. was elected president I secured a 1988 meeting at the White House with the new president, some of his key staffers, and the new treasury secretary. I recruited five other participants from finan-cial institutions, CEOs the new president knew. Yes, I had been out of the Fed vice chairmanship for two years, partnering with former Treasury Secretary Bill Simon Sr. in acquiring three sick S&Ls and one healthy one, so this wasn't a meeting about the economy.

I was briefing them about a piece of pending disastrous legislation, disastrous for homebuilding, inner city redevelopment, and the financial institutions industry. Together, the six of us communicated how costly the implementation of this proposed legislation would be to U.S. taxpayers. "As much as $200 billion cost, Mr. President," I warned. (My estimates were too low!)

This monstrous bill was the congressionally proposed FIRREA, the Financial Institu-tions Reform, Recovery and Enforcement Act of 1989. Passage of this Act would breach hundreds of contracts entered into by the federal government with investor groups. There were long negotiated contracts with the money raisers like Bill Simon Sr. and me, who would invest in, buy, and fix up broken banks and thrifts. (The act was enacted August 8, 1989—we didn't convince the Whitehousers nor the "Pres.") Several economists have lately estimated that the costs to us taxpayers will amount to $250 billion! More later on the history of "FIRREA." Now back to the Fed.

Independent Streak

The Fed has built a reputation for independent monetary policymaking and has bene-fited from strong chairmen to maintain the independence, sometimes to the displeas-ure of the sitting administration. In Chapter 3, we talked about previous Chairman Marriner Eccles. He was an ex-chairman and a governor by the time he defied President Truman in a battle between the Fed and the Treasury, a crucial battle that the Fed ultimately won.

During the Vietnam War President Lyndon Johnson didn't want his economic stimu-lus policies to be undermined by higher interest rates. The administration needed cheap money to finance the war and the Great Society programs. Fed Chair William McChesney Martin favored an increase in the discount rate as a measure to contain higher inflation.

> **CAUTION**
>
> **Ups and Downs** _____
>
> A showdown occurred at the December 3, 1965, FOMC meeting. President Johnson and key administration officials tried to influence Chairman Bill Martin and other members of the FOMC to vote against an interest rate hike. The committee voted four to three to raise the discount rate, demonstrating the increasing independence of the FRB. (Important? You probably know that LBJ's long career road was covered by the footprints of winning. He "ran the Senate," didn't he?)

There is no formal reporting between the president and the chairman of the FRB. The legislative mandates are between the FRB and the Congress, but the president and the chairman do meet informally, generally without any agendas or announce-ments after the meetings and at other times when major financial crises strike. Don't forget the Fed is the "lender of last resort" when the financial weather gets really heavy. When that happens, you know now to watch the media discussion of what is happening at the Fed Bank of New York and the Fed Board.

Grilling the Chairman Looks Great on TV

As we have discussed before, the Fed is a creature of Congress. Through a variety of legislative initiatives (discussed in previous chapters) the Congress has defined the

Fed's monetary policy goals and objectives in broader and broader terms—maximum employment, stable prices, and moderate long-term interest rates, functioning domestic and international financial markets, and community reinvestment. No central bank, not the Bank of Japan, the Bank of England, not even the Eurobank, has the wide responsibility and authority the Fed has.

Congress has also required twice yearly reporting by the chairman to Congress on monetary goals and objectives. Although law does not require this any longer, the FRB has found it useful in keeping Congress informed as to the current economic well-being of the country. In addition to the twice-yearly testimony, the chairman and other members of the FRB frequently testify to various Congressional committees on topics ranging from the availability of credit to small businesses to antiterrorism initiatives.

Congressional Impacts

So how does Congress impact monetary policy? One of the most obvious ways is by confirming or not confirming appointees to the Board. Individual senators can hold up nominations in an attempt to influence policy and appointments. The latter years of Clinton's second term were marked by Congressional inaction on more than one candidate for Fed Board membership. Political power splits are especially evident when the president and the Senate majority leadership are from different political parties and explain in part why there have been vacancies on the Board in recent years.

In difficult economic conditions, members of Congress always try to influence monetary policy. (That's their job, right?) For example, from 1983 to 1985, the late Rep. Henry Gonzalez (D-TX) introduced resolutions to impeach Fed Chairman Paul Volcker and members of the FOMC in an attempt to influence the Fed to reduce interest rates. I was serving then, and I assure you that, not surprisingly, the resolutions didn't make it out of committee. Similar legislative efforts to change the regulatory attitudes and implementations of the Fed have had minimal results. Other regulators are not quite so independent, but all resist Congressional pressures stemming from their constituents.

FIRREA Disaster

A major example? It was very difficult for the Congress and the FHLB board to resist FIRREA, the "tear up the contracts" law we discussed, because so many S&Ls were failing or near-failure in the 1980s and 1990s. Let's take a closer look at that.

The FIRREA legislation, together with 1986 amendments to the Internal Revenue Code, severely restricted the whole real estate lending process in the United States.

Many of the law's proponents emphasized the "bad guys," whom history would reveal made up a very small proportion of mortgage lenders in the country. The legislation thus commanded major media attention and promoted many reelection successes for its proponents. Its contraction of housing financing and home building commanded little media or political attention.

Let me share with you an analysis by Peat Marwick Main and Co., a leading CPA firm working with one of Simon and Martin holdings companies, WESPAR Financial Services, Inc. (Wespar). Our question to the accounting firm was what were the potential effects on the 2,550 FSLIC-insured thrifts that were "solvent under generally accepted accounting principles"?

Peat Marwick's study found a "traditional thrift" was well capitalized and had the overwhelming percentage of its assets in home and multifamily mortgage loans and other residential and small business financing, including construction loans. As was typical of thrifts in 1989, there was a substantial portion of its assets in mortgage-backed securities (MBSs). The case study S&L has "well capitalized equity," and was a good borrower from its district FHLB Bank, which comprised 20 percent of the total of liabilities and equity.

This "typical" S&L had $2.2 billion in assets and 27 branches. It had acquired troubled thrifts in its last five years, some at the urging of the FHLB and of the local office of the deposit insurer, the FSLIC. These owners also had affiliates that did real estate appraisal, real estate developing (housing), insurance brokerage, and title insurance. Wouldn't you call these folks "financial services firms"? Yes.

So what did Peat warn us the effects of FIRREA would be when it passed later in the year? First, that the one thrift example described above should be easily capable of complying with those new guidelines. Peat said, "You already have sufficient capital." (In that one example, not in all of them.) "The expectation is that it will continue to have positive earnings." Then here came the negatives:

♦ Current returns will not attract new investors.

♦ Future earnings will not provide enough capital to fund additional acquisitions.

♦ The limits to this kind of (healthy) thrifts growth imply that the segment of the industry it represents will not be able to fill the void in housing investment left by other thrift industry segments.

So I took the Peat Marwick study and much information regarding sick and sicker thrifts to the White House, to a group of the House Banking Committee members and to an S&L and housing conference in Utah. The FDIC under the direction of

William Seidman was sending examiners into certain S&Ls, borrowing examiners from the Fed, the Comptroller, and the FSLIC. (You can see that when it is necessary, the several financial regulators work together.) In many cases, the result was closing the bank or the S&L and paying off the depositors.

Deposit liabilities of the thrifts in *conservatorship* were sold off to banks, many of whom had modest home mortgage portfolios, and housing development crashed to a 10-year low.

You can see that this story of a historic Congressional policy blunder continues, at the expense of us taxpayers. "Act Three" is a history of the Treasury and the Fed policies after Congress ordered them to "go get them"—the good guys and the bad guys.

Now that we've looked at the Congress and the Fed, let's move to the relationship between the Treasury Department and the Fed.

Fiscal Facts

A conservatorship of sick savings and loans was established when they were unable to manage their property and investments. Once a conservatorship was put in place, all income and disbursements were managed by the conservator, which in the case of S&Ls was the FSLIC or FDIC.

Uneasy Allies: The Fed and the Treasury Department

The Fed and the Treasury are necessary allies during periods of widespread bank and thrift failures. The 1987–1990 epoch was one of those times, and the Reagan administration struggled to meet the financial demands of its two deposit insurers: the FSLIC and the FDIC. Early in 1987, it appeared as though the FDIC would be required to spend $4 billion in that year to settle cases of failing banks, with the FSLIC spending over $3.7 billion on its failures, according to the banking industry's newspaper, *The American Banker*, in an article on January 6, 1987.

By midyear, 1985, the rising failure rate pushed the Treasury secretary to enlist the Fed chairman's support for a $10.825 capital infusion into the FSLIC, as the failures and the government takeovers PM mounted. Unfortunately, Treasury also supported legislative proposals to "sunset" the "regulatory forbearance" sections of the existing legal infrastructure. What did that mean? Rescinding the contracts the government (the FDIC and the FSLIC) had entered into giving "on paper" net worth accounts to groups willing to takeover the cleanups. The "on paper" capital accounts were called "regulatory capital."

The chaos in the savings and loan industry was not a major issue in the 1988 presidential campaign. This disturbing development was hardly mentioned. Both candidates for the presidency understood that the thrift crisis would be a major task, but there was almost no discussion of the matter during the campaign. Similarly, the "refinance, reregulate act" (FIRREA) which was enacted shortly after the election had bipartisan support.

The Bank Board (my old mortgage central bank) was dissolved and replaced by an Office of Thrift Supervision (OTS) under the guidance of the Treasury, like the Office of the Comptroller of the Currency, S&Ls would have to boost their capital and eschew some of their accounting atrocities and devote a higher share of their investments to residential housing. The FSLIC would also be closed and be replaced by a Savings Association Fund that would be operated as part of the FDIC. The enlarged FDIC would have power to examine all state-chartered S&Ls and to deny insurance to S&Ls that sought to exercise powers the federal agency believed might endanger the insurance fund—even if a state that chartered the S&L approved them.

Preston's Points

Meanwhile, Bill Simon Sr., our partners, and I continued with our efforts to restore four ailing savings and loans: Hon Fed Bank in Hawaii; Western Federal in Playa del Rey, California; Southern California Federal in Beverly Hills, California; and Bell S&L in San Mateo, California. We "repaired" Hon Fed Bank and sold it to Bank of America. How do you "repair" a sick financial institution? New capital, new management, sales of bad assets, and selling off losing branches. You can merge sick ones into healthy ones. FHLBB insisted we acquire Bell S&L, and after more than a year negotiating with the board by our able partner Larry Thrall, we capitulated. Bell was merged into healthy Western Federal (making it much less healthy). So Cal was imbued with new management and new business plans, and it disposed of many of its worst assets.

So you can see from all this that the Fed is only one of the key players in Washington, and its advice is not always heeded. Now we'll move on to the Fed and its relationship with other international money powers.

The Least You Need to Know

- The relationship between the White House and the Fed can be characterized by one of distance ... presidents have learned it is not wise to pressure the Fed to act.

- The Fed does have reporting responsibilities to the U.S. Congress and is frequently called to testify on pending legislation.

- The Fed and the U.S. Treasury may battle occasionally, but when a crisis strikes they work closely together.

Chapter 17

Going International

In This Chapter

- ◆ Exchanging money
- ◆ Foreign banking
- ◆ World money powers
- ◆ Emerging roles

Today we live in a "global economy" in which that Dell computer you bought was made in Taiwan, and your new neighbors moved in after living in the United States just three years. Their English has a heavy Spanish accent, but their kids attend the same school yours do, and they are doing well.

My car wasn't made in Detroit, but in Germany, and that movie we saw last Saturday was spoken in French, with English subtitles. Wasn't it great to take that cruise down the Rhine and Danube rivers with our university alumni friends? We paid for some of the local shopping in that new currency, the "euro," not in dollars (pictures of dead U.S. presidents). Well, no shopkeeper refused to accept dollars for payment, it just meant you had to keep in mind how many dollars it took to pay for that clothing your wife loved, when the price was in that European currency.

Twenty-seven major U.S. banks operate in Europe ("the European Union"), with assets totaling more than $650 billion. Their Euro competitors, 66 of them, provide competitive financial services in the United States, and their assets here are more than $1.7 trillion according to Governor Mark W. Olson when he testified before the Committee on Financial Services of the House of Representatives, May 22, 2002.

Let's take a look at the roles the Federal Reserve plays in the international arena as to interest rate stabilization, keeping money flowing, developing improved international bank supervision, participating in world banking institutions, and helping emerging countries strengthen their financial systems.

European Banking Center

Neither Paris nor London is the meeting center for international banking negotiations dealing with bank supervision and regulation. Basel, Switzerland is. I made many a voyage to tacky old Basel (look at all those train stations!) during my vice chairmanship. Most of the attendees were from what they call the "European Union," so we Americans and the Japanese bankers attending did not "have the floor" most of the time, they did (or the Brits did).

You know how Europeans love those get-togethers. They call their "bible" The Financial Services Action Plan of the European Union (FSAP). It implements policy on the following:

♦ Money laundering

♦ Investment services

♦ Capital standards and measurement

♦ International capital standards

♦ Banks, the Europeans never fell into the regulatory trap of our 1930s, isolating banking from other financial services)

> **Fiscal Facts**
>
> In Europe, a bank from one country can establish branches in any other "EU" country under the authority and supervision of its home country rules called the "European passport." Of course U.S. banks follow this path—first establish a bank in country "A," then utilize the "passport" for branches in countries B, C, and D.

The Basel Capital Accord of 1988 with its standards for supervising banks, adopted in 1992, were the product of decades of negotiation and the leadership of New York Fed President Bill McDonough. He led his Fed colleagues and all those central bankers from around the planet (nine Euro central bankers) to reach agreement on the issues we have listed previously.

Of course there is more to do. (There always is, right?) McDonough and company (only kidding) are working on shaping up the Basel Capital Accord with a better system of evaluating a financial institution's capital adequacy. What is that old media cliché, "more coming"?

Other cooperative Basel Accord organizations that bring U.S. and Euro regulators together include the International Organization of Securities Commissioners (IOSCO) and the International Association of Insurance Supervisors (IAIS). Do you have any doubt that your finances are "global" today?

Balancing World Money

No one has to remind you of how "open" our economy is today, open as to trade and financing. If you add the big dollar amounts of real exports and imports they total almost 30 percent of our GDP compared to about 10 percent in the early 1960s.

We've talked about how the Federal Reserve's monetary policy impacts interest rates in the United States. In the international arena the Fed's monetary policy can influence foreign exchange rates, as well as domestic interest rates. That is, as the dollar weakens compared to the euro, what should the Fed do? Or not do?

Fiscal Facts

Our international trading in securities is larger than trade in goods and services! Let me give you an example. In 1999, gross U.S. international transactions in securities totaled twice our GDP. Since 1995, investors from overseas have provided an average of 35 percent of the total credit raised by U.S. nonfinancial organizations.

Preston's Points

How often do international considerations affect the discount rate or the domestic policy directive for Fed Open Market Operations? My experience at FOMCs was that we spent time considering international developments, but these were related to their domestic impact—you know, all those exporters and their businesses. Yes, in the 1985–1986 period the international setbacks leaned us toward "looser" policies.

Treasury and the Fed

During the Reagan administration, Treasury Secretary James Baker led an international program to restore the dollar's value. Should the Fed be doing that in this millennium? The emergence of a weaker dollar and a relatively slow U.S. recovery has a global effect. We are by far the world's largest importer, have the world's largest negative balance of payments (imports over exports), and the biggest importer of overseas capital.

At a Senate hearing in May 2002, Alan Greenspan was asked question after question about how the Fed was charting the dollar's course in foreign exchange markets. Like, "Mr. Chairman, why had the dollar been declining in those markets and what is the Fed doing about that?" Fedspeak came flowing, but its message was "nothing, except maintaining orderly currency market behavior."

The Senate Committee summoned Greenspan and Treasury Security Paul O'Neill right after May 1, 2002, following three months of decline in the dollar. Unemployment had risen to 6 percent. Several of the senators' questions strongly implied that their business supporters were making the case that the strong dollar was "killing them." Question: "Doesn't it look as though a weaker dollar is necessary to sustain this weak economic recovery?" O'Neill's response argued that a strong dollar was in the best interest of the United States.

The U.S. Department of Treasury has primary responsibility for international financial policy, but the Treasury consults closely with the Fed and it's up to the Fed to implement whatever policy is adopted. When interest rates are changed in this country, it can affect the *foreign exchange* (*FX*) value of the dollar. So when the foreign exchange value of the dollar plunged to new lows in the late 1970s, the Fed cut the discount rate by 100 basis points (yes, 100), the largest reduction in 45 years. Then the Fed raised reserve requirements and bumped up the discount rate.

Money Meanings

The **foreign exchange** (**FX**) system was established by international leaders at the Bretton Woods Conference in July 1944. The system was developed to ensure a stable post-war international economic environment. Initially the value of gold as well as the value of the dollar determined the exchange rates of currencies. In 1973, Nixon dropped the gold standard without asking Congressional approval. Well, Congress didn't disapprove, either! The gold standard was dropped and today exchange rates are based on the supply and demand of different currencies in international markets. Remember, there are still many who feel the United States should go back on the gold standard.

Intervention

If the Treasury and the Fed decide deliberately to change the dollar's value, they carry out a function called "intervention." If the Fed wants to support the value of the U.S.

dollar, the New York Fed will buy dollars and sell foreign currency. Sometimes the Treasury and the Fed will decide to reduce the value of the dollar. To do this, the New York Fed would sell dollars and buy foreign currency.

Why does the value of the dollar matter? Basically these changes impact the import and export of products and services. When the dollar's value drops in the foreign markets, it will cost more to buy all that huge volume of goods imported into the United States. That lovely vacation in Paris and Rome will cost Americans more, also. It will be cheaper for people outside the United States to buy exported U.S. products. When the dollar value increases, the reverse happens. Imports become cheaper in this county, but our export goods are more expensive to buy.

The Federal Reserve doesn't buy or sell a large volume of dollars when it wants to intervene in FX markets. Instead, interventions are used to signal other foreign countries and bankers that there is a desire for exchange rate movement. Usually an intervention is coordinated with the central bank of the country whose currency is involved in the transaction.

Interventions are not common today. While in 1995, the U.S. monetary authorities intervened in the FX market eight times, the United States acted to intervene only once in the next three years. U.S. foreign exchange intervention has always occurred on a very modest scale compared with the total domestic and foreign "interventions." These transactions are performed by the New York Fed, but the Treasury can order the New York Fed to intervene on its behalf. Other countries will also use intervention more significantly to shift the standing of their currency on the FX.

Economic Wisdom

"The turmoil in the European Exchange Rate mechanism in 1992, the plunge in the exchange value of the Mexican peso at the end of 1994 and early 1995, and the recent sharp exchange rate adjustments in a number of Asian economies have shown how the new world of financial trading can punish policy misalignments, actual or perceived, with amazing alacrity. This is new. Even as recently as fifteen or twenty years ago, the size of the international financial system was a fraction of what it is today. Contagion effects were more limited, and, thus, breakdowns carried fewer negative consequences." Almost nobody talked about "LDC" (less developed country) debt. Came the 1980s, virtually every financial "player" did.

—Alan Greenspan in a speech at the 15th Annual Monetary Conference of the Cato Institute in Washington, D.C., October 14, 1997

Devaluation

You probably hear more frequently about some developing nation devaluing their currency. Devaluation is the deliberate downward adjustment in the official exchange rate, which reduces the currency's value. Usually this happens when a country does not have sufficient resources to support its currency or pay its debts. By devaluing the currency, a country's exports become very cheap on world markets, but its imports become very expensive at home. Devaluation may increase demand for a country's goods, which could increase the demand for its products and create jobs.

There are two dangers of devaluing currency:

- ◆ The economic stimulus of job creation could aggravate inflation.

- ◆ Devaluation raises questions about a country's creditworthiness and could hurt the country's ability to entice foreign investment.

We'll talk more about the economic difficulties developing countries face and the international institutions that aid these countries in the following sections.

First let's take a look at the other international services the Federal Reserve offers to foreign banks.

Banking Foreign Assets

Intervention, while it may be the most visible part of the Fed's job in the international arena, is actually a very small part of what the Fed does in conjunction with foreign governments. The Fed offers a wide variety of services to more than 200 foreign governments and their banks, as well as other international institutions such as the International Money Fund (we'll talk more about the IMF later). These services can include *demand deposit transactions*, investments, custodial and safekeeping services, and FX operations.

Money Meanings

A **demand deposit transaction** is a deposit that can be drawn at any time without prior written notice to the institution holding the money. A checking account is the most common example of a demand deposit.

An official foreign financial institution can send its checks drawn on U.S. dollars to the New York Fed for collection. The Fed collects the funds and deposits them into the foreign institution's account at the Fed. We're talking big bucks here. In 2001, demand deposit transactions totaled about $8.5 trillion for foreign official accounts. The New York Fed also arranges for shipments of U.S. currency to foreign central banks or makes the pickup of that currency from the Fed possible.

The Fed doesn't only help foreign banks and institutions collect the funds due them. Foreign banks also count on the Fed to invest money for them. These investment services can include trade in federal funds, U.S. Treasury bills, or other securities. No, the Fed doesn't serve as an investment advisor. The foreign countries have to figure out investing strategies on their own. In 2001, the New York Fed invested about $9.5 trillion on behalf of foreign institutions. Wouldn't you like to be the broker for them?

Most of the foreign official accounts hold their funds in the form of marketable U.S. government securities, which totaled $750 billion at the end of 2001. The Fed also is the repository of the largest concentration of monetary gold in the world—even larger than Fort Knox, but it's not owned by the U.S. government. In 2001, Fed's vaults held about $64 billion of monetary gold. All this gold is kept in Fed vault facilities for foreign countries and international official institutions. The Fed keeps the identities of its depositors secret and does not charge for storing the gold. There are charges when the Fed first receives the gold and when the institution wants to take some out.

 **Fiscal Facts**

Foreign banking is big business in the United States. In fact, foreign banks controlled about 19 percent ($912 billion) of total commercial banking assets in the United States as of June 2000. Foreign banking organizations operated or controlled 348 branches, 111 agencies, and 79 U.S. commercial banks in December 2000.

Then there is the question of U.S. policy regarding foreign investment in the United States. Our country is the leading attractor of foreign investment in every kind of securities, especially equities. In those years, when our exports account for as much as 40 percent of our economic growth, the Fed is compelled to pay close attention in its policy making. When I served there in the 1980s and we went through more than one "debt crisis," the director of the Division of International Finance was often the lead-off presenter at the FOMC meeting. When you check out those reports of FOMC meetings, note the extensive references to international developments.

Supervising Foreign Banks

In addition to the services offered to foreign banks and institutions, the Fed also has responsibility for supervising and regulating foreign banks that operate in this country. The Fed assesses the parent bank's financial condition as well as the bank's U.S. branches.

What can the Fed do if it finds a problem? If the problem isn't that serious, the Fed can take what is called "informal action" by requiring a letter of commitment from the bank that details when and how the problem will be fixed. If the problem isn't fixed or is more serious, the Fed can terminate the U.S. activities of a foreign bank.

A foreign bank can be federally or state licensed and may provide a full range of banking services. They can make long- and short-term loans, invest people's money, and accept deposits of any size, as long as they are from foreigners. As a U.S. citizen, you can only make deposits in excess of $100,000. Foreign bank branches established after December 19, 1991, are not covered by U.S. deposit insurance, which is now available only to U.S.–chartered depository institutions.

Federal Reserve approval is required to establish any foreign banking institution in the United States. Foreign banks must also get regulatory approval from the U.S. Treasury Department's Office of the Comptroller of the Currency or the state banking supervisor before establishing new branches and agencies.

In addition to the Fed's services for foreign banks and institutions operating in the United States, as we have reviewed, the Fed works closely with international agencies to help assure that international financial markets operate smoothly. Let's take a quick look at some of the other international monetary power brokers.

Sharing International Money Power

At the center of the international money establishment is the Bank for International Settlements (BIS) in Basel, Switzerland. We have reviewed how this international organization fosters cooperation among the world's central bankers and financial agencies. Also, BIS serves as a bank for central banks, providing a broad range of financial services. BIS offers its facilities for international monetary meetings among central bankers and operates the Financial Stability Institute, which focuses on effective bank supervision.

Cooperation is critical, as world economies have become more intertwined. The war on terrorism certainly has brought regulators even closer together as they realized how much yet needs to be done to understand how terrorists groups use international monetary facilities to finance their gruesome work.

But, getting back to the more mundane activities of the financial power brokers, helping the world's banks to operate more efficiently and effectively with proper supervision in the key goal of international banking organizations. In addition to setting up international standards, the Fed works with these other money power centers to help train bankers in other countries to establish more solid banking structures.

Another major player we have discussed in the international arena is the Economic Money Union. This union includes 11 countries—Austria, Belgium, Finland, France,

Germany, Ireland, Italy, Luxembourg, the Netherlands, Portugal, and Spain. These countries yielded their ability to conduct monetary policy to the European Central Bank (ECB) located in Frankfurt, Germany. The new combined currency is the euro and for the participating countries this is the only currency they use, beginning in 2002.

How powerful a player this new international currency, the euro, will become is yet to be seen. Currently, the U.S. dollar is involved in 80 percent of all foreign exchange transactions and represents 60 percent of the world currency reserves, according to the Fed. If the U.S. dollar's power and value is reduced in the foreign exchange markets, this could put upward pressure on import prices in the United States—in other words, prices increase on foreign goods and services. Right now the countries involved with the start up of the euro are concentrating on promoting European growth and a more efficient international monetary system. Next time you go to Europe you will be spending and paying for things with the new euro currency!

In addition to the key international banks and banking institutions, politics play a critical role in how well the international money arena operates. The international money political power base rests with the *G*-7 finance ministers and central bank governors. This financial power group was formed in 1986, at the G-7 Leaders Summit in Tokyo and now meets four times a year.

Money Tips

There are 16 major central banks in addition to the Fed. Countries with central banks include Austria, Australia, Brazil, Canada, Finland, France, Germany, Italy, Japan, Netherlands, Norway, South Africa, Spain, Sweden, Turkey, and the United Kingdom. If you would like to learn more about any central banks, there are links to them at the Fed site (www.federalreserve. gov/centralbanks.htm).

Money Meanings

The **G-7,** which is a group of foreign and financial ministers from the United States, France, Germany, England, Japan, Italy, and Canada, was formed in 1976. The idea for the group was formulated at a 1973 meeting called by then President Richard Nixon, which included finance ministers from France, Germany, England, and French president Georges Pompidou, British prime minister Edward Heath, and German chancellor Willy Brandt. This initial group was reacting to the need for international monetary control after the monetary instability that was caused by taking the world's monetary system off the gold standard in August 1971. Speculative investors were buying and selling large amounts of a country's currency to make a profit with little regard for the impact on that country's monetary system. Today the G-7 periodically becomes G-8, when Russia is involved in economic discussions.

The G-7 finance group seeks to improve communications among finance ministers and central bankers and works on key issues of economic and financial growth and stability, inflation, and currency developments. In 1997, the G-7 Leaders Summit added Russia as a participant and became known as G-8, but Russia is not a full member of the G-7 finance ministers process even though it does take part in some G-7 meetings primarily when discussion centers around the Russian economy. Russia also participates in discussion about ways to combat the financing of terrorism.

G-7 finance ministers have a pre-summit ministerial meeting before being joined by the G-7 central bank governors. Two meetings are hosted on a rotational basis by member countries. The other two meetings are held in Washington, D.C. in conjunction with meetings of the International Monetary Fund (IMF) and the World Bank in the spring and fall.

Let's take a look at the roles of IMF and World Bank. Both institutions have responsibilities to aid developing countries.

Helping Emerging Countries

The role of the Federal Reserve, or for that matter of any central bank in this global economy, is no longer exercised in isolation. The world economy is so intertwined that central bankers and finance ministers or treasury secretaries all need to work closely together to strengthen all the world's resources.

The World Bank

The World Bank was founded in 1944 and is one of the world's largest sources of development assistance. In 2001, the World Bank Group provided a total of $17.3 billion to its client countries, which included more than 100 developing nations. The World Bank's goals are to "improve living standards and eliminate the worst forms of poverty."

Fiscal Facts

The United States controls 16.45 percent of the voting power and Japan controls 7.89 percent of the voting power within the World Bank Group's International Bank of Reconstruction and Development (IBRD), which is the largest entity under the World Bank umbrella. Germany, France, and the United Kingdom each control slightly more than 4 percent of the World Bank voting power of the IBRD. The World Bank's president by tradition is a national of the largest shareholder, the United States.

The World Bank Group is owned by more than 180 member countries. Member countries are shareholders who carry ultimate decision-making power in the World Bank, which is run by a board of governors and a Washington-based board of directors. Each member country has a certain amount of voting power. The big money contributors have the most power based on their shares of ownership.

The International Bank of Reconstruction and Development (IBRD) is the largest of the World Bank Group's institutions. There are four additional parts of the World Bank that specialize in different aspects of development. These include:

- The International Development Association (IDA)

- The International Finance Corporation (IFC)

- The Multilateral Investment Guarantee Agency (MIGA)

- The International Centre for Settlement of Investment Disputes (ICSID)

Economic Wisdom

"Just think of the dynamics of our current world. Our current world has six billion people in it. Five billion of them live in developing countries. One billion of them live in the OECD countries. So we have one-sixth of the world with 80 percent of the global income, and we have five-sixths of the world with 20 percent of the global income. You have three billion people that live on under $2 a day. You have a billion two hundred million people that live on under $1 a day. And you have one and a half billion people that don't have access to water or to sewerage, and you have 125 million kids that are not in school. I could go on and on, but will neither test my memory nor your patience. But let it be simply said that the issue of equity in our world is not one that we've addressed very well. That's what we're trying to do at the Bank."

—James D. Wolfensohn, president of The World Bank Group, at the 14th International Frankfurt Banking Evening, Frankfurt, Germany, May 7, 2002

Funding for the World Bank Group is raised by tapping the world's capital markets, as well as through contributions from its wealthier member governments. The World Bank focuses on numerous developmental projects in the areas of health, education, social development, governance, poverty reduction, environment, private business development, and governmental and financial reforms.

The International Monetary Fund (IMF)

The other major financial player in the developing world is the International Monetary Fund (IMF), which has 183 member countries. The IMF also was conceived in 1944 at Bretton Woods and began financial operations in 1947. The goal of the founders was to prevent a reoccurrence of the economic disasters created by the Great Depression. Its primary purposes are to promote international monetary cooperation and exchange stability and orderly exchange arrangements. It also works to promote economic growth and high levels of employment. Its lending services are directed to poverty reduction, debt relief, and emergency assistance.

The board of governors of the IMF includes ministers of finance and heads of central banks (or other officials of similar rank) from each of the 183 member countries. That would be a rather unwieldy group to get anything done, so the day-to-day operations are run by an executive board of 24 executive directors representing the member countries. In 2002, eight executive directors represent individual countries: China, France, Germany, Japan, Russia, Saudi Arabia, the United Kingdom, and the United States. The 16 other executive directors each represent groupings of the remaining countries. The executive board usually relies on consensus among its members rather than formal voting.

The day-to-day activities fall into three key areas:

◆ **Surveillance.** This is a policy dialogue with each of the IMG members through yearly appraisals of members' exchange rate policies within their overall framework of the country's economic policies. The goal is to maintain strong and consistent domestic economic policies that will lead to stable exchange rates and a prosperous world economy.

◆ **Financial Assistance.** Credits and loans are provided to member countries that have balance of payments problems. As of February 28, 2002, the IMF's credits and loans total $77 billion to a total of 88 countries. Additional assistance is offered to a country that cannot meet its debt burden provided the country develops a plan to fix the problem that is approved by the IMF. Some say these fixes sometimes make the problems worse.

◆ **Technical Assistance.** Various assistance and training programs are offered to help countries develop sound fiscal and monetary policies in addition to helping to develop statistical analysis tools.

Working Closely

The Basel Committee and the BIS work closely with the IMF and the World Bank to provide needed training and technical assistance to developing countries. The Basel Committee also provides expertise and resources to supplement and advise World Bank and IMF staff.

Economic Wisdom

"... [B]ank supervisors have a special role in maintaining financial stability. That role is to facilitate a resolution of banking problems so that the depository institutions will continue to provide the vital lifeline of credit to businesses and consumers. Past experience in many countries suggests that even severe problems can be overcome with decisive action by banks to identify problems quickly, recognize losses, strengthen the capital base, and execute sound, forward-looking business strategy."

—William McDonough before the 10th International Conference of Banking Supervisors, Sydney, Australia, October 22, 1998

In addition to sharing money power with the rest of the world, the Fed also shares its responsibilities with other money power brokers within the United States as well. In the next chapter, we'll take a look at the other Washington money power brokers.

The Least You Need to Know

◆ Money changes hands around the world every day through the foreign exchange system initially designed at Bretton Woods in 1944.

◆ The value of a country's currency in the foreign exchange system will impact the costs of goods exported to other countries, as well as the cost of goods imported.

◆ Trillions of dollars are handled each year by the Fed for foreign banks and institutions.

◆ World banking institutions work closely together to develop more effective and efficient banking regulations and improve economic conditions worldwide.

◆ Developing nations are assisted through the efforts of the World Bank Group and the International Monetary Fund.

The Regulators: Other Washington Money Powers

In This Chapter

- ◆ Money watchers
- ◆ Potpourri of banking regulators
- ◆ Insuring funds
- ◆ Nonbanking regulators

You may think the Federal Reserve has control of the entire banking system, but that isn't so. Our country has a dual banking system, federal and state. Almost all banks fall under the regulatory authority of more than one agency. In fact, the Federal Reserve has direct supervisory responsibility of its state licensed member banks as well as bank and financial holding companies. Then there are the regulators of the other "financial services providers," the thrifts, the insurance companies, the investment servicers, and the credit union people. Quite a matrix, isn't it?

Did you know that there are 8,000 commercial banks in this country? Eight thousand, and three or four hundred new banks are licensed in most years? New ones can be federally licensed or state licensed, of course. So don't believe those media stories that argue that most or all your banking will be done on the computer, you know, "e-banking." No. And is there any reason why you shouldn't do financial service business with a branch of a bank headquartered in another state? No, they are regulated, too.

We'll explore the world of banking regulation in this chapter. Since we covered the Fed's regulatory responsibilities in Chapter 11, we'll be concentrating on the other regulators in this chapter.

Picking Your Authority

Banks must answer to their chartering authority, which can either be the Office of Comptroller of the Currency (OCC) if it is a national bank, or the state banking authority if it is a state bank. The banker can choose its regulator, avoiding what he or she sees as unreasonable regulatory implementation. Most banks also have Federal Deposit Insurance and must abide by FDIC regulations and supervision. Banks face even more regulators if they spread their wings and sell insurance or securities or take on nonbanking activities. That good ol' 1999 Gramm-Leach-Bliley Act we keep telling you about mitigated the line between "banks" and other financial service providers mightily.

Economic Wisdom

"Our country's founders established a federal system of government, dividing power and responsibilities between the state governments and the central government. Perhaps less well known to the public is that, since the Civil War, our banking system has developed along similar lines. State banks were, of course, first. But the dynamic tension between centralization and decentralization in U.S. banking is as old as the debate between Thomas Jefferson and Alexander Hamilton over the First Bank of the United States."

—Fed Governor Mark W. Olson at the Annual Meeting of the Conference of State Bank Supervisors, Salt Lake City, Utah, May 31, 2002

In addition to banks, other service providers fall under federal and state regulation including credit unions and thrift associations (such as savings banks and savings and loan associations). Today, the thrift regulators are called the Office of Thrift Supervision (OTS) and the Federal Housing Finance Board (FHFB).

Another model? The deposits ("savings accounts") were at first insured by a new entity, the Federal Savings and Loan Insurance Corporation (FSLIC). (Don't you love that Washington jargon? Congress did it. "Fizlick," as it was called, was a brother to the bank deposit insurer, FDIC.) Now let's see how all the regulators are organized.

Getting Organized

You may be thinking that with all these regulators a bank, credit union, or thrift institution spends a good part of its time answering to examiners. In reality it's not as bad as that, unless the institution shows signs of getting into trouble. The federal regulatory agencies coordinate their examination efforts under the umbrella of the *Federal Financial Institutions Examination Council (FFIEC)*. This interagency body was given the power to develop uniform principles, standards, and report forms for the federal examination of financial institutions. These apply, whether the examination is conducted by the Board of Governors of the Federal Reserve System (FRB), or the Federal Deposit Insurance Corporation (FDIC).

> **Money Meanings**
>
> The **Federal Financial Institutions Examination Council (FFIEC)** was established on March 10, 1979. The council is a formal interagency body empowered to prescribe uniform principles, standards, and report forms for the federal examination of financial institutions. It makes recommendations to promote uniformity in the supervision of financial institutions. The council was given additional statutory responsibilities as part of the Housing and Community Development Act of 1980. This facilitates public access to data that depository institutions must disclose under the Home Mortgage Disclosure Act of 1975. The council also has an advisory State Liaison Committee composed of five representatives of state supervisory agencies.

The FDIC today examines both the banks and the S&Ls, working with one of the Federal Home Loan Banks (FHLBs), the National Credit Union Administration (NCUA), the Office of the Comptroller of the Currency (OCC), or the Office of Thrift Supervision (OTS). FFIEC also makes recommendations to promote uniformity in the supervision of financial institutions. These federal institutions coordinate examinations with state authorities, including S&L commissioners.

One of the key tools developed by FFIEC is the Uniform Bank Performance Report (UBPR), which is used to measure how well a bank is doing. This analytical tool was created for bank supervisory, examination, and management purposes. It shows the impact of management decisions and economic conditions on a bank's performance and balance-sheet composition. The information gathered by this tool and the report generated can be used as an aid in evaluating the adequacy of earnings, liquidity, capital, asset and liability management, and growth management. Bankers and examiners use this report to get a better understanding of a bank's financial condition.

You can see that financial condition is not the only thing examiners are concerned about. The Community Reinvestment Act (CRA) also requires examiners to assess an institution's efforts to meet the credit needs of its community. CRA evaluations compare the performance of an institution based on its capacity, constraints, and business strategies with the performance of its competitors and peers.

Within a community data is collected on demographics, the economy, lending practices, investment practices, and service opportunities. Institutions are rated on a four-tiered system—outstanding, satisfactory, needs to improve, and substantial noncompliance.

Preston's Points

We have all seen the community programs and efforts to "bring back" our older urban neighborhoods and their homes, schools, medical facilities, religious institutions, or what President George W. Bush styled "faith-based" organizations. To our credit there are many community organizations working with their banks to achieve the "comeback communities." I had the honor to participate in the start-ups of Neighborhood Housing Services of America (NHSA) and Social Compact, and to serve on the board of Operation HOPE. The thousands of banks and thrifts are providing a large volume of home loans and small business financing, and many of their employees are working pro bono.

For interstate banks, the federal bank supervisory agencies must evaluate an institution's CRA in each state and metropolitan statistical area in which it has a branch. The supervisor then gives the institution an overall rating for its performance. Prior to 1995, there were 12 assessment factors. These were substantially revised in 1995 to put greater emphasis on performance and establish different evaluation tests based on the size and purpose of the institutions. Today financial institutions are grouped into seven performance evaluation categories:

◆ Large institution

◆ Small institution

◆ Strategic plan

- Community development—limited purpose or wholesale

- Hybrid

- Assessment factor

- Not reported (The method is not available for this examination.)

The assessment method used to evaluate the institution's "community" performance and the format of the evaluation will vary depending on the types of criteria used. Is this just some more of that ubiquitous government "reg"? No, moderate/low family income lending is changing some (not all) neighborhoods for the good or better (okay, not the best).

> **Money Tips**
>
> You can find out how well an institution in your area is doing to meet communities needs by checking their CRA rating and their slow pay counseling. The FFIEC has a database you can use to search online at www.ffiec.gov/cracf/crarating/main.cfm. You can use this search engine to find the latest CRA ratings of financial institutions supervised by the Federal Reserve, Office of the Comptroller of the Currency, Federal Deposit Insurance Corporation, or Office of Thrift Supervision. Examinations are not made public until 45 to 60 days after an examination is finished.

Now that you know the basics of how examinations are coordinated, let's review the responsibilities of each of the other key regulators.

Office of the Comptroller of the Currency

The Office of the Comptroller of the Currency (OCC) is the oldest of the regulators. The OCC was established in 1863, as a bureau of the U.S. Department of Treasury. The comptroller, who heads the office, is appointed by the president for a five-year term, but must be confirmed by the Senate. He also serves as a director of the FDIC and of the Neighborhood Reinvestment Corporation.

The OCC's primary responsibility is to charter, regulate, and supervise all national banks. Its headquarters are in Washington, D.C., but it also has six district offices plus an office in London to supervise international activities of national banks.

The OCC's examiners supervise domestic and international activities of national banks and perform corporate analyses. Examiners analyze a bank's loan and investment port-folios, funds management, capital, earnings, liquidity, sensitivity to market risk, and compliance with consumer banking laws, including the Community Reinvestment Act. They review the bank's internal controls, internal and external audit, and compliance with law. They also evaluate bank management's ability to identify and control risk. In addition to conducting examinations, the OCC issues rules, legal interpretations, and corporate decisions concerning banking, bank investments, bank community development activities, and other aspects of bank operations.

The OCC's powers include more than just bank examination. Other key duties are as follows:

> **Money Tips**
>
> If you have a complaint about a national bank and cannot resolve it with the institution, you can turn to the OCC for help. Call the OCC Customer Assistance Group at 1-800-613-6743 or contact them by e-mail at customer.assistance@occ.treas.gov.

- Approve or deny applications for new charters, branches, capital, or other changes in corporate or banking structure.

- Take supervisory actions against banks that do not comply with laws and regulations or that otherwise engage in unsound banking practices. The agency can remove officers and directors, negotiate agreements to change banking practices, and issue cease and desist orders as well as civil money penalties.

- Issue rules and regulations governing bank investments, lending, and other practices.

Funding for the OCC is generated primarily by assessment of national banks. Congress does not appropriate any money to pay for its activities. The OCC also receives revenue from its investment income, primarily from U.S. Treasury securities.

Federal Deposit Insurance Corporation

The Federal Deposit Insurance Corporation (FDIC) has been insuring deposits and promoting safe and sound banking practices since 1934. The FDIC is an independent federal agency managed by a five-member board of directors appointed by the president and confirmed by the Senate. The FDIC is audited by the General Accounting Office, and Congress also has oversight duties.

The FDIC receives no Congressional appropriations to carry out its mission as a deposit insurer and banking regulator. The money for these purposes comes from deposit insurance premiums paid by banks and savings associations and from earnings on investments in U.S. Treasury securities. The FDIC separately manages the FSLIC Resolution Fund (FRF), which was created by Congress in 1989 in response to the thrift industry crisis of the 1980s. The FRF, which is funded by Congressional appropriations, is responsible for wrapping up the obligations of the former FSLIC and the former Resolution Trust Corporation (RTC).

Fiscal Facts

There are actually two federal deposit insurance funds. The Bank Insurance Fund (BIF) and the Savings Association Insurance Fund (SAIF). Deposits in most commercial banks and many savings banks are insured by the BIF. In 1989, Congress created the SAIF to succeed the Federal Savings and Loan Insurance Corporation (FSLIC) when it was disbanded in 1989 after the savings and loan crisis was so badly mismanaged by the Congress' legislative failures. The SAIF is managed by the FDIC. Both the BIF and SAIF deposit insurance programs are backed by the full faith and credit of the U.S. government, which means if there isn't enough money to pay all insured depositors, the federal government gets to step in or not to, if the Congress enacts another FIRREA.

Today the FDIC insures virtually all U.S. banks and savings associations (formally called savings and loan associations or S&Ls) deposits up to $100,000. Legislation to increase that insurance to $130,000 may be making its way through Congress. There also is a provision in the bill to insure retirement savings up to $260,000.

In addition the FDIC is the primary federal regulator for more than 5,000 state-chartered "nonmember" banks—commercial and savings banks that are not members of the Federal Reserve System.

Economic Wisdom

"But today, in our judgment, neither financial stability, nor depositories are being disadvantaged by the current (insured deposit) ceiling. Raising the ceiling now would extend the safety net, increase the government subsidy to banking, expand moral hazard, and reduce the incentive for market discipline, without providing any real evident public benefits."

—Alan Greenspan testifying against raising the FDIC insurance limit before the Senate Banking Committee hearing, April 2002

When FDIC insurance started in 1934, only $2,500 per depositor was insured. Today the $100,000 insurance is based on a depositor's combined savings, checking, and other accounts within an individual financial institution. Single and joint accounts may be separately insured. Retirement accounts are generally insured separately as well. Insurance does not include securities, mutual funds, or similar types of investments that may be offered for sale at FDIC-insured banks and savings associations.

When a federal financial institution fails, and is not purchased by a stronger, well capitalized institution, it is generally closed by its chartering authority—the state regulator, the Office of the Comptroller of the Currency, or the Office of Thrift Supervision. The FDIC's job involves paying depositors up to the $100,000 insurance limit and recovering as much money as possible from the failed institution's assets (primarily loans, real estate, and securities).

The FDIC has several options for resolving failed institutions, but by law it must use the least-costly approach in each case. The option generally used is called a "purchase-and-assumption agreement," in which the FDIC arranges for an existing or newly chartered institution to assume either the insured deposits or all of the deposits (insured and uninsured) of the failed institution plus some of the loans and other assets. Customers of the failed institution automatically become customers of the assuming institution.

By maintaining banking services at most or all of the failed institution's offices, the purchase-and-assumption approach is less disruptive to the community than other options available to the FDIC. The assuming institution also usually pays a premium to the FDIC, which helps reduce the agency's costs of handling the failed institution.

Sometimes the FDIC is not able to find an institution that wants to assume the remaining assets and to trust the government to honor its contracts. When that happens payments are made directly to insured depositors. No matter which option the FDIC uses, funds within the $100,000 insurance limit are always fully protected.

The FDIC attempts to return the assets of the failed institution to the private sector as quickly as possible, and most of the assets are sold to healthy institutions soon after the troubled institution is closed. It may be necessary for the FDIC to retain and manage some of the less-desirable assets. Proceeds from asset sales are used to reimburse the insurance funds and to pay uninsured depositors, to the extent possible. General creditors are paid to the extent possible only after all depositors are paid in full. Shareholders of the failed institution receive any residual value, although there usually is none.

Office of Thrift Supervision

The Office of Thrift Supervision was established by Congress on August 9, 1989, as a bureau of the Department of Treasury after the S&L scandals and failures. Its primary responsibilities include chartering, examining, supervising, and regulating federal savings associations and federal savings banks. The states have their S&L commissioners. OTS also has regulatory responsibility to examine, supervise, and regulate state-chartered savings associations belonging to the SAIF. In addition, OTS oversees the holding companies of savings associations as well.

The Gramm-Leach-Bliley Act (GLBA) of 1999 at last was passed to modernize financial activities. The GLBA is prompting changes at OTS. New regulations are needed and old ones are being reviewed. The act prevents new affiliations between commercial firms and thrifts and places significant restrictions on the sharing of nonpublic customer information with unaffiliated third parties.

National Credit Union Administration

The National Credit Union Administration (NCUA) is an independent federal agency that supervises and insures 6,566 federal credit unions and 4,062 state-chartered credit unions. Credit unions are growing rapidly and expanding their offering of services. NCUA is headquartered in Virginia, plus it has six regional offices. The NCUA also works closely with state regulators with regard to state-charted credit unions.

The NCUA is both a regulator and insurer. For federally chartered credit unions, the NCUA has primary supervisory responsibility, as well as responsibility for insuring deposits. For state-chartered credit unions, the NCUA serves as insurer of their deposits.

State Banking Authorities

Each state has its own regulatory agency that charters and supervises state banks. Commonly, the agency that supervises banks also supervises other types of financial institutions.

State banks must follow the rules and regulations of the states plus, if they take out federal deposit insurance, they are subject to supervision from the FDIC. The Federal Reserve gets into the act if the state bank chooses to become a member of the Fed system.

> **Money Tips**
>
> You can find out how to get in contact with your state banking authority at a website operated by the Federal Consumer Information Center (www. pueblo.gsa.gov/crh/banking.htm). In addition to mailing addresses and telephone contact information, the website includes links to each state's individual website.

State regulatory agencies can issue bank charters, conduct bank examinations, construct and enforce bank regulations, and rule on proposed branch and merger applications. They can also revoke a state bank's charter for unsound banking practices. Many states also give their banking agencies the right to remove bank officials and levy fines.

Other Regulatory Agencies

In addition to the banking regulators mentioned, there are others that get involved in bank regulations including the Department of Justice, the Securities and Exchange Commission, the State Insurance Commissions, and the Federal Trade Commission. Whether a bank is subject to actions by these agencies depends upon the actual types of businesses and services offered by the financial institution.

The Department of Justice gets involved when there are questions about antitrust issues. This happens most often when there are questions about the potential competitive effect of a bank merger or holding company consolidation.

The Securities and Exchange Commission (SEC) gets involved in a number of different scenarios. Large bank holding companies must follow SEC registration and reporting requirements when they publicly issue stock. The SEC also gets involved in areas related to the accuracy of *bank loan loss reserves* and other financial disclosures, accounting and disclosure rules on insider loans, insider stock trading, and bank mutual fund activities. The SEC also has primary responsibility for activities conducted by a securities subsidiary of the bank or holding company.

Money Meanings

Bank loan loss reserves are maintained to absorb losses arising from the business of banking. Equity capital, which includes retained earnings and funds paid-in by shareholders, serves as the last line of defense for the deposit insurance funds. This is the primary means by which regulators can ensure that the insurance funds will not be depleted, necessitating a call for taxpayer dollars.

State insurance commissions jump into the mix if the bank or its affiliates get involved in insurance activities. As with state banking authorities, each state has an insurance commissioner or insurance department. If a bank does get involved in insurance sales, it must be licensed by the state and abide by state insurance laws.

The Federal Trade Commission (FTC) shares responsibility with the other federal regulatory agencies for the enforcement of the Truth in Lending Act and other consumer protection legislation. The FTC has primary enforcement responsibilities only with regards to activity by nondepository lending institutions.

Your head is probably spinning with all the various regulators that get involved in monitoring banking activities. You can imagine what bank officers go through to be sure they are meeting their regulatory obligations.

Now that you've got a good idea of how the Federal Reserve and other government entities make sure banks are doing what they should be doing legally, we'll take a look at how the Federal Reserve and its member banks serve the community.

The Least You Need to Know

♦ The Federal Reserve is not the only regulator with responsibility for monitoring banks.

♦ Federal bank and savings association regulators coordinate their examinations through the Federal Financial Institutions Examination Council, which also coordinates with state examiners.

♦ The Federal Deposit Insurance Corporation not only insures deposits, it also supervises banks that are not part of the Federal Reserve System but offer FDIC insurance to their depositors.

♦ Banks that spread their wings beyond traditional banking activities increase the number of regulators they must answer to at the both the federal and state levels.

Part **6**

The Money Machine Comes Home

We wouldn't have a strong economy without communities that generate business activity and house the people. We take a look at the Fed's role in helping to keep America's communities strong.

We look at ways the Fed guarantees your consumer rights, privacy, credit, and savings.

Chapter **19**

Developing Our Communities

In This Chapter

- ◆ Community money
- ◆ Inner workings
- ◆ Getting advances
- ◆ Affordable housing

Financial institutions of all kinds are vital contributors to the growth and stability of the communities they serve. Economic growth has a "bottoms up" path. Community after community creates new activities and new employment. In our increasingly diverse society, financial services experience must be utilized to serve our complicated communities. A financial institution has to build on its past experience to respond creatively to the needs of today's consumers and organizations. The Federal Reserve encourages its member banks to work with community organizations to promote local economic development as part of its responsibilities under the Community Reinvestment Act of 1977 (CRA), as we discussed in Chapter 18.

The Federal Reserve is just one of many institutions that promote community development. There is a long list of government agencies that get into the mix, including the Federal Home Loan Bank System (FHLB), Department of Housing and Urban Development (HUD), the Department of Agriculture's Rural Housing Services to develop housing, and the Small Business Association to assist business startups.

In addition to looking at mortgage and small business lending programs, the Fed also looks closely at ways to improve business, particularly small business and startup business access to capital. Business credit for women, minorities, and small business are a key objective for the Fed. Let's take a look at some of the communities programs provided through the Fed and its federal partners.

Funding for Community Projects

The Fed does not have the key responsibility for actually raising the funds for community development and redevelopment. That job belongs to the Federal Home Loan Bank System, which Congress established in 1932 to fill a need for a stable source of funds for residential mortgages. The Great Depression had undermined the existing banking system, and with it, Americans who wanted to purchase homes. The mission of the Federal Home Loan Banks is to support its members residential-mortgage and economic-development lending activities.

The Federal Home Loan Banks (FHLB) are wholesale banks, places where community financial institutions turn for funds. Although the FHLB System has been around since 1932, its role in our economy has never been more crucial than it is today.

That's because the explosive popularity of mutual funds, money markets, and other instruments in the 1980s and 1990s triggered a profound change in financial consumer behavior. Millions of Americans moved their money from depository institutions to other investments. Core deposits declined in the late 1980s, 1990s, and 2000s, forcing banks and thrifts to turn to new sources of money. The key source the community banks, credit unions, and thrifts turned to was the FHLB System.

Even though community development is not a key role of the Fed, the Fed does have regulatory responsibility in overlapping consumer areas, so we'll cover the FHLB briefly here.

How the FHLB Works

The FHLB provides financial institutions with loans known as advances (more about those later). As we've discussed, the Gramm-Leach-Bliley Act (GLB) expanded the collateral that FHLB member institutions could use in obtaining advances. In addition to traditional mortgage loans, now financial institutions can also put up rural, agricultural, and small business loans as advance collateral.

These two major developments—national demand for a reliable source of liquidity and the expansion of eligible collateral—has made the FHLB the lifeblood of community banking in the United States. Their pivotal role is apparent in the increased demand for advances over the past decade.

Money Tips

Which FHLB district do you live in? The regional structure of the Federal Home Loan Banks is similar to the Fed as you can see from the map on its website www.fhlbanks.com/Pages/template1.asp?P=5.

So what is a Federal Home Loan Bank? Federal Home Loan Banks are privately owned wholesale banks that provide readily available, low-cost funding, known as advances, and other credit products to more than 7,901 stockholder members. FHLB System members include commercial banks, savings institutions, credit unions, and insurance companies. Each member belongs to one of 12 regional FHLBs, which serve different regions of the country. Sound like the Fed? Yes, many banks belong to the Fed and to the FHLB! Federal Home Loan Banks are government-sponsored enterprises, federally chartered but privately capitalized and independently managed.

Each Federal Home Loan Bank is governed by a board of directors made up of industry leaders elected by member institutions and public-interest directors appointed by the system's federal regulator, the Federal Housing Finance Board (FHFB, formerly called the Federal Home Loan Bank Board). Each Federal Home Loan Bank is capitalized by the capital-stock investments of its members and its retained earnings. Members purchase stock in proportion to their borrowings from the Federal Home Loan Bank, their holdings of mortgages and mortgage securities, and their other assets.

FHLB banks meet all their costs from earnings, including the costs of raising funds jointly in the capital markets. In addition, they are assessed for the full costs of the Finance Board (the system regulator). No tax dollars are involved in the operation of the Federal Home Loan Bank System. The Federal Home Loan Banks raise funds by issuing debt instruments (bonds and notes) in the capital markets. Because these instruments have "AAA" credit ratings, the Federal Home Loan Banks can borrow at very favorable rates and terms. However, the U.S. government does not guarantee Federal Home Loan Bank debt.

While the Federal Home Loan Banks are not subject to federal income tax, they do pay 20 percent of their net earnings to fund a portion of the interest on the

Resolution Funding Corporation (REFCorp) debt. These obligations were issued for the resolution (takeover) of all those insolvent savings and loans in the late 1980s. In addition, the Federal Home Loan Banks contribute the greater of 10 percent of their net income or $100 million toward the Affordable Housing Program, which awards grants and rate-subsidized loans for housing serving very low- to moderate-income families and individuals. We'll discuss those in depth a little later in this chapter.

In a time when cash deposits in community banks are dwindling, the funds provided by the Federal Home Loan Banks to member banks guarantees a stable source of funds for mortgages and community lending. Without the Federal Home Loan Banks, most depository institutions would not have access to medium- and long-term sources of funding.

Making Advances

Advances are the key FHLB product. An "advance" is simply the FHLB word for "loan." Advances are fully collateralized loans. Member banks can pledge a range of assets against their advances, including home mortgages, small business, and rural and agricultural loans.

FHLB advances are made at lower rates than are available in the commercial market. They are not only a reliable low-cost source of funds, they also reflect the changing needs of today's community bankers. Advances range in duration from overnights to 20-year loans and come with fixed, floating, and adjustable rates. Payments can be made either as one-time bullets or amortized over time. And they can be structured either as convertible instruments or with a floating cap rate. (Flexible enough, Mr. banker?)

The use of FHLB advances has grown markedly in recent years, due in large part to the lack of deposit growth and because of the safe, reliable, and low-cost nature of the loans. The low cost of advances helps member banks provide consumers with lower cost loans and mortgages. Now let's look at the programs for which advances are used.

Funding Affordable Housing Program (AHP)

The Financial Institutions Reform, Recovery, and Enforcement Act of 1989 (FIR-REA) established the Affordable Housing Program (AHP). The purpose of the AHP is to subsidize the interest rate for advances (loans) and to provide direct subsidies to the FHLB System member institutions engaged in lending for long-term, low and moderate-income, owner-occupied and affordable rental housing. The program is designed to encourage members to undertake creative efforts and increase their participation in and support for efforts directed toward increasing the supply of affordable housing in the members' FHLB district. The "comeback communities."

> **Fiscal Facts** _____
>
> The FHLB System reported that it paid $777 million in 2001, approximately one third of its net earnings, to the Affordable Housing Program (AHP) and REFCorp. Of that, $239 million went to AHP, bringing total contributions since the program's inception in 1991 to more than $1.4 billion. Ten percent of FHLB net earnings are used each year to support AHP which helps member banks meet housing and community development needs in the low and low-to-moderate income sectors.

Advances under this program may be used in conjunction with other sources of funds, such as the FHLB System's Community Investment Program (CIP), Low-Income Housing Tax Credits, as well as other federal, state, local, or private assistance programs. Subsidies under the AHP must be used for the following:

♦ To finance the purchase, construction, or rehabilitation of owner-occupied housing for very low and moderate-income households

♦ To finance the purchase, construction, or rehabilitation of rental housing, at least 20 percent of the units of which will be occupied by and affordable to very low-income households for at least 15 years

FHLBs have contributed $1.2 billion to AHP since the program's inception and a total of $218 million in subsidies for 41,000 families awarded in just one year, 2000. The system has a record of 275,000 units of housing funded since 1989. They hold another record, as the largest single contributor to Habitat for Humanity Affiliates. (Remember seeing President Jimmy Carter, hammer in hand, working at Habitat home building projects?)

Each FHLB administers its own AHP. I pitched the good U.S. experience from the program to 100 or so UN members from around the world at UN headquarters in New York City eight days after the September 11 disaster.

Fostering Community Investment

The Community Investment Program (CIP) is a targeted housing and economic development loan program authorized under the Financial Institutions Reform,

Recovery, and Enforcement Act of 1989. The purpose of the CIP is to provide funding for community-oriented mortgage lending, which means providing loans ...

♦ To finance home purchases by families whose incomes do not exceed 115 percent of the area median income.

♦ To finance the purchase or rehabilitation of housing for occupancy by families whose incomes do not exceed 115 percent of the area median income.

♦ To finance commercial and economic development activities that benefit low- and moderate-income (defined as 80 percent of the area median income) households, or activities that are located in low- and moderate-income neighborhoods (defined as a neighborhood in which 51 percent or more of the households are low- to moderate-income households).

♦ To finance projects that include a combination of these activities.

CIP is a flexible program that members have used to finance a wide range of targeted housing and economic development projects, including day care centers, special needs housing, health care facilities, single family housing, and multi-family housing. The FHLB has provided more than $20 billion in advances to fund various community development projects.

Other Services

FHLB System banks can provide stand-by, direct-pay, and confirming triple-A rated letters of credit (LOCs) to assist members with their funding needs. The FHLB can issue or confirm these LOCs to facilitate residential housing finance, to facilitate community lending, to assist members with asset/liability management, and to provide members with liquidity or other funding.

Many FHLB System banks provide their members with an array of back-office and operational services, including the following:

♦ Cash management

♦ Electronic funds transfer

♦ Deposit processing

♦ Check processing

♦ Coin and currency management

These services help small member banks provide their customers with the wide variety of activities they have come to expect from larger institutions.

Most FHLB System banks act as custodial agents for their members, providing reliable securities safekeeping. This service enables member banks to offer their customers an important feature, thus keeping customers' business in-house, rather than turning to a broker or a competitor for custodial functions. FHLB System banks generally handle a full range of securities.

Some of these banks provide member financial institutions with research and library services, such as online searching, periodicals, and demographic data. This gives small banks all the informational advantages that big banks enjoy without the cost and added personnel.

Member banks that need advice on investing or risk management can often turn to the FHLB for assistance. Some even provide financial consulting services, offering guidance on portfolio management, interest rates, and other forms of risk.

Purchasing Mortgages

Mortgage Purchase Programs (MPP) are one of the newest FHLB products, helping to expand home ownership by giving financial institutions an alternative, flexible approach to mortgage funding. The Chicago FHLB should get credit, along with the New York FHLB, for leading this development in the system with their "Pilot Program." As of mid-2000, eight of the FHLBs participated. Although the specific details of MPP vary from bank to bank, in general this product allows banks to split the risks from fixed-rate mortgages between the lender and the FHLB. The lending member assumes the credit and customer relationship risks, while the FHLB manages the funding, interest rate, liquidity, and prepayment risks.

MPPs are designed to benefit local financial institutions and home buyers by increasing competition and efficiency in the secondary (resale) mortgage market for conventional and FHA/VA mortgages. With almost $2 trillion in outstanding mortgage loans, the secondary mortgage market is one of the largest credit markets in the world and the most important to American families.

The program addresses a need outlined in a recent Congressional Research Service report (Government Sponsored Enterprises: The Issue of Expansion into Mission-Related Business, January 19, 1999). The report suggests encouraging competition among the housing Government Sponsored Enterprises (GSEs) (Fannie Mae, Freddie Mac, and the FHLBs) so that "competition among them increases and subsidies are forced through to intended customers."

At the Federal Home Loan Bank Board, my colleagues and I found that our financial system had grown like some complicated organism that behaved before. We had to be creative to come up with new methods of meeting the housing demand and new ways of attracting more savings deposits to the beleaguered home loan industry.

So what does all of this history tell us? Why should tomorrow's mortgage originators pay any attention to the past and why is there a need for the FHLB to develop new services and products? The "complicated organism" that my colleagues and I managed in the 1970s has grown increasingly more complicated. We need to be alert to new opportunities to serve our neighbors and communities. The "new products" and "new services" of this millennium will succeed in many instances because we build on our past experiences to creatively respond to the needs of today's diverse families and their communities.

The Least You Need to Know

- Many commercial banks, savings associations, and credit unions get their money for providing mortgages from the Federal Home Loan Bank System.

- The Federal Home Loan Bank System was started in 1932 after the Great Depression to help with the job of rebuilding our communities.

- Today almost 8,000 financial institutions are members of the FHLB System.

- The FHLB provides most of its money through advances, which is just FHLB jargon for a loan.

Chapter 20

Protecting Consumers

In This Chapter

- ◆ Credit rules
- ◆ Housing acts
- ◆ Leasing laws
- ◆ Time to complain
- ◆ Legal recourse

Today we take for granted all the consumer protection laws in place. In fact, many of us even complain about all the extra paperwork we must sign when taking out a new loan. Well, it was long ago that none of this existed and people signed loan papers never really understanding the interest rates they were actually going to pay and other loan terms like appraisal costs and closing costs that would ultimately affect their costs of borrowing.

Consumer credit protection laws didn't exist until 1968, when the Consumer Credit Protection Act was first passed. This act launched the requirement for Truth in Lending Disclosures. This legislation made it a requirement for creditors to actually tell borrowers in common language the full cost of borrowing and give consumers a better chance to be able to compare their loan costs and shop for the best deal.

Many laws have been passed since that time that not only guarantee "truth in lending," but also seek to encourage "fair" and "equal" lending processes. The Federal Reserve has the responsibility to develop regulations for banks and other lending institutions based on these laws. Let's take a look at how these laws work and what the Federal Reserve does to ensure their enforcement.

Protecting Your Credit

Purchasing on credit for many consumers has become a way of life. For some, it has become the only way to meet their monthly needs. There are so many different types of loan products out there, the first step in your line of consumer credit defense is to learn about your credit options and be sure to shop carefully for the loan products you ultimately decide to use.

Before even starting to shop for a loan, you should figure out how much you can afford and how quickly you will be able to pay it back. This will give you the best opportunity to shop for your most beneficial loan terms. There are two laws that help you when loan shopping:

- **Truth in Lending.** Requires creditors to give you basic information about the cost of buying on credit or taking out a loan.

- **Consumer Leasing Act of 1977.** Consumer leasing disclosures required under this act help you compare the cost of several leases by requiring the same basic information be provided about leasing terms.

Truth in Lending regulations require a lender to tell you in writing, and before you sign the loan documents, the finance charge and the annual percentage rate (APR) of the loan. The finance charge, which is the total dollar amount you pay to use credit, includes interest costs as well as other costs, such as service charges, points, and some credit-related insurance premiums. This information is presented in a standard form so it is easier for you to compare loans and find the best deal. If you've closed on a house recently, you know how astronomical these numbers can look when your 30 years of payments are totaled on this form.

Just to give you an idea of how to compare loans, let's look at an example from the Federal Reserve's consumer protection handbook. In this example, a $7,500 car loan is being compared. The consumer plans to put down $1,500 and finance $6,000. Here are some common loan options for this scenario:

Creditor	APR	Length of Loan	Monthly Payment	Total Finance Charge	Total of Payments
Creditor A	14%	3 years	$205.07	$1,382.52	$7,382,52
Creditor B	14%	4 years	$163.96	$1,870.08	$7,870.08
Creditor C	15%	4 years	$166.98	$2,015.04	$8,015.04

You can see the consumer can select the lowest monthly payment from Creditor B, which might look the best because it's about $40 less monthly than the loan offered by Creditor A, but look at total costs. Since Creditor A is offering a three-year loan, the total costs of that loan are actually $488 less. When paying a mortgage, just ¼ percent difference in interest can be a huge savings over 30 years.

The type of loan we just considered has a set term with a set interest rate. For this type of loan you borrow the amount that you need all at one time and pay it off over a set number of years. Another way to borrow on credit is to use open-end credit, which includes basic credit cards from your bank or department store, equity lines, and overdraft protection. With these types of loans you have a credit limit and can spend up to that amount as the need arises. Truth in Lending also applies here because the creditors must tell you the terms of the credit plan to enable you to shop and compare costs.

When you are shopping for credit cards you not only need to compare the APR and finance charges, but you also should look at how the credit company sets its billing policy. Many creditors will give you a certain number of days called a grace period during which no interest will be charged provided you pay the loan amount in full.

Do you know how your finance charges are calculated for your credit cards? If not check it out. You may find that a card which you think has a lower interest rate starts charging interest on all new purchases immediately and your total interest costs are lower on a card with a higher interest rate that doesn't start charging new purchases until the next billing cycle, giving you more days free of interest.

The Truth in Lending laws do not set the rates a creditor can charge or the method the creditor can use to calculate your finance charges, it only requires that you be informed about what the charges will be. Be sure you understand the charges and how they are calculated so you can compare costs. If you are not sure you understand the terms, be sure to ask for clarification before signing on the dotted line.

Your Credit History

When you apply for credit, you know how important your credit history can be to getting the credit you want. There are actually two laws that help protect your credit history—the Equal Credit Opportunity Act and the Fair Credit Reporting Act.

The Equal Credit Opportunity Act requires lenders to report to credit bureaus in the names of both husband and wife if both use the account or are responsible for paying the debt. This is particularly important to women who become divorced or widowed. Prior to this protection being in place, women could be left with no credit history and no ability to get new loans after a divorce or death of a spouse.

Under the law creditors are also required to consider spouses separately if an account is only held in one spouse's name. This can be critically important if a spouse or ex-spouse has a bad credit rating. The spouse with a good credit rating must be permitted to clear his or her record of a bad credit rating if he or she can prove that the bad record is not a reflection of his or her own creditworthiness. Many couples will hold separate credit accounts to maintain two distinct credit histories.

The Fair Credit Reporting Act protects you if mistakes were made on your credit file. The act requires credit bureaus to tell you what is on your credit file and provide you with a method to correct those mistakes.

If you apply for credit and are rejected because of negative information on your file, you have the right to get the name and address of the agency that made that report. If you can request that information within 60 days of being rejected for credit, you must get a copy of your report for free. After reviewing the report if you see any error, you should notify the credit bureau. The bureau must investigate your claim and resolve any dispute within 30 days of receiving your notice. If you disagree with the findings you can ask that a short statement of explanation be attached to your record to give your side of the story.

CAUTION

Ups and Downs

If you believe there is an error on your bill, don't just ignore it. You must act in order to protect yourself. You must notify your creditor within 60 days of a billing error.

Sometimes errors are actually related to billing problems you are having with a company. In these cases the Fair Credit Billing Act comes to the rescue. This law requires creditors to promptly credit your payments and correct billings mistakes. It also allows you to withhold payments on defective goods. Be sure you document any problems in writing so you can build a strong case if a negative report is filed with a credit bureau.

The Federal Reserve recommends you take these three steps in its consumer protection information:

1. Notify the creditor in writing within 60 days after the first bill was mailed that showed the error. Be sure to write to the address the creditor lists for billing inquiries and include your name and account number, the billing error, and why you believe it is wrong, and the date and suspected amount of the error or item that you want explained.

2. Pay all parts of the bill that are not in dispute. You do not have to pay the amount being questioned or the minimum payments or finance charges that apply to that amount. Your creditor must acknowledge your letter within 30 days unless the problem can be resolved within that time. The creditor has two billing periods, but no longer than 90 days, to correct the error or tell you why the creditor believes that the bill is correct. You will not have to pay any finance charges on the amount questioned if there is an error. The account must be corrected with a statement regarding any amount you still owe. If the creditor finds there is no error, you must be sent an explanation for that finding with a statement of what is owed. In a case where there is no error you will owe finance charges and any minimum payments missed during the time you disputed the bill.

3. If you still are not satisfied, you should notify the creditor in writing within the time allowed to pay your bill.

While you are disputing a billing error, a creditor cannot report to credit bureaus or other creditors anything that would hurt your reputation. Once the creditor has explained the bill, if you don't pay in time then the creditor can take actions to collect the money and report your late payment to credit bureaus. If you still dispute the amount, you can attach a statement to your credit report giving your side of the story.

Sometimes there are errors on your bill or credit history because of a lost or stolen credit card. If your credit cards are lost or stolen, you do not have to pay for any unauthorized charges made once you notify the credit card company of the loss or theft. The most you will have to pay for unauthorized charges is $50 on each card even if someone runs up several hundred dollars worth of charges before you report a card missing, but be sure to report any lost or stolen cards as quickly as possible.

Not-So-Perfect Credit?

So what can you do if your credit rating isn't "perfect"? Well, there are "subprime" mortgage loans that you can use to buy a coop, condo, or even home. Subprime mortgage lending has skyrocketed in recent years. Its roots are found in two pieces of 1980 legislation (which several of us supported with all our might!): the Depository Institutions Deregulation and Monetary Control Act of 1980 (DIDMCA) and the Tax Reform Act of 1986. If you decide that your family needs could be best served by a "home" purchase even though you have had less than perfect credit experience, then think about getting a subprime loan to improve your housing. You also may be rated subprime if you are carrying an unusually large amount of debt. (Don't we all? No.)

> **Money Tips**
>
> Don't think you will be the only "subprimer." Subprime lending has grown substantially in recent years, to $140 billion in 2000, up from $34 billion in 1994, according to "Subprime Mortgage Lending and the Capital Markets," Federal Reserve Bank of San Francisco Economic Letter, December 28, 2001.

Subprime loans require a higher interest rate and higher processing fees than ordinary mortgage loans. In the 1998–2001 period you would pay 3.7 percent more than the prime borrower. For example, a prime borrower may pay 7 percent per annum, while a subprime borrower may pay 10.7 percent. A subprime lender will even build in a so-called prepayment penalty charge he requires to avoid reinvesting at a much lower rate of interest.

Electronic Age

Today credit cards are not the only way to make purchases. Many people are making use of systems that enable electronic funds transfers (EFTs). You probably do this most often when using an ATM (Automated Teller Machine) card to get cash at a 24-hour banking machine. Another common use of EFTs is check cards that allow you to pay directly from your checking account when making a purchase.

Paying bills using EFTs is also becoming a more common practice. Most people do this by preauthorizing money to be transferred from their account to a service provider, such as your electric company. Others use an online bill paying service to make arrangements for electronic transfers.

You may also be taking advantage of EFTs when you use direct deposit for your paycheck or other types of payments into your checking account. Isn't it great not to have to run to the bank every week or two to deposit your check?

This new type of funds transfer of course resulted in the need for another new law to be passed by Congress and new regulations to be developed by the Fed. The Electronic Fund Transfer Act protects consumers in a number of ways. Unfortunately, if there is an error or you are the victim of theft or fraud, you will find it more difficult to correct a problem. The biggest problem is that if there is an error with an EFT, the money is out of your account and it can take weeks to get it back.

The Federal Reserve recommends the following steps for fixing an EFT error:

1. Write or call your financial institution immediately if possible, but no later than 60 days from the date the first statement that you think shows an error was mailed to you. Give your name and account number and explain why you believe there is an error, what kind of error, and the dollar amount and date in question. If you call, you may be asked to send this information in writing within 10 business days.

2. The financial institution must promptly investigate an error and resolve it within 45 days. For errors involving new accounts (opened in the last 30 days), POS transactions, and foreign transactions, the institution may take up to 90 days to investigate the error. However, if the financial institution takes longer than 10 business days to complete its investigation, generally it must put back into your account the amount in question while it finishes the investigation. For new accounts, the financial institution may take up to 20 business days to credit your account for the amount you think is in error.

3. The financial institution must notify you of the results of its investigation. If there was an error, the institution must correct it promptly. If it finds no error, the financial institution must explain in writing why it believes no error occurred. If money was redeposited in your account, the bank will take it out if the investigation finds no error. You may ask for copies of documents relied on in the investigation.

CAUTION

Ups and Downs _____

   Loss and theft risks for EFTs are greater than with credit cards. You can lose more than $50. Here are the rules:

- ◆ Your loss is limited to $50 if you notify the financial institution within two business days after learning of the loss or theft of your card or code.

- ◆ You could lose as much as $500 if you do not tell the card issuer within two business days after learning of the loss or theft.

- ◆ If you do not report an unauthorized transfer that appears on your statement within 60 days after the statement is mailed to you, you could lose all the money in your account plus your maximum overdraft line of credit, if any.

With all the additional risks of EFTs, you may wonder if you have to use electronic transfers. The EFT Act does not allow a creditor to force you to use EFTs when you repay a loan or other credit bill except in the case of overdraft checking plans. An employer can require you to receive your salary by electronic transfer provided you get to choose the institution into which the money gets deposited. This is also true for governmental agencies that pay government benefits.

Discriminating Yeses and Nos

In addition to protecting your credit history, the Equal Credit Opportunity Act also guarantees that you cannot be rejected for certain personal characteristics. Creditors are able to reject for some personal reasons though. Basically Fed regulations allow creditors to consider the three "C's"—capacity, character, and collateral—when you apply for credit. Here's what the Fed allows by law:

- **Capacity.** Can you repay the debt? Creditors may ask for employment information, such as your occupation, how long you've worked, and how much you earn. They also can ask about your expenses, how many dependents you have, whether you pay alimony or child support, and the amount of your other obligations.

- **Character.** Will you repay the debt? Creditors can look at your credit history to find out how much you owe, how often you borrow, whether you pay bills on time, and whether you live within your means. They can also review how long you've lived at your present address, whether you own or rent your home, and the length of your present employment.

- **Collateral.** Is the creditor fully protected if you fail to repay? Creditors can find out if you have the resources to back up or secure your loan and other resources you have for repaying debt in addition to income, such as savings, investments, or property.

While creditors are allowed to collect information based on the three C's, they don't have carte blanche to collect and use any personal information they find. They also must apply any credit tests they develop fairly and impartially without regard to age, gender, marital status, race, color, religion, and national origin. The act also bars discrimination because you receive public income, such as veterans' benefits, welfare or social security, or because you exercise your rights under federal credit laws, such as filing a billing error notice with a creditor.

Let's take a closer look at some of the more common discrimination protections. Age is a big factor and will become of even greater concern as the baby boomers move into retirement. Before the Equal Credit Opportunity Act was passed many older persons complained they were denied credit because of their age. Today a creditor may ask your age, but as long as you can sign a binding contract (usually 18 or 21 years old depending on state law), a creditor may not do the following:

- ◆ Turn you down, offer you less credit, or offer you less favorable credit terms because of your age

- ◆ Ignore your retirement income in evaluating your application.

- ◆ Close your credit account or require you to reapply for it because you reach a certain age or retire

- ◆ Deny you credit or close your account because credit life insurance or other credit-related insurance is not available to a person your age

Creditors may "score" your age in a credit-scoring system, but if you are 62 or older you must be given at least as many points for age as any person under 62.

Another common area where discrimination can sometimes be a factor is for people receiving public assistance. You cannot be denied credit just because you receive Social Security or other public assistance.

The Equal Credit Opportunity Act also protects you when you want to buy a home. The act bars discrimination based on the race or national origin of people living in a neighborhood. Creditors cannot use any property appraisal that considers the race of the people in the neighborhood. If you think discrimination may have occurred, request a copy of the appraisal. You are entitled to get a copy of that report. You paid for it!

Women also sometimes face discrimination when applying for credit. Here are some of the credit protections now in place for women as part of the Equal Credit Opportunity Act:

- ◆ **Gender and Marital Status.** Generally, creditors cannot ask for your gender on an application form. One exception is on a loan to buy or build a home. You do not have to use Miss, Mrs., or Ms. with your name on a credit application. But in some cases, a creditor may ask whether you are married, unmarried, or separated (unmarried includes single, divorced, and widowed).

- ◆ **Childbearing Plans.** Creditors may not ask about your birth-control practices or your plans to have children, and they may not assume anything about those plans.

- ◆ **Income and Alimony.** The creditor must count all of your income, even income from part-time employment. Child support and alimony payments are a source of income for many women. You don't have to disclose these kinds of income, but if you do, creditors must count them.

- **Telephones.** Creditors may not consider whether you have a telephone listing in your name because this factor would discriminate against many married women. (However, you may be asked if there's a telephone in your home.)

- **Change in Marital Status.** Creditors may not make you reapply for credit because you marry or become widowed or divorced. Nor may they close your account or change the terms of your account on these grounds. There must be some sign that your creditworthiness has changed. For example, creditors may ask you to reapply if you relied on your ex-husband's income to get credit in the first place.

If you are denied credit and you think some form of discrimination played a factor, don't hesitate to ask for a full explanation of why you were turned down for credit. If you think the reason given is discriminatory, cite the law to the creditor. If the creditor still says no without a satisfactory explanation, you may want to contact a federal enforcement agency for assistance. The federal agency you should contact should be included in the notice you receive from the creditor. Contact information for the key federal agencies is given later in the chapter.

Money for Your Home

Buying a home is one of the most important investments most consumers make. In addition to the discrimination laws that are part of the Equal Credit Opportunity Act, home buyers are protected by the Fair Housing Act, which prohibits discrimination in housing sales or loans on the basis of race, religion, color, national origin, sex, familial status (having children under the age of 18), or handicap.

> **Money Tips**
>
> You can get a copy of HUD's booklet, "Buying Your Home: Settlement Costs and Information," by writing to:
>
> Deputy Assistant Secretary for Housing
> Attention: RESPA Enforcement
> U.S. Department of Housing and Urban Development
> 451 Seventh Street, S.W. Room 9416
> Washington, DC 20410

Home buyers also have additional credit protections because purchasing a home on credit is one of the most complicated types of loans. In addition to the rules under the Truth in Lending Law, home buyers are also protected by the Real Estate Settlement Procedures Act, which is administered by the Department of Housing and Urban Development.

If you've closed on a home recently, you should have received a copy of HUD's booklet, "Buying Your

Home: Settlement Costs and Information." If you are like most folks you probably threw it away without reading it. But, there is some critical information in there you should know about your credit protection, especially with regards to the costs you will pay when you close a home loan and how to shop for lower settlement costs.

Homeowners also have additional protections when they use their home as security to get credit. For example, if you are planning to do a major renovation and use your home as security to finance the costs of that work, you have three business days, usually after you sign a contract, to think about the transaction and cancel it if you wish. You must be given notification of your right to cancel (also known as right of rescission). But, if you do decide to cancel, you must inform the creditor within that three-day window. The creditor must then return all fees paid and cancel the security interest in your home. The creditor also cannot start work on your home during this three-day period. If the money to be borrowed or work to be done is needed for emergency purposes, you do have the right to cancel your three-day rescission period by writing an explanation of the circumstances.

This law also protects you if you get a second mortgage or equity line, but does not protect you if you are getting a mortgage to finance the purchase of your home. When making an initial purchase, you do commit yourself as soon as you sign the mortgage contract.

Rules for Leasing

You'll also find there is a special law for leasing called the Consumer Leasing Act. This law covers the long-term leasing of cars, furniture, and appliances, but it does not cover daily rentals of cars or apartment leases. This law requires a leasing agent to give you the facts about the costs and terms in the contract to help you make a good leasing decision.

You must be given certain information about costs and terms in a designated format, including the costs you pay at the beginning of the lease upon signing or delivery of the leased item, such as a car; the monthly or periodic payments; and any other charges you will face. Plus, you must be told about the total amount you will pay over the lease term.

Other key disclosures include showing how the payment was determined and termination information, such as charges for early termination, excess wear and use, mileage limits and excess mileage charges, and any purchase option at the end of the lease.

Filing Complaints

Now that you know more about consumer protection laws, you may believe your bank or creditor is not complying with the law. If you do, you should first contact your creditor or bank to give them a chance to resolve the problem. If you are not satisfied with the response, you can file a complaint with the federal agencies that enforce the law.

> **Money Tips**
>
> You can file a complaint with the Federal Reserve in writing and send it to the Division of Consumer and Community Affairs, Board of Governors of the Federal Reserve System, Washington, DC 20551. Be sure to provide the complete name and address of the bank, a brief description of your complaint, and any documentation that may help the Fed investigate your complaint. Be sure to send copies of your information and not the original documents. You'll get a response from the Federal Reserve within 15 business days. The Fed will let you know whether a Federal Reserve bank will investigate your complaint or if it will be forwarded to another federal agency for attention.

If your complaint is with a bank or other financial institution, the Federal Reserve System will either investigate the complaint if they have jurisdiction or send it on to the proper federal agency. The Fed will let you know where your complaint has been sent if the investigation will not be handled by one of its banks.

You also have the option of filing a lawsuit against a creditor if you believe a consumer law has been broken. If you win, the creditor may have to pay you penalties as well as restore your money. Here are some of the penalties under the key consumer laws:

- **Truth in Lending and Consumer Leasing Acts.** If a creditor fails to disclose information required under these acts, or gives inaccurate information, or does not comply with the rules about credit cards or the right to cancel certain home-secured loans, you may sue for actual damages and any money loss you suffer. In addition, you can sue for twice the finance charge in the case of certain credit disclosures, or if a lease is concerned, 25 percent of total monthly payments. In either case, the least the court may award you if you win is $100, and the most is $1,000. In any lawsuit that you win, you are entitled to reimbursement for court costs and attorney's fees. Class action suits are also permitted.

- **Equal Credit Opportunity Act.** If you think you can prove that a creditor has discriminated against you for any reason prohibited by this act, you may sue for actual damages plus punitive damages—that is, damages for the fact that the law has been violated—of up to $10,000. In a successful lawsuit, the court will award you court costs and a reasonable amount for attorney's fees. Class action suits are also permitted.

♦ **Fair Credit Billing Act.** A creditor who breaks the rules for the correction of billing errors automatically loses the amount owed on the item in question and any finance charges on it, up to a combined total of $50 even if the bill was correct. You may also sue for actual damages plus twice the amount of any finance charges, but in any case not less than $100 nor more than $1,000. You are also entitled to court costs and attorney's fees in a successful lawsuit. Class action suits are also permitted.

♦ **Fair Credit Reporting Act.** You may sue any credit-reporting agency or creditor for breaking the rules about who may see your credit records or for not correcting errors in your file. Again, you are entitled to actual damages, plus punitive damages that the court may allow if the violation is proved to have been intentional. In any successful lawsuit, you will also be awarded court costs and attorney's fees. A person who obtains a credit report without proper authorization or an employee of a credit-reporting agency who gives a credit report to unauthorized persons may be fined up to $5,000 or imprisoned for one year or both.

♦ **Electronic Fund Transfer Act.** If a financial institution does not follow the provisions of the EFT Act, you may sue for actual damages (or in certain cases when the institution fails to correct an error or recredit an account, for three times actual damages) plus punitive damages of not less than $100 nor more than $1,000. You are also entitled to court costs and attorney's fees in a successful lawsuit. Class action suits are also permitted. If an institution fails to make an electronic fund transfer or to stop payment of a preauthorized transfer when properly instructed by you to do so, you may sue for all damages that result from failure.

Who to Contact

Different federal agencies have responsibility for enforcing these laws. Here is the contact information for the key agencies:

The Department of Housing and Urban Development (HUD) has primary responsibility for implementing the Fair Housing Act. You can contact them by calling 1-800-424-8590 or visiting their website at www.hud.gov/complaints/housediscrim.cfm.

Compliance by lenders is monitored by federal agencies based on the type of financial institution.

For national banks contact:

> Office of the Comptroller of the Currency
> 1-800-613-6743
> www.occ.treas.gov

For state banks that are members of the Federal Reserve System contact:

> Division of Consumer and Community Affairs
> 202-452-3693
> www.federalreserve.gov

For nonmember federally insured state banks contact:

> Federal Deposit Insurance Corporation
> 202-942-3100 or
> 1-800-934-FDIC (1-800-934-3342)
> www.fdic.gov

For savings and loan associations contact:

> Office of Thrift Supervision
> 202-906-6237 or
> 1-800-842-6929
> www.ots.treas.gov

For credit unions contact:

> Federal Credit Unions
> National Credit Union Administration
> 703-518-6330
> www.ncua.gov

For other lenders contact:

> Federal Trade Commission
> 202-326-3758 or
> 1-877-FTC-HELP (1-877-382-4357)
> www.ftc.gov

You also can contact the Department of Justice:

> Department of Justice
> 202-514-3301
> www.usdoj.gov

We've just taken a tour of the federal laws that protect you and your credit, but there are also laws to protect your savings. We'll take closer look at those laws in the next chapter. We'll also look at how you can protect your privacy and your identification.

The Least You Need to Know

- ◆ The Federal Reserve is responsible for developing consumer banking regulations and monitoring their implementation.

- ◆ If you have a credit problem, you must notify your creditor within a set time frame to get credit protection.

- ◆ Creditors cannot discriminate because of age, race, or religion just to name a few of the discrimination no-nos.

- ◆ If you think a financial institution is not abiding by federal consumer regulations, there are a number of federal agencies you can contact for help depending on the type of institution.

Chapter 21

Are We Saving Enough?

In This Chapter

- ◆ Teaching about money
- ◆ Saving for retirement
- ◆ Maintaining privacy
- ◆ Protecting your identity

The simple answer to the question, "Are we saving enough?" is no. In fact national savings when measured as a share of national input not consumed by households or the government dropped over 4 percent between the 1970s and 1990s, according to research by the Federal Reserve. National savings averaged well over 9 percent during the 1960s and 1970s, but dropped to 6 percent in the 1980s and 4.7 percent in the 1990s. In fact, personal savings reached an all-time low of 2.4 percent in 1999.

While the actual numbers dropped household wealth did not. The Fed reported that during the 1990s household wealth jumped from less than $21 trillion to about $40 trillion. These numbers are based on the Survey of Consumer Finances, which is done by the Fed every three years. The most recent survey doesn't reflect the stock market crash of 2000 because it was completed in December 1998. The next survey that will be released in January 2003 will reflect consumer finances as of December 2001. Wonder how much the number will drop?

"About 80 percent of the increase in wealth over the past decade was attributable to capital gains, only 20 percent to saving," Federal Reserve Governor Edward Gramlich told the National Savings Forum in Washington, D.C., in June 2001. I'm sure it won't take much convincing to get you to believe those savings numbers will be dramatically lower given the anemic growth of the stock market since the crash.

If people aren't saving, where is all the money going? That, too, is a simple answer—personal consumption. People have been consuming more on a steady upward trend since the 1960s. Personal consumption rose from 68.3 percent during the 1960s to 77.2 percent in 1999 according to Fed research.

We're going to look at the initiatives being taken by the Federal Reserve to reverse these savings and spending patterns. Then we'll look at some of the key issues surrounding savings for retirement. Finally, we'll review how you can secure your financial assets through financial privacy rules and strategies for protecting your financial identity.

Educating the Public

All Federal Reserve banks are looking for ways to help their member banks develop good consumer education programs. Programs sponsored by the Fed banks include competitions on economic principles for high-school students and workshops on home ownership. There are also programs developed to help consumers develop wealth-building strategies.

> **Money Tips**
>
> You can take a tour of the Fed's education programs on its website at www.federalreserveeducation.org.

The Federal Reserve banks of Dallas, Cleveland, and Chicago have developed the most extensive programs.

The Dallas Fed provides an excellent program called "Building Wealth: A Beginner's Guide to Saving for Your Financial Future" (www.dallasfed.org/htm/wealth/introlhtml). You can use this online tool to develop your own financial plan. Sections include "Wealth Creation," "Learn the Language," "Budget to Save," "Save and Invest," and "Take Control of Debt." When you finish entering your personal information, you can print out your draft plan.

This tool was developed to help even people at low-income levels become knowledgeable about wealth creation. There are examples used throughout the tool that show people with limited income ways to take control of their finances and save. There are also tips on how to avoid *predatory lending* schemes and reduce credit card debt.

After you finish developing your wealth building plan, you may want to check out the Fed bank of Cleveland (www.clev.frb.org/Education/index. htm). The U.S. Department of Treasury worked with the Cleveland Fed to develop a national program called "America Saves." Other partners in the effort include the Consumer Federation of America (CFA), Consumer Credit Counseling Services of Northeast Ohio (CCCS), community-based Working for Empowerment through Community Organizing (WECO), and over 100 local business, bank, and community leaders.

Money Meanings

Predatory lending is a practice where lenders, usually nondepository institutions, offer high cost loans to the elderly, low-income earners, minorities, or women. Frequently these loans are home-secured and when the consumer can't make the payments they are encouraged to refinance the loan into another expensive option to avoid losing their home.

This program was developed to motivate low- and moderate-income households to build wealth through savings. Programs were developed to be used in workplaces, schools and at local banks. Participants are called "Cleveland Savers." They attend motivational workshops filled with information on how to reach wealth-building goals. A network of employers, nonprofit organizations, and religious institutions was formed to encourage their employees and members to join the program. To support the initiative further, many Cleveland-area financial institutions developed low- or no-minimum-balance and no-fee savings accounts for the program participants. Cleveland Savers also have the option of joining a Savers Club that offers peer encouragement and support. The participants' progress toward their goals is tracked to measure the program's effectiveness.

Economic Wisdom

"Consumers with a basic knowledge of lending programs, of the credit process, and of their rights, may be better able to protect themselves against bad credit situations. Consumer education alone may not be the sole answer to predatory lending, but it is certainly an essential part of the solution."

—Fed Governor Edward M. Gramlich at the Financial Literacy Teaching Training Workshop, University of Illinois at Chicago, May 2, 2002

Economic Wisdom

"Financial literacy can empower consumers to be better shoppers, allowing them to obtain goods and services at lower cost. This effectively increases their household budgets, providing more opportunity to consume and save or invest. In addition, comprehensive education can help provide individuals with the financial knowledge necessary to create household budgets, initiate savings plans, manage debt, and make strategic investment decisions for their retirement or their children's education. Having these basic financial planning skills can help families to meet their near-term obligations and to maximize their longer-term financial well-being."

—Chairman Alan Greenspan testifying before the Committee on Banking, Housing, and Urban Affairs, U.S. Senate, February 5, 2002

Money Tips

Kids may have a good time playing "Peanuts and Crackerjacks" at the Federal Reserve bank of Boston site. This baseball simulation helps kids learn about economics. There are also good resources for teachers as part of the game. Check it out: www.bos.frb.org/peanuts/leadpgs/intro.htm.

The third very innovative program was developed by the Federal Reserve bank of Chicago called "Project MoneySmart" (www.chicagofed.org/consumerinformation/projectmoneysmart/index.cfm). This site provides extensive consumer information on a wide variety of financial topics. You'll find excellent articles and tools on spending money, using credit wisely, avoiding frauds and scams, and understanding mortgages. You'll also be able to create personal budgets online with a key emphasis on saving strategies.

Getting Ready for Retirement

Why all the emphasis on savings? Well in addition to the reasons already mentioned above, another key goal of the Fed is to help people get ready for retirement. You've certainly seen many stories about Social Security and whether there will be enough left when you get to retire.

You may not be aware that Alan Greenspan spearheaded the effort to save Social Security in the early 1980s before he became chairman of the Fed. Greenspan still plays an integral part in promoting efforts to secure the future of Social Security.

Social Security wasn't designed to be a person's only retirement income. In fact, it only replaces an average of 40 percent of your pre-retirement income. Other income is needed from pension plans, 401(k)s, IRAs, or other earnings in order to maintain your standard of living in retirement. Greenspan never passes up an opportunity to encourage increased savings not only by individuals, but also by the government as well.

> ## Economic Wisdom
>
> "If we move now to shore up the social security program, or replace it, in part or in whole, with a private system, and subsequently find that we had been too pessimistic in our projections, the costs to our society would be few. If we assume more optimistic scenarios and they prove wrong, the imbalances could become overwhelming, and finding a solution would be even more divisive than today's problem."
>
> —Chairman Alan Greenspan before the Committee on the Budget, U.S. Senate, January 28, 1999

The crucial problem Social Security is facing is the fact that when the baby boomers retire fewer workers will be contributing to Social Security and the number of beneficiaries will increase dramatically. Social Security is a pay-as-go system. In other words about 85 percent of the Social Security taxes currently being taken out of your paycheck go toward paying current beneficiaries. When there are fewer workers and more retirees it will become much more difficult for the government to make these payments unless efforts are made now to save more money in the trust funds.

There are numerous options being considered including raising taxes, cutting benefits, and increasing the retirement age. While privatization is being discussed, so far no plan has been put forward for which this option will not drain current Social Security trust funds even faster and cut deeply into general tax revenues. The problem is that putting even part of the current Social Security taxes into private accounts means payments to current beneficiaries either need to be cut or less money will have to go into trust funds for beneficiaries unless Social Security taxes are raised or general tax revenues are used. You can find more detailed discussion of Social Security's future in author Lita Epstein's book, *The Complete Idiot's Guide to Social Security* (Alpha Books, 2002).

Another option being considered is investing the trust funds in stocks. Right now the trust funds are invested in government bonds. Greenspan has spoken in opposition to the stock investment option numerous times. He stated it most strongly in testimony before the Senate Budget Committee in January 1999, "I do not believe that it is politically feasible to insulate such huge funds from governmental influence, investing Social Security trust fund assets in equities compromises the efficient allocation of our capital—which, as the past few years have demonstrated, is so essential to raising our standards of living."

The president's Commission to Reform Social Security proposed three alternatives for Social Security privatization using personal accounts. The Congress will probably take up the issue in 2003 after the 2002 elections. No one wants to deal with the political hot potato going into an election year.

Money Tips

Saving for retirement is a critical task for all Americans. You can find out more about savings options through the "Choose to Save" program (www. choosetosave.com) sponsored jointly by the American Savings Education Council and the Employees Benefit Research Institute.

Even with all the publicity about saving for retirement, the Employees Benefit Research Institute found that the percentage of the population doing retirement planning actually dropped between 2000 and 2002 according to EBRI's twelfth annual Retirement Confidence Survey. EBRI found that only 32 percent of people surveyed in 2002 calculated their future retirement needs. That number is down 7 percent from the percentage who did retirement planning in 2001. The percentage of people who saved for retirement also dropped in 2001. In 2000, 74 percent of respondents said they saved for retirement. Only 69 percent had retirement savings in 2002.

The Fed doesn't have direct responsibility for people's savings habits, but obviously its member banks benefit from increased savings. The Fed does regulate savings as part of the Truth in Savings Act of 1991. The law requires that depository institutions disclose information about annual percentage yield and how interest is calculated. The Fed also regulates advertising of savings accounts.

Economic Wisdom

"One of the most complex economic calculations that most workers will ever undertake is, without doubt, deciding how much to save for retirement. At every stage of life, individuals ought to make judgments about their likely earnings before retirement and their desired lifestyle in retirement. Also implicit in such decisions are assumptions about prospective rates of return, life expectancy, and the possible accumulation of a nest egg for one's children. The difficulty that individuals face in making these projections and choices is compounded by the need to forecast personal and economic events many years into the future."

—Chairman Alan Greenspan at the 2002 National Summit on Retirement Savings, the Department of Labor, Washington, D.C., February 28, 2002

In addition to savings responsibility, the Fed regulates your financial privacy. In the Right to Financial Privacy Act of 1978, Congress mandated certain protection for bank customer accounts. The Fed developed regulations to protect you from unlawful scrutiny of your financial records by federal agencies. Government agencies must follow a set of rules developed by the Fed in order to access your financial records.

Keeping Things Private

The Federal Reserve also develops rules that your banks and other financial companies must follow to keep your financial records private based on legislation passed by Congress. There are two acts that regulate how your information can be shared. The Federal Credit Reporting Act and the Gramm-Leach-Bliley Act (GLB). GLB requires financial companies to tell you about their policies regarding the privacy of your personal financial information. We discussed the Credit Reporting Act in Chapter 20.

You may wonder how private your financial situation actually is when you see your mailboxes fill up with solicitations for credit, insurance, and investments. You probably also received a bunch of privacy notices about how your information will be kept private. Today most companies that provide financial services must send you notices about their privacy practices. These include the following:

- Banks, savings and loans, and credit unions

- Insurance companies

- Securities and commodities brokerage firms

- Retailers that directly issue their own credit cards (such as department stores or gas stations)

- Mortgage brokers

- Automobile dealerships that extend or arrange financing or leasing

- Check cashers and payday lenders

- Financial advisors and credit counseling services

- Sellers of money orders or travelers checks

You've probably found these privacy notices are printed in documents with tiny, hard-to-read type. I hope you have taken the time to read the fine print though. They are telling you how your financial information will be used and giving you an opportunity to opt out of various information-sharing plans. These notices should explain:

♦ What personal financial information the company collects

♦ Whether the company intends to share your personal financial information with other companies

♦ What you can do, if the company intends to share your personal financial information, to limit some of that sharing

♦ How the company protects your personal financial information

It's very important that you read these privacy notices, find out how the company plans to share your financial information and what your choices may be to keep your information private. In some cases you have the right to opt out of information-sharing with companies in the same corporate group as your financial company or with companies not part of your financial institution's corporate group. Remember, as we discussed in Chapter 14, many banks are now part of large holding companies that hold numerous types of financial service companies, such as stock and insurance brokers.

Even if you do opt out of information sharing, the law does permit financial companies to share certain information even without your permission. Some of the key things that can be shared include:

♦ Information about you to firms that help promote and market the company's own products or products offered under a joint agreement between two financial companies

♦ Records of your transactions—such as your loan payments, credit card or debit card purchases, and checking and savings account statements—to firms that provide data processing and mailing services for your company

♦ Information about you in response to a court order

♦ Your payment history on loans and credit cards to credit bureaus

Even what they can share adds to the junk mail you get. If you are like me, you would like to cut down the flow of your personal information to others as well as the junk mail that information sharing likely will generate. One of the best ways to do this is to opt out of whatever you can.

You are usually given about 30 days to opt out after you get the privacy mailing. If you don't respond the financial institution can then start sharing certain parts of your personal financial information. If you threw away the notice and now want to opt out, all is not lost. You can always change your mind and opt out later. Just contact your financial institution to get information about opting out of information-sharing.

Ups and Downs _____

Financial institutions are not the only ones that can share or sell information about your financial status. Credit bureaus can and do frequently sell your financial information to lenders and insurers. That's how you get most of your unsolicited mail for credit cards or insurance policies. You'll probably find that most of those notices say you have been "prescreened." You can opt out of receiving these prescreened offers by calling 1-888-567-8688.

There are three types of privacy notices you could receive from your financial institutions:

+ **Initial Privacy Notice.** Usually given to you when you open an account or become a customer of a financial company. If you open an account over the phone, this may be mailed at a later time.

+ **Annual Privacy Notices.** These must be sent each year by every financial company at which you have an ongoing relationship including your bank where you have a checking account, your credit card company, or a company that services your loans.

+ **Notice of Changes in Privacy Policies.** These must be sent whenever a financial institution revises its privacy policy. The company can opt to send the change notice with your annual notice.

You can be sent these notices as part of your monthly statement or bill or the notice can be sent separately. Electronic delivery of the notice is permitted if you have given the financial institution permission to send you notices by e-mail or via the company website.

If after reading the notices you want to opt out, then follow the instructions given in the notice. If you don't like an institution's privacy policy, your only other option is to switch to a financial institution that will maintain your privacy in the way that you do like—if you can find one.

You can contact related federal regulators if you think a company is not living up to the privacy rules. Who you contact will depend upon the type of financial institution involved. Here are the key contact points:

Board of Governors of the Federal Reserve System for chartered banks that are members of the Federal Reserve System, bank holding companies, and branches of foreign banks contact:

Division of Consumer and Community Affairs, Stop 801
20th and C Streets, NW
Washington, DC 20551
202-452-3693
www.federalreserve.gov

Commodity Futures Trading Commission for commodity brokers, commodity trading advisors, commodity pools, and introducing brokers contact:

Privacy Officer, Office of Chief Counsel
Division of Trading and Markets
Three Lafayette Center
1155 21st Street, NW
Washington, DC 20581
202-418-5430
www.cftc.gov

Federal Deposit Insurance Corporation for state-chartered banks that are not members of the Federal Reserve System contact:

Division of Compliance and Consumer Affairs
550 17th Street, NW
Washington, DC 20429
1-877-ASK-FDIC (1-877-275-3342)
www.fdic.gov

Federal Trade Commission for any financial company not covered by the other federal regulators such as mortgage brokers, tax and investment services, finance companies, credit bureaus, nonbank lenders, auto dealers, leasing companies, appraisers, real estate settlement services, credit counseling services, and collection agency services contact:

Consumer Response Center
600 Pennsylvania Avenue, NW
Washington, DC 20580
1-877-FTC-HELP (1-877-382-4357)
www.ftc.gov or www.consumer.gov/idtheft/

National Credit Union Administration for federally chartered credit unions contact:

Office of Public and Congressional Affairs
1775 Duke Street
Alexandria, VA 22314-3428
703-518-6330
www.ncua.gov

Office of the Comptroller of the Currency for national banks, District of Columbia banks, federal branches and federal agencies of foreign banks, and subsidiaries of such entities. These typically include banks with "national" or "N.A." in their names.

Customer Assistance Group
1301 McKinney Street
Suite 3710
Houston, TX 77010
1-800-613-6743
www.occ.treas.gov

Office of Thrift Supervision for federal savings and loan associations and federal savings banks contact:

Consumer Programs
1700 G Street, NW
Washington, DC 20552
1-800-842-6929
www.ots.treas.gov

Securities and Exchange Commission for brokerage firms, mutual fund companies, and investment advisors contact:

Office of Investor Education and Assistance
450 5th Street, NW
Washington, DC 20549-0213
Fax: 202-942-9634
www.sec.gov/complaint.shtml

You can see there is a lot to learn about your savings options and maintaining your privacy. This information is critical for your and your family's financial safety.

The Least You Need to Know

- ◆ Savings in the United States have decreased steadily since the 1960s and hit an all-time low of 2.4 percent in 1999.

- ◆ Improving financial literacy is the best way to help people get control of their financial future and increase savings.

- ◆ Saving for retirement in addition to expected Social Security payments is critical if you want to maintain your standard of living in retirement.

- ◆ Your financial records are not always private and can be shared with other financial entities. You can opt out of some financial information sharing.

Part 7

The Money Machine's Future

Some folks would like to see the Fed disbanded, but most support its work. We discuss issues facing the Fed in the near and long-term future.

We also introduce you to ways you can work at the Fed as a full-time staffer or through volunteering on its advisory councils.

Chapter 22

The World of Tomorrow

In This Chapter

- ◆ Money policies
- ◆ Questions of trust
- ◆ Regulations anew
- ◆ Looking global

Albert Einstein expressed it well: "I never think about the future. It comes soon enough."

Easy for that Nobel Prize recipient to respond. Not for me, not for you. We must look down that long, winding road, right?

This coming decade challenges us to sit back and think about the future of our economy and our very society. The good life for you and yours requires you to wrench your mind away from the next few hours and from tomorrow and peer out into the future.

We face almost unprecedented challenges and opportunities in the remaining years of the decade 2000 through 2010. Those first two years, 2001 and 2002 were challenging, weren't they? Alright, what should we focus on? Let's take a look at the key issues facing us and the role the Fed may play.

Monetary Policy in Our Future

Remembering my four years on the Fed board, and our rather mixed, but positive results, I give today's Fed high marks for their policy contributions to our last decade's growth and relative stability.

Will Sir Alan Greenspan pull his knightly sword out of its scabbard and prod economic growth? (Queen Elizabeth II bestowed upon him the honorific "A Knight Commander of the British Empire" in 2002.) Well, the Parliament really did the honor, in Britain the "lords" decide and the royalty carries things out). "Alan the Lionhearted" (did I get that right?) won't serve forever. Will President Bush choose instead one of his four fine Federal Reserve Board appointees—Susan Bies, Mark W. Olson, Don Kohn, and Princeton's Ben Bernanke—when Greenspan's current term ends in June 2004?

Less than two years remain of Sir Alan's term as Chairman, and with his 16 year record and his "connections" he could be reappointed. Yes, but presidents tend to appoint their "own" chairman. No, we have reviewed the reality, in previous chapters, appointees do not do the president's bidding. Nevertheless, one of Bush's appointees could receive the "coronation."

Ups and Downs

Look at the "Greenspan board's" fine policy record. The best example is the most recent 2001 to 2002 period: 12 federal funds rate reductions, to 1.75 percent (a 41 year low), and increases in the M3 money supply. Regulatory policy has been balanced. Negotiations and loan loss reserve requirements strong, but none of the "wipe 'em out, seize them" over-regulation we savings and loan owners and managers faced in the early 1990s.

Yes, every institution's projections change from report to report. In today's "informational" and "global" environments there is no historic period the forecasters can pick up and replicate. No, we don't live in a fully "new economy" as some argued after nearly 10 years of "dot-com" growth (and prior to the 2001 three-quarter mild recession). Yes, a significant segment of our economy is "new" in its informational availability, productivity increases and its speedy changes in employee utilization. Global? Your local manufacturer opened a plant where? In southeast China?

Today's Federal Reserve recognizes the importance and the effects of market trends and volatility, but it has refrained from using its tool of "margin requirements" to restrain or cut back market prices. The Fed's margin requirements require PMa percent of cash you have to put up when you are buying those stocks. The 50 percent requirement has been in place for many years.

Greenspan didn't spend all those years working in New York without "getting it." Listen to his September 1996 comments at an FOMC meeting, "I recognize that there is a stock bubble at this point with the possibility of increasing margin requirements. I guarantee that if you want to get rid of the bubble, whatever it is, that will do it." The chairman went on (correctly) to remind his colleagues, "… it was very difficult to definitively identify a bubble until after the fact—that is, when its bursting confirmed its existence." (Good Fedspeak, right?)

Fed thinking regarding using margin requirement increases to restrain or deflate stock prices hasn't changed. Reacting to media criticism in 2002, "Sir Alan" repeated the admonition, "the notion that a well tuned incremental tightening could have been calibrated to prevent the late 1990s bubble is almost surely an illusion."

Well, give the chairman credit. The Fed doubled interest rates in the 1994–1996 stock market boom "to break the cocoon of capital gains speculation," the FOMC argued at the time. Stocks moved sideways, not down, as the FOMC raised rates. After a period, stocks resumed their rise, Greenspan told the central bankers at their annual Jackson Hole, Wyoming, conclave that "even if a central bank identifies a bubble as it forms—a difficult task raising interest rates wouldn't deflate it unless they also tipped the economy into recession—the very outcome we would be seeking to avoid." You can guess that no central banker shouted, "Sir Alan, how about your margin requirements!"

Rebuilding Trust

No one would reasonably argue that the scandals and giant sweetheart loans to corporate CEOs and CFOs were ethical or that investors and employees weren't exploited in dozens of ventures. They were. Did the scandals and takings add to the speculative bubble, to the "irrational exuberance"? Of course they did.

The corporate malfeasance we experienced recently has had substantial market impacts, particularly driving the technology heavy NASDAQ down almost 75 percent.

I lived through a similar set of setbacks in the 1990s as chairman of three savings and loan holding companies. I watched a few of my competitors out-gushing corporate money around the world from their corporate airplanes and their big private yachts. Did my partner Bill Simon Sr. and I suck up your companies' money? Not at all.

Economic Wisdom

"Almost by nature, this wealth aggrandization breeds corruption in three forms—financial, political and philosophical. One caveat: the considerable parallels between contemporary excesses and those of seventy years ago don't warrant any firm conclusion about the next one, two or five years. History frequently repeats, but only in broad outline. ... The terrorist attack of 9/11 may have already pushed the United States into another wartime stimulus situation, although the new U.S. vulnerability could also lead into a negative economic watershed. We just don't know."

—Kevin Phillips, *Wealth and Democracy: A Political History of the American Rich*

What Simon and I did as owners was, and will be, typical corporate governance, not anything like the Adelphia, WorldCom, Global Crossing, Inclone, Xerox, and Arthur Andersen shenanigans. Dishonest execs and their fishy accountants are a small minority of the 17,000 listed corporations. But don't make the error of assuming most boards, most compensation committees, most audit committees of companies and most accountants are crooks. They aren't. We weren't!

Yes, Congress, the regulators and the president stepped up the disclosures and the rules of the corporate game to avoid future corporate fraudulent behavior. The Sarbanes-Oxley (August, 2002 Reform Act) was needed. Yes, the TV and the print media loved showing those handcuffed execs being led away arm to arm. Fine. But that does not signal the inevitability of a recession.

Preston's Points

I recently prepared year 2002 testimony in federal claims court for the years of time and investments we made to reconstruct our three ailing S&Ls under contracts with the Federal Government. I went over the multiyear CPA work and the long monthly board preparations analyses we made with the outside auditor firms. Yes, we took notes at the get-togethers with each company's CFO without "his honor" the CEO present. Yes, I recall the years of three board member checks we gave back to our company treasurers, each month—We weren't the only "good guys," but no, we didn't use options for compensation with only a few minor exceptions. You may already be serving on one or more boards. When you do, do your homework, line by line. Don't be "gentlemanly," be information demanding!

The probable impacts are slow real economic growth, 3 percent or 5 percent and a "jobless recovery." No, the new jobs will be coming! Don't let the media fool you. "Show trials" on the media will deliver the "shape up" message to the corporate world. Pay attention to all those CEOs who aren't working "there" anymore. And their lawyers aren't getting those huge fees, either.

The corporate messes do not inevitably bring on recession. Yes, they pull down the stock markets and the mutual fund holdings. Half of us will still own stock or mutual fund stock funds when the corporate reforms are accomplished, when the financial restatements are completed and the market reactions are done. Half!

So what will all those investors who are dumping their stocks do with the money? The stock dumpers will still take on buying that SUV with its no initial interest rate loan. Their neighbors will still refinance that home mortgage at a 6-plus rate for 20 years. The corporate binge is over for now, and the private economy is correcting itself (with a lot of government help). We investors are "on our guards" now, aren't we? Good ol' financial orthodoxy and corporate reportorial honesty will be celebrated and rewarded.

Keeping Up with Technology

With the world becoming more Internet savvy it is important that banks be innovative to remain competitive with each other as well as with nonbank competitors. Charles Schwab, for example, offers an access account that allows customers to use their investment accounts to write checks, receive and pay bills online and withdraw cash from ATMs. Sounds like a checking account to me!

Today's consumers can track their financial activities real time—on their PCs or they can even go wireless with a PDA (personal digital assistant like the Palm Pilot) or a cell phone. Routine online offerings from banks include real time access to account balances, bill payment, bill presentment, balance transfers, applying for a credit card, auto loan or even a mortgage. More and more banks are offering brokerage trading capabilities and insurance services. Consumers expect to have all of these services available when and where they need them.

To remain competitive, banks of the future will need to be full-service financial services institutions. This will require considerable investment in technology and a combination of "clicks & bricks" customer service. Convenient customer access to information and services as well as consumer centric customer service available when and where the customer wants it.

Today millions of Americans choose to do their banking electronically. The number will surely grow each year. The anthrax scare in late 2001 actually sent large numbers of Americans to online paying systems so as to reduce the amount of contact with potentially tainted mail. So as Americans move to do more of their banking electronically, technology and the security of their financial information are important factors.

As the Umbrella Regulator, the Fed will play a key role in shaping the future in technology in the financial services industry.

New Regulations

The Washington bureaucracy is waking up to its regulatory responsibility. It is well known that President Bush appointed Harvey Pitt, an experienced accounting and financial person to run the SEC. Yes, and "over regulation" will probably happen in this decade.

Don't read every article about the new Sarbanes-Oxley law. Pre-Enron, the corporate governance regulatory laws were already on the books for outright fraud prosecution, but they weren't pursued enough. Yes, the pre-Harvey Pitt SEC was way understaffed by Congress and it little used a 1934 law (Sec. 21[a]), which had required written statements by CEOs under oath, including their most recent annual report and quarterly statements. Not enforced, nor applied.

The Financial Accounting Standards Board (FASB) went along with ever greater reporting "flexibility." FASB encouraged the most positive revenue recognition and "earnings" creation and earnings momentum. For quite a time the clever "earnings creators" shuffled the books of a number of corporations. (Not the majority). The "gremlins" assured their bosses or their clients, "don't worry, growth will bail you out." (Shouldn't have used the term "bail.")

Then came the mega waves of reality in the new millennium. Boom became possible bust. Possible. All of the U.S. equity market measures fell. Corporate earnings became harder to project, hitting capital spending and technology demand. Employment additions became outsourced or part-timers. Then the "bust" burst! Individual and family wealth fell lower in the United States, Japan, and Germany, among many other countries.

Here is what the CEO and the CFO must certify today under Sarbanes-Oxley:

> "To the best of my knowledge, based upon a review of the covered reports of [company name]:

> ◆ "No covered report contained an untrue statement of a material fact as of the end of the period covered by such report."

> ◆ "No covered report omitted to state a material fact necessary to make the statements in the covered report, in light of the circumstances under which they were made, not misleading as of the end of the period covered by such report."

The many results should be understood. Corporate CEOs and CFOs (and their directors) will have augmented accountability and liability with pages of financial information. Don't take any generalizations by management as gospel. Read every line of the report they send you. Then think about it!

Penalties under the new law are stiff:

- When they catch that crook bilking the books he or she could be put away for up to 25 years.

- Another regulatory hook: 20 years in the pokey if he or she is proven "destroying, altering, or fabricating (like that term?) records in federal investigations or any scheme or artifice to defraud shareholders." (Today's lawyers are a bit "Shakespearean" in their language, aren't they? Well, they don't have to confine themselves to the Globe Theatre, you know. The world is their stage.)

- Increases CEO and CFO penalties to a $5 million fine and a 20-year prison term for false statements to the SEC or failing to certify financial statements.

- Requires "preservation" of "key" financial audit documents and e-mail for five years. Violate this: Ten years! (Don't shred 'em anymore!)

- Mail fraud, wire fraud max 20 years, but defrauding pension funds max 10 years.

The immediate effect? Threefold: revisions, revisions, revisions. Now SEC Chairman Harvey Pitt is using his new and old powers, partly retroactively. You may be sure that necessary actions will provide a good number of sleepless nights! The legislation gives the SEC responsibility over a new five-member oversight board with powers to investigate and to discipline when it finds accounting fraud.

Next, the SEC's proposal that the CPA chief must "rotate" (i.e., change) the "lead" partner auditing that company every five years. The SEC was understaffed and underfinanced (thank you, Congress). New larger funding was voted. The good ol' boy stock exchange NYSE, and OTC supervisors didn't supervise did they? Now they and the government regulators will. We have to restore trust, with a capital "T."

No, that doesn't mean the deliriously exuberant stock markets will be on comeback trails (for a long while). Don't feel you have to join the stampeding mindless herd selling everything but your home! Re-regulation contributed to the slow economic recovery we experienced in 2002. No, "re-reg" does not bring on a recession, but re-regulation was one of several factors contributing to gradualism in 2000–2010 growth. The major increase in the SEC's budget, and the updraft in federal terrorist security measures (like 65,000 airport hires) are not the only spending bubbles; Total federal outlays in second quarter of 2002 were up 7.4 percent, and rising!

Other considerations make the recent financial market's ups and downs even more important to your future. All those major American and foreign companies that have gone through financial scandals now are going through agonizing restructuring. Yes, some major corporate failures! Any projections you read or see about where our economy is going will carry question marks. Even all those "geniuses" on Wall Street can't really repeatedly forecast correctly.

Government Spending

Another big forecasting PM question mark is government spending. Larger federal programs (and large deficits) are continuing to push economic growth upward. Government spending is a wide mixture. Federal spending was rising, up 7.5 percent just in 2002's second quarter. We taxpayers are "going" for more military (with or without Saddam Hussein war-removal), more security (new home defense, including new agency, maybe 65,000 airport controllers), and you have read of several other federal programs increasing spending. "Reaganomics," reducing government and deregulation, is not alive and well today. The United States has swung from large budget surpluses to deficits. Post–September 11 defense spending has risen significantly.

How much defense spending will there be? A major unknown is the threat of warfare and of terrorist attacks in the United States and elsewhere around the planet.

Billions more! Homeland defense spending is a vital necessity in today's world. Remember President Franklin Delano Roosevelt's reminder in the 1930s: "The only thing we have to fear is fear itself." U.S. military activities are virtually impossible to predict, but you know that we will have massive needs for rising defense (and homeland defense) expenditures. Massive!

> **CAUTION**
>
> **Ups and Downs**
>
> Defense spending will continue to accelerate when the United States is serving as the planet's "enforcer of last resort." With the slow recovery persisting in 2002, the federal deficit was estimated at $165 billion, and fiscal year 2003's "guesstimate" at $190 billion. Neither of these "guesses" by research institutes programmed in a real war with Iran, or other "rogues."

Retirement Needs

No one has to remind you of the baby boomers' retirement costs mounting nor of unemployment compensation or government medical costs payments. And the 2002 flood damages and their costs were not confined to the "good ol' USA." The many billions of dollars in damages from the European floods will significantly distort fiscal polices on the continent, spending amounts that will be long in occurring.

Well, you can't just leave consideration of those kinds of future projections to the president, the congressional committees, the courtrooms and Wall Street, can you? No, you are not just a "voter," but a "supporter" (financially speaking). Your family's financial future and your kids' opportunities and challenges are right out there in front of you.

These are ever changing "global" times, aren't they? Even the Fed has to change its projections periodically. Especially today, the United States is the major player in the world markets, but it is the leading one of many. Today's economy is a matrix of economic and political pushes and pulls, of industry—ups and downs.

Global Views

Think about our country's leadership in the global economy. Our country and its overseas economic partners are confronting not just their domestic goals. We face such challenges and opportunities around the planet!

The United States is doing the hard work of the world leader, economically, socially, and militarily. These roles do not become easier over time, do they? Did you ever think you would see those stories on the TV every night dealing with global incentives to restructure the Middle East? Is foreign aid really "aid" or raw American assertiveness? Did you ever imagine that the dollar would become the world currency, bouncing up and down around the euro, the yen, the British pound, and all those other means of payment?

When our markets become as volatile as they are in the first few years of this millennium, it is no surprise that the value of the dollar dropped in 2002, and some of the many, many billions of foreign investments drifted home—and not just the Saudi billions. The good news was the flood of German investment in U.S. companies when Germany permitted it.

International Demand

One very important economic force in 2002, 2003 and the rest of the decade is our international trade and investment. What is all this "global" stuff the TV talking heads keep warning about?

The overseas markets for U.S. services and goods is a mixture of plusses and minuses which, on balance remains substantially positive. China and Taiwan are plusses, Germany a minus, and Japan a question mark with a plus sign.

The TV talking heads keep referring to the "contagion" which could spread to our economy from Latin America, citing the "Asian contagion" and the "Russian rampage" of a few years ago. Our advice? Don't ignore, but don't believe all the media gloom and doom.

> **Economic Wisdom**
>
> "'You can always rely on America to do the right thing,' quipped Winston Churchill, one of America's greatest 20th century fans, 'once it has exhausted the alternatives.'"
>
> —*The Economist,* June 29, 2002

The other good news: The United States is taking big steps to freer trade. Our trade with other countries is a huge combination of goods and services, in and out. The problem early in this millennium was that we bought $358 billion more than the very large amounts we sold and delivered. Talk about global volume! Our giant trade deficit exceeds very substantial exports of our goods and services, deficits of $266 billion in services and $56 billion in farm products, both in year 2001!

Remember that economics has always been called the "dismal science." Yes, the 2002–2003 economy had more than its share of negatives, as we have reviewed. However, consumer spending and federal government program expansion would seem to outweigh slow business investment and the up-and-down waltz of business inventories.

Our overseas customers haven't abandoned American services and products. The 2002 falling dollar value gave them more bang for the euro (no, not the "buck"). U.S. consumption, more gradual spending growth, at 3 percent to 4 percent (inflation adjusted), would appear to represent our most probable future.

Now let's turn our attention to how you can become more involved in future money policy.

The Least You Need to Know

♦ One of the biggest questions for future monetary policy is whether President Bush will reappoint Alan Greenspan or name his own chairman of the Fed in 2004.

♦ The Fed, working with the other regulatory agencies in Washington, will need to concentrate on rebuilding trust in American business.

♦ A key challenge for banks will be finding ways to keep up with ever changing technology to meet customers needs.

♦ The U.S. economy is increasingly dependent on the global economy, so the Fed will need to keep a careful balance of meeting U.S. needs without negatively impacting our partners.

23

You, Too, Can Work at the Fed

In This Chapter

- ◆ Budding economists
- ◆ Business gurus
- ◆ Computer geeks
- ◆ Summer vacationing

You may think that you have to be an economist to get a job at the Fed board or a Fed bank, but that is only one type of position at the Fed. In addition to economists, the Fed recruits folks with training in business administration, accounting, finance, information technology, consumer economics, consumer behavior, as well as folks with legal training. Remember that this central bank and umbrella regulator has many functions, so it brings in a medley of colleagues. Yes, "colleagues" who work together in one of the least bureaucratic of government entities I either worked for or dealt with when I was running private companies.

Even if you are a nurse or media specialist there could be openings in Washington or at one of the Fed banks. Essentially, just about any job you find in the day-to-day operations of U.S. bank corporations exists at the Fed. You won't find tellers though. People can't just open up an individual account at the Fed, it's the "banker's bank" as you know so well.

We'll take a quick look at the types of jobs and qualifications unique to the Fed, but if the Fed is a place you would like to work and you don't have any of these skills, you still may find opportunities there.

Opportunities for Economists

Economists in Washington staff three divisions out of the fourteen divisions and "offices." These are the divisions that carry out research and policy analysis on domestic and international issues. The Fed banks have regional economists, too. You'll primarily find economists in the board divisions of research and statistics, monetary affairs, and international finance. These three divisions have 450 staff members and about half of the staff have Ph.D.s in various economic disciplines. Some Ph.D. statisticians are also on these staffs. Economists without Ph.D.s have substantial postgraduate training.

> **Economic Wisdom**
>
> "This structure and these responsibilities have attracted to the Federal Reserve System men and women of high intellectual capabilities and deep knowledge of the relevant subjects. Naturally, and fortunately, these people often disagree. Disagreements, however, are largely over evidence and analysis, not goals and objectives. To be sure, Federal Reserve decisions often emerge as a broad consensus of policymakers. But forming that consensus involves considerable give and take, with many people influencing the outcome."
>
> —Chairman Alan Greenspan before the Committee on Banking, Housing, and Urban Affairs, U.S. Senate, January 26, 2000

Even in these board and bank divisions people with specialties in systems analysis, programming, and research are needed, so they aren't all economists. Each of the Fed banks have their economic research groups, so economists are on staff there as well.

What does the Fed look for when it is hiring an economist? Quoting from it's career opportunities page: "At the entry level, the primary concern is that individuals have a strong grounding in economic theory and quantitative methods; specialized course work or research in an area closely related to the divisions' areas of activity is desirable."

Enthusiasm about applying one's knowledge to real-world issues and an ability to communicate clearly both orally and in writing are important, as are personal energy, (the ability to interface, to "listen,") "initiative, and collegiality."

Economists working at the Fed can either specialize in one area and build their expertise in a particular field or move from section to section. In addition to developing research and working papers, Fed staff also is sometimes called on to testify in Congress about their specialty areas. The Fed says that it "offers a work environment that minimizes bureaucratic constraints, encourages creative thought, and stimulates the lively and free exchange of ideas."

One thing that the Fed is not known for is paying competitive salaries. Economists usually take a drop in salary if they are coming from the private sector. Let me make my pitch. Service there is worth drawing on your savings to pay those high Washington, D.C., living expenses. I did just that for eight years, and it was worth "every nickel," to use a 1930s expression.

Now let's take a closer look at the jobs available at the Fed if you are not an economist. (Yes, they will talk to you if you're working there!)

Money Tips

You can find out more about the job opportunities at the Fed by visiting its Career Opportunities pages.

For openings in Washington, D.C., go to: www.federalreserve.gov/careers/default.cfm.

For openings at one of the Federal Reserve banks, go to: www.federalreserve.gov/careers/info.cfm?WhichCategory=11.

Researchers' Haven

Applicants for Research Assistant positions generally have training in econometrics, mathematical statistics, or both. They must also be able to work with statistical packages such as *SAS* or a programming language such as C. In addition, most positions require training in economics through the intermediate theory level plus some study in areas such as money and banking, finance, and international trade theory as well. Well, this is a "central bank" dealing with financial specialists from around your bank district, or around the world.

Typically, research assistants work at the board for about two years before going on to graduate

Money Meanings

SAS is a computer software product that is used for collecting and analyzing business data. Its capabilities include data access, data management, data analysis, and data presentation.

programs or careers in economics, business, or related disciplines. Then some of them return for other assignments. Once you've worked at the Fed it "gets into your blood." When I was serving those four years as vice chairman I recruited an economist from one of the Fed banks, and added an intern in the summers.

You can get a research job at the Fed if you only have an undergraduate degree. The Fed primarily hires researchers with an economics degree, but also considers applicants with related fields such as statistics, mathematics, finance, or computer science. Extensive coursework in mathematics also would be useful, as would study in such areas as money and banking, finance, and international trade theory. Research assistants apply quantitative skills to both real world policy issues and to high-level research projects.

Research assistants in the Consumer Policies Section conduct statistical analyses on a variety of consumer issues such as credit, electronic banking, mortgage market analysis and consumer behavior patterns. Staffers may be asked to present studies at conferences, Fed bank advisory meetings, and seminars. Most positions require training in microeconomics through the intermediate theory level. In addition, study in areas such as consumer economics, consumer behavior, policy analysis, money and banking, and finance is helpful for landing a job.

Jobs for Business Specialists

If you want to work as a financial analyst or bank examiner, get a degree in business administration with a concentration in accounting or finance. Work experience in banking financial analysis also will help you get a job at the Fed. You should learn a lot about the laws and regulations governing banks and bank holding companies. The following three Fed board divisions hire examiners and analysts:

- **Division of Banking Supervision and Regulation.** Financial analysts review applications seeking Fed board approvals for formation of new banks (a couple hundred are chartered per year, state and federal). More frequently the analysis is needed for startups, or expansion of banks, or bank branches. Analysts also monitor the condition of state member banks and bank holding companies and their affiliates under the GLB authority. Staffers help develop supervisory policy and examination and inspection practices.

- **Division of Reserve Bank Operations and Payment Systems.** Analysts oversee the efficiency, effectiveness, and adequacy of controls over Reserve bank financial services, fiscal agency services, and certain significant Reserve bank support functions, such as accounting, human resources, information technology, and internal audit. Analysts also conduct research and studies on various payments issues (not just e-banking) and participate in the development of board policies and regulations that foster the efficiency and integrity of the U.S. payments system.

◆ **Division of Consumer and Community Affairs.** Analysts and examiners work to protect consumer rights and to implement laws to help communities meet their financial needs. They are concerned primarily with laws such as the Truth in Lending, Equal Credit Opportunity, and Community Reinvestment Acts. Responsibilities include reviewing the results of examinations of banks that are subject to the board's credit regulations.

In the field at the Federal Reserve banks, examiners carry out inspections of the member banks and analysis of their financial results and conditions. The advantage those examiners and supervisors have is intimate knowledge of the regional economics in which the bank and its affiliates operate. Look at those reports you have seen regarding the decreasing population in some of our regions, even whole states in this country.

The Fed's supervisory people work with their peers in the other financial regulatory offices. From time to time there is a Joint Release from the Office of the Comptroller of the Currency, the Fed board, the FDIC and the Conference of State Bank Supervisors, even at times adding the Office of Thrift Supervision.

Technology Folks Needed

If you are a computer guru and have a degree in computer science, engineering, or information science, you could work for the Fed's information services division. You have a better chance of getting a job if you also have knowledge of economics, finance or accounting. The Fed board produces information to help consumers better understand the "Information World" in which they live. Electronic check conversion transactions is one example of the work in this area.

Information technology professionals develop mainframe and distributed computing systems, implement local and wide-area network services, construct intranet and public websites, and evaluate and introduce innovative information

> **Money Tips**
>
> The Fed developed an excellent guide to electronic check conversion called "When is Your Check Not a Check? Electronic Check Conversion." You can order it from Publications Services, Mail Stop 127, Board of Governors of the Federal Reserve System, Washington, DC, 20551.

technology. Staff members also provide technical training, database administration, graphic support, and computer security and operate analytical and statistical systems.

At the board, communications analysts design, deploy, and support telecommunications networks. Computer applications analysts, drawing on knowledge of economics and finance, design and develop systems using contemporary database management systems. Financial systems analysts use statistical techniques to ensure that data used for decision-making are accurate. The technologies used at the board include Powerbuilder, C++, Windows NT, Lotus Notes, Unix, Visual Basic, web technologies, and advanced IBM mainframe databases and languages.

Opportunities for Legal Eagles

Recent law school graduates and experienced attorneys can find opportunities at the Fed, too. Recent grads have their best shot if they can show excellent scholastic records plus law review experience. Experienced attorneys should be members of an accredited bar. Attorneys counsel the board on commercial, corporate, antitrust, administrative, and banking law and administer the board's statutory responsibilities in consumer credit protection. There are three divisions that hire attorneys:

- **Legal Division.** Attorneys provide analysis and counsel on all aspects of the statutory and regulatory responsibilities of the Fed. They prepare rules, regulations and interpretations for consideration by the Board of Governors. They also prepare proposals for legislation, draft bills, report on pending bills, and provide opinions on the legal basis and effect of proposed actions. In addition, attorneys in the Legal Division participate, on behalf of the board, in administrative proceedings under the Bank Holding Company Act, the Bank Merger Act, and all those other statutes. They also prepare the board's orders, statements, and briefs and participate in litigation involving the board.

- **Division of Banking Supervision and Regulation.** Attorneys are primarily responsible for providing the board with specialized advice on formal supervisory actions against institutions regulated by the Federal Reserve and against individuals associated with such institutions. They are responsible for the board's program concerning money laundering (you know, passing those bundles of federal reserve notes in and out of foreign hands). Attorneys also are responsible for preparing the documents relating to cases of bank fraud.

- **Division of Consumer and Community Affairs.** Attorneys help administer the board's statutory responsibilities in the area of consumer credit protection. Attorneys in this division help formulate policy recommendations, draft legislative proposals, prepare board testimony for congressional hearings, and write briefs when "invited" by the court. They also work closely with the Federal Reserve banks and other federal agencies on matters involving the administration of consumer laws.

Giving It a Try

Are you still in school and think the Federal Reserve might be just what you are looking for career-wise? You can give it a try while finishing your studies through summer internships offered by the Fed. I had very good experience with those interns when my assistants temporarily recruited them for my vice chairman's office staff.

The board's summer internship program is designed to provide valuable work experience for undergraduate and graduate students considering careers in economics, finance, and computer science. Paid and unpaid internships are available. Interns are expected to work from approximately June 1 to September 1. Three of the board's divisions regularly offer internships:

- ◆ **Division of Banking Supervision and Regulation.** Offers unpaid summer internships to college sophomores, juniors, or seniors who are majoring in finance, economics, or a related discipline. Interns help support the operations of the division.

- ◆ **Division of Research and Statistics.** Offers paid summer intern positions to qualified graduate students working toward their doctoral degrees in economics. There are also paid summer intern positions for undergraduates majoring in economics, finance, mathematics, statistics, or computer science. Selected applicants are assigned to assist in research projects conducted by economists at the board.

- ◆ **Division of Information Technology.** Offers internships to college students who have completed their sophomore, junior, or senior years with majors in computer science, economics, business administration, finance, or related disciplines. Interns may write and test software, assist with the installation of hardware and software, design web pages and Powerpoint presentations, review test results, or write technical documentation.

As you can see there are many different specialties needed at the Fed. If you're interested in the work of the Fed but don't want to work there full time, you may also want to consider volunteering for one of its advisory councils. We'll talk about how you can get involved that way in the next chapter.

Economic Wisdom

"Policymakers are in turn supported by outstanding staff at the Board and the Reserve Banks. Many, perhaps most, of the policymakers and staff could be making substantially more income in the private sector, but, attracted by the character of their colleagues, the nature and importance of issues they deal with, and the atmosphere in which those issues are addressed, they chose to exercise their considerable talents within the Federal Reserve."

—Chairman Alan Greenspan before the Committee on Banking, Housing, and Urban Affairs, U.S. Senate on January 26, 2000

The Least You Need to Know

◆ Economists are not the only types of professionals who work at the Federal Reserve.

◆ People with degrees in business administration, finance, law, and information services are also among the key staff of the Fed.

◆ Lawyers can work in regulation, bank supervision, or consumer rights.

◆ You can try out working for the Fed during the summer months while you are going to school.

◆ You can serve the moderate- and low-income families and individuals in your community by working with the CRA (community reinvestment) staffers. Just ask yourself, "what am I on this planet for?"

Chapter **24**

Can You Advise the Fed?

In This Chapter

- ◆ Serving nationally
- ◆ Regional voices
- ◆ Changes proposed
- ◆ Moving in shadows

The Fed's design includes a number of advisory councils that are supposed to give the public a voice inside the bank, but in reality these advisory councils are not very public. Our original intention for this chapter was to introduce you to the national and regional councils on which you can serve and how to go about volunteering to serve.

In reality the selection for these councils is done within a closed network of organizations known to the regional and national Fed board members or their staffs. If you do not move in these close circles, you have little chance of serving on a Fed advisory council. So, get to know the staffers and the officers of your Fed, or the Fed branch office in your vicinity. Does your working experience give you knowledge of the regional, the state, the national or the international business or financial goings-on? If "yes," inform them, nag them!

We'll take a look at the advisory council structure and how members are chosen for the councils. Then we'll explore the shadow councils that have developed.

Keeping Secrets

In 1972, Congress passed the Federal Advisors Committee Act requiring federal advisory committees to hold open meetings and publicly release records of their activities. Two governmental agencies were exempted from the Act—the CIA and the Fed.

No secrets will get out of either of those agencies through their advisory councils. In fact the Fed's Federal Advisory Council (FAC) is more secretive than the FOMC. FOMC minutes are released after a five-year lag. The Fed's FAC never releases its minutes and only releases summaries after a three-year lag.

National Councils

The Fed has three councils that advise governors and staff at the national level—the Federal Advisory Council, FAC, the Consumer Advisory Council (CAC) and the Thrift Institutions Advisory Council (TIAC). Each Fed bank has its advisory council, also.

Law established the FAC and CAC. The Federal Reserve Board created the TIAC.

Preston's Points
Volcker assigned me to managing the TIAC because of my former tenure as chairman of the Federal Home Loan Bank Board (now known as the Federal Housing Finance Board). Now the Fed board had a channel to communicate our regulatory moves to avoid a financial panic among their millions of depositors. Remember in those days there were more than 5,000 of these "thrifts" everywhere!

Federal Advisory Council

Twelve representatives of the banking industry serve on the Federal Advisory Council (FAC), which consults with and advises the board on all matters within the board's jurisdiction. The council meets four times a year, which is the minimum number of meetings required by the Federal Reserve Act. These meetings are held in Washington, D.C., usually on the first Friday of February, May, September, and December.

Each Federal Reserve bank has its own advisory council, whose meetings are held at the Fed bank's headquarters. If you are appointed, unless you have a calendar conflict, never miss one of those meetings! I didn't. Each year, each Reserve bank chooses one person to represent its district on the FAC, and members customarily serve three one-year terms. They love it.

Economic Wisdom

Political scientist John Woolley found in his research that there was disdain among some Fed officials for the council, "Bankers don't know anything about monetary policy. They don't have the foggiest notion about how it works," one former board staffer told Woolley during his research. Another told him that, "no member of the Board would ever ask a banker [for advice] about monetary policy."

—"Banker's Advice," from the Fed Archives of the Financial Markets Center (www.fmcenter.org/fmc_superpage.asp?ID=6)

Here are some examples of the types of questions that may be asked of council members:

- How do council members assess the economic situation, especially in your specific region and industry?
- What do you consider to be the major economic risks from this point forward?
- Have you observed recent changes in labor market or wage trends that have affected your industry?
- Have you experienced recent changes in price trends in your region or industry?
- How are changes in the value of the dollar and in international trade patterns affecting your business or industry?
- What special factors are affecting agricultural trade?
- What is your perception of the current availability and cost of credit?
- Are credit risks increasing?

Let us give you one more reason for considering serving on the Fed bank board or the Fed bank "advisory." You are able to interrogate the Fed bank president and his (or her) key staff members at the Fed bank meetings, with the Fed bank's president sitting right there in the room. He can't escape! Here's the type of questions you can throw at them:

- We had 11 interest rate reductions over 11 months, lowering the Federal funds rate from 6 percent to 1 percent. What are the greatest risks to the recovery?

- Are the debt levels of consumers and businesses high and are they rising faster than economic activity?

- Will banking regulators' increased concern about credit quality affect the availability of credit?

- China's admission to the World Trade Organization led to optimism that trade with China would increase. Has this occurred?

> **Money Tips**
>
> If you would like to find out more about the types of people chosen for the regional councils, here's a press release from the San Francisco Fed bank announcing it's newest members and describing the section process: www.frbsf.org/federalreserve/perspectives/readall99/board.html.

There have been attempts by Congress to make the FAC membership more diverse, but these have failed. In 1961, a congressionally appointed Commission on Money and Credit recommended replacing the 12-member FAC with a council appointed by the Fed board of the same size. Three years later the House Banking Committee recommended a much larger council with as many as 50 members representing different interests. This larger council would have included the Comptroller of the Currency and chairman of the Federal Deposit Insurance Corporation. We're not aware of any current moves to make a change.

Consumer Advisory Council

The CAC, which was established in 1976, advises the Fed board on issues relating to the Consumer Credit Protection Act and on other matters in the consumer financial services area. The council membership represents interests of consumers, communities, and the finance services industry. Members are appointed by the Board of Governors and serve staggered three-year terms. The council meets three times a year in Washington, D.C., and the meetings are open to the public.

The CAC is the most public of the advisory councils, but you won't find many grassroots consumer advocates serving in its ranks. Membership is drawn primarily from bank executives, community development organizations, academicians, and attorneys.

In its most recent call for nominations for members to serve three-year terms beginning January 2002, nominations had to include the following:

- Complete name, title, address, and telephone and fax numbers

- Organization name, brief description of organization, address, and telephone number

- Past and present positions

- Knowledge, interests or experience related to community reinvestment, consumer protection regulations, consumer credit, or other consumer financial services

- Positions held in community and banking associations, councils, and boards

Thrift Institutions Advisory Council

The Thrift Institutions Advisory Council (TIAC) was established in 1980 by the Board of Governors during the thrift crisis. The council advises the Fed board on the special needs and problems of thrift institutions. TIAC (pronounced *tee-ack*) meets with the board in Washington, D.C., three times a year. Its 12 members are representatives from savings and loan institutions, mutual savings banks, and credit unions. Members are appointed by the Board of Governors and generally serve for two years.

Let's take a closer look at the advisory councils at regional banks.

Regional Councils

In addition to these national councils, each Federal Reserve bank has advisory councils. These councils advise the bank on matters of importance in the bank's district, such as agriculture and small business. Two representatives of each committee meet once a year in Washington, D.C., with the Federal Reserve Board.

The party line from the national press office is that individuals who want to serve on these regional councils or committees should contact the local Reserve bank for membership criteria and upcoming vacancies, but after making contact with each regional bank, I still don't have membership criteria to put in this chapter, so I doubt you'll have much luck getting it either.

The official line is that council members are active in their respective communities via trade or professional associations and come to the attention of the banks that way. As a general rule, they look for people who have an in-depth knowledge of their organization and the issues facing the industry, as well as a broader awareness of the local, regional and national economies.

No Formal Process

There is no formal application process and the selection process varies from bank to bank. Council members are reimbursed for actual out-of-pocket expenses and some districts even pay their council members $100 per day to attend meetings. The councils must hold at least two meetings per year. Some meet more frequently.

Congress urged the Fed to organize these regional councils and the governors and bank presidents finally agreed in 1984. By early 1985, councils were in place at all 12 banks, but they are not required by law.

Serving in Atlanta

The Atlanta Federal Reserve bank gave the most complete explanation of how its members were chosen. The Federal Reserve bank of Atlanta's advisory group is the Small Business, Agriculture and Labor Advisory Council (SBAL). The SBAL advises the Atlanta Fed's president on economic conditions, issues and trends facing small business owners, agricultural groups, including farmers, and labor groups.

The SBAL consists of 15 members: 4 representing agriculture, 8 representing small business, and 3 representing labor. The council meets twice a year with the bank's president as well as other senior management. In addition to the two meetings per year, SBAL members may also be contacted individually to provide economic information as part of the bank's economic research efforts.

> **Money Tips**
>
> While there is no requirement on how the Atlanta Fed selects individuals for this council, members can be nominated in a variety of ways. For instance, the bank actively seeks nominations by contacting industry or professional associations, such as the Alabama Cattleman's Association, Tennessee Farm Bureau, or the National Association of Women Business Owners. In addition, the bank may receive nominations from members of the Atlanta Fed's head office board of directors or from one of the bank's five branch boards of directors. If you are not affiliated with an industry or professional organization but are interested in nominating yourself or someone else, you can contact the Atlanta Fed's Corporate Secretary's office by calling 404-498-8500.

The Atlanta Fed's president then evaluates the nominations and selects the members for the SBAL. In evaluating the membership nominations, the bank strives to find representation from throughout the Sixth Federal Reserve District, which includes

Alabama, Florida, Georgia, and portions of Louisiana, Mississippi, and Tennessee. The bank also strives to have diverse economic representation on the board. SBAL members can serve up to three one-year terms.

Redesigning the Councils

So far no serious redesign of the councils has made significant progress through Congress, but here are some of the changes the Financial Markets Center recommends for the councils:

♦ Open up the advisory councils to full public scrutiny.

♦ Make the CAC's mission as broad as the FAC and remove creditor interests from the panel since they already monopolize the FAC and Thrift Advisory Council. An alternative to this could be a new 12-member Public Advisory Council composed of grassroots representatives from each Reserve district.

♦ Open up the selection process for membership in advisory councils to encourage civic participation.

♦ Strengthen the advisory councils or committees at the Fed's regional banks to include more representation from labor, consumer and civic organizations.

Preston's Points

I have one other piece of advice for the Fed. In today's diverse society with tomorrow's 50 million or so new immigrants, it is very important to listen and act to preserve and build up those old neighborhoods, urban and rural. I've enjoyed the opportunities to found or help grow the Neighborhood Housing Services of America Social Compact and Operation HOPE. The Fed Reserve board and the 12 Fed banks should set up a formal organization like TIAC to share visions. Vice Chairman Roger Ferguson has been outstanding in his interface (I've been at those get-togethers at the board). Now, Mr. Senate Finance Committee Chairman: we strongly suggest that the Congress legislate a Community Renaissance Board, with quarterly meetings with the board and its staff. Mr. Fed bank president: duplicate your advisory committee with an Urban Growth Group.

Shadow Councils

Academicians have formed their own shadow committees to develop their own series of recommendations for the Fed and other central banks. These committees exist in the United States and several European countries, including Germany, France, the

United Kingdom, and Spain. There are also shadow committees that discuss banking and financial regulation in the United States, Europe, Latin America, and Japan.

Shadow Open Market Committee

The first of these formed was the Shadow Open Market Committee, which was founded in 1973 by professor Karl Brunner of the University of Rochester and professor Allan Meltzer of Carnegie-Mellon University. The original objective was to evaluate the policy choices and actions of the Federal Reserve Open Market Committee.

Economic Wisdom

"There are costs of maintaining inflation and costs of ending inflation, but there is no way to end inflation without cost. Sharp and sudden swings between extremes, attempts to break expectations, false promises, ringing statements of commitment to anti-inflationary policy and controls have not succeeded during the past eight years. Less dramatic policies will cost less and will, perhaps, be more effective. They are unlikely to be less effective."

—First Statement of SOMC, September 14, 1973

Since its founding, the SOMC has met on a regular basis to discuss economic policy including issues ranging from monetary and fiscal policy to international trade and tax policy. Four years after founding the SOMC, Meltzer and Brunner created a companion group, the Shadow European Economic Policy Committee, to badger policymakers in Britain, France, Germany, Italy, and the OECD.

The SOMC meets semi-annually. Committee members prepare papers on a variety of economic and public policy topics. Based on these papers and the committee's deliberations, a policy statement is prepared summarizing the most important policy recommendations of the committee. Today the committee is an independent organization with members from academic and private institutions.

Shadow Financial Regulatory Committee

The Shadow Financial Regulatory Committee is a group of independent experts on the financial services industry and its regulatory structure. The committee was founded in 1986.

The purposes of the committee are as follows:

♦ To identify and analyze developing trends and ongoing events that promise to affect the efficiency and safe operation of sectors of the financial services industry

♦ To explore the spectrum of short- and long-term implications of emerging problems and policy changes

♦ To help develop appropriate private, regulatory and legislative responses to such problems

♦ To assess and respond to proposed and actual public policy initiatives with respect to their impact on the public interest

The results of the committee's deliberations are intended to increase the awareness and sensitivity of members of the financial services industry, public policy markets, the communications media and the general public to the importance and implications of current problems, events and policy initiatives affecting the industry.

Members of the Shadow Financial Regulatory Committee are drawn from academic institutions and private organizations and reflect a wide range of views. The committee is independent of any of the members' affiliated institutions or of sponsoring organizations.

The Shadow Financial Regulatory Committee meets quarterly. Following these meetings the committee issues a policy statement at a press conference and sends the statements to policymakers, regulators and the media.

> **Ups and Downs** ____
>
> The recommendations of the Shadow Financial Regulatory Committee are its own. The only common denominators of the members are their public recognition as experts on the industry and their preferences for market solutions to problems. All believe in a minimum degree of government regulation consistent with efficiency and safety.

A Latin American Shadow Financial Regulatory Committee was organized in 2000. Its first meeting was held in December 2000 in Sao Paulo, Brazil. This committee joins the other two international committees—the European and Japanese Shadow Committees—which were both organized in 1998. All four committees operate independently, but keep each other informed of their activities and meet jointly once a year. The membership and activities of all the committees are posted on the U.S. committee's website—www.aei.org/shdw/shdw.htm.

You can see there is a lot of work to do if you believe there should be more public involvement in the workings of the Fed. You can contact your nearest regional bank, but you may have more success of helping to change the situation by contacting your congressional representative.

You've now visited all the parts of the Federal Reserve money machine. We hope you now have a better understanding of how the Fed works and how to read between the lines of Fedspeak. Get involved in your local Fed and learn more about how the money machine works.

No one has to remind you that we live in a constantly changing world. Our thinking regarding financial matters is vital for both our individual and our family's future. Most important is your understanding and keeping up with our central bank, the Fed. What are they doing? Really? Let us remind you again that your financial future and that of your family depends on your planning and action. You don't have to perish in the avalanche of facts and figures the media keep retelling you. Make more of an effort to understand finance and what the Federal Reserve is telling you.

Again, our decisions about spending or saving, risky investments or safer ones will make or unmake your future. How vital it is to think and plan to meet both your family's current needs and needs of all those retirement years (We're living longer, right?) The Fed board is "future oriented." "Listen to them!" Think about your financial future! Get up and turn off that TV and "do something" (many somethings) to make the "good life" more possible, even probable!

The Least You Need to Know

♦ The Federal Reserve has numerous advisory councils, but its work is primarily conducted behind closed doors.

♦ Only two of the national advisory councils are mandated by law—the Federal Advisory Council and the Consumer Advisory Council.

♦ Shadow advisory committees have cropped up within academia to develop recommendations for the Fed's monetary and regulatory process.

♦ Shadow committees also exist on an international level to offer advice to central banks in Europe, Japan, and Latin America.

Glossary

adjusted balance method   When calculating interest expense on a credit card, the creditor considers the amount owed at the start of the billing cycle, subtracts payments made during that cycle, and calculates the interest to be charged. In this method new purchases are not counted when figuring interest rate charges.

average daily balance method   When calculating interest expense on a credit card, creditors add your balances for each day of the billing cycle and divide the total by the number of days in the cycle. In some cases new purchases are considered, in other cases they are not.

bank holding companies   These circumvent geographic and business restrictions normally applied to individual banks. They are large, multifaceted institutions that initially faced less regulation than the banks enjoyed. The Bank Holding Company Act of 1956 put the Federal Reserve System in charge of supervising multibank holding companies. The BHC Act of 1956 was amended in 1970 to include one-bank holding companies.

bank loan loss reserves   Maintained to absorb losses arising from the business of banking. Equity capital, which includes retained earnings and funds paid-in by shareholders, serves as the last line of defense for the deposit insurance funds. This is the primary means by which regulators can ensure that the insurance funds will not be depleted, necessitating a call for taxpayer dollars.

bank reserves   All commercial banks and thrifts in the United States must meet reserve requirements on their customer checking deposits. The amount of reserves required is based on an average of money held over a 14-day period. These reserve requirements are supposed to ensure that a bank can meet its customer's daily withdrawal habits. Banks don't earn interest on the amount they keep in their reserves, so they always try to keep the reserve amount to its bare minimum. Reserves can include cash in the vault, as well as the money on deposit at the Fed.

Beige Book The key document prepared before every FOMC meeting to give committee members of snapshot of current economic conditions in the United States. Each bank reports on its regional economic status. You can read current and archived Beige Books in news reports and at www.federalreserve.gov/FOMC/BeigeBook/2002/.

bias or "leanings" The way the FOMC announces its perspective on the future state of inflation in the economy. It is a statement that indicates how the Fed is leaning in terms of its next interest rate move.

capital requirements The amount of money a bank or thrift institution must have on hand to meet regulations.

chain-type index Calculation method that enables the comparison of nonadjacent years. First a calculation is made to determine the real changes between adjacent years. Annual rates of real changes are then chained (multiplied) together to find the rate of real change between nonadjacent years. Chained dollars are preferred to constant dollar because they capture the effect of changes in the components of the GDP, while constant dollars only reflect overall price inflation.

chief risk officer (CRO) A senior executive who is charged with independently monitoring risk identification, measurement, mitigation, and controls. They do that risk reporting to the CEO, the board and to the examiners when they are there.

clearing houses Responsible for stabilizing currency fluctuations and processing exchange of drafts among banks until the Fed was formed in 1913. The New York Clearing House was the first one established in October 1853. The first exchanges through the Clearing House involved 52 banks on October 11, 1853. If you want to learn more about the history of these institutions go to www.nych.org/files/nych_hist. pdf. The New York Clearing House is still in operation today.

conservatorship The conservatorship of sick savings and loans was established when they were unable to manage their property and investments. Once a conservatorship was put in place all income and disbursements were managed by the conservator, which in the case of S&Ls was the FSLIC or FDIC.

counterparty risks The risks that a financial institution on the opposite side of a transaction may not be able to fulfill its obligations. In the case of LTCM this involved buyers, sellers, and hedgers on the other side of LTCM transactions. The institutions that helped to rescue LTCM were the "counterparties" at risk.

deflation A decline in the prices of goods and services rather than in the rate of inflation.

demand deposit transaction A deposit that can be drawn at any time without prior written notice to the institution holding the money. A checking account is the most common example of a demand deposit.

depression   A period of economic crisis in commerce, finance, and industry. It is a time of falling prices, restriction of credit, low output and investment, numerous bankruptcies, and a high level of unemployment. The Great Depression of the 1930s is the most recent one we've seen in the United States.

discount rate   The rate that the Federal Reserve bank charges when it lends deposits to member banks. This is a short-term (usually overnight or weekend) loan to depository institutions facing unexpected outflows of deposits or insufficient reserves in the money market. The Federal Reserve banks set their rates, but the approval for the change must come from the Board of Governors (BOG).

disinflation   A decrease in the rate of inflation.

economic indicators   Various types of statistical data used to measure the general trends in the economy. Common examples you'll see regularly in the newspaper include unemployment, housing starts, Consumer Price Index, industrial production, and stock market prices.

econometric modeling   A way to apply the use of statistics and mathematical methods to key economic forces such as capital, interest, and labor to make economic forecasts.

economy   Comprises an entire system of production, distribution, and consumption. An economy's boundaries can be set by a geographic area, such as a nation (the U.S. economy) or group of nations (such as the European economy). Sometimes economies are designated by types, such as an agrarian or industrial economy.

Employment Cost Index   Tracks the compensation for civilian workers. The index reflects the changes in wages, salaries, and benefits. Another key measurement is how many people are choosing to change jobs.

Fed funds rate   The rate one bank charges another if it wants to borrow reserves or deposits with its Federal Reserve Bank, usually overnight.

Federal Financial Institutions Examination Council   Established on March 10, 1979, the council is a formal interagency body empowered to prescribe uniform principles, standards, and report forms for the federal examination of financial institutions and to make recommendations to promote uniformity in the supervision of financial institutions. The Council was given additional statutory responsibilities as part of the Housing and Community Development Act of 1980 to facilitate public access to data that depository institutions must disclose under the Home Mortgage Disclosure Act of 1975. The Council also has an advisory State Liaison Committee composed of five representatives of state supervisory agencies.

Fedwire   An electronic transfer system that enables financial institutions to transfer funds and securities nationwide. In addition to serving the needs of the Fed banks, the U.S. Treasury and other government agencies, Fedwire connects more than 9,000 online and offline depository institutions. Most large-dollar international funds transfers are handled through Fedwire, or a private sector funds transfer network called CHIPS.

Foreign Exchange (FX) System   Established by international leaders at the Bretton Woods Conference in July 1944. The system was developed to ensure a stable post-war international economic environment. Initially, the value of gold as well as the value of the dollar determined the exchange rates of currencies. In 1973, Nixon dropped the gold standard without asking for congressional approval. Well, Congress didn't disapprove, either! The gold standard was dropped and today exchange rates are based on the supply and demand of different currencies in international markets. Remember, there are still many who feel the United States should go back on the gold standard.

government securities   Debt obligations of the U.S. government. They can be treasury bonds (mature in seven years or more), treasury notes (have a maturity of one to seven years), or treasury bills (also called "T-bills," having maturities of one year or less). They are sold at public auctions on a regular schedule published by the U.S. Treasury Department.

gross domestic product (GDP)   The market value of all final goods and services produced annually in the United States. These goods can be produced in the United States by a U.S. company or a foreign company. We used the term "final goods" because only goods that are being sold for final use are used in the calculation. Goods that are purchased for the purpose of further processing or manufacture are not included.

hedge funds   Specialized institutions providing forward looking financial contracts which investors use to manage risks. Included in such risks are interest rate changes, financial asset market price changes and other market risks. They are aimed at high returns for institutions and "wealthy" individuals. The "funds" are not subject to significant government regulation and disclosures of their finances may be minimal if their management so chooses.

Humphrey-Hawkins Act or Full Employment and Balanced Growth Act of 1978   Mandated a twice yearly briefing to Congress by the Federal Reserve on the state of the American economy and the outlook for monetary policy. The act expired in 2000 but the briefings have become an important indicator of the health of the American economy. The Fed has continued the briefings, changing the name to the Monetary Policy Report to the Congress. It is delivered twice yearly, in February and July.

hyperinflation   Inflation in which rates are rising very rapidly.

inflation   The rate at which the general level of prices for goods and services is rising.

"leanings" or bias   *See* bias.

matched sale-purchase transaction   A transaction that is immediately followed by the sale of treasury bills by the Trading Desk at the New York Federal Reserve Bank. The New York Fed sells T-bills to the system portfolio to dealers, at the same time it agrees to purchase the same obligations generally in one to seven days.

monetarism   The process of managing the economy by controlling the flow of money. This means changing the "Ms" to impact inflation, deflation, and economic growth. The old Friedman theory says that the faster the money supply is increased, the more economic growth is stimulated and the more danger there is of inflation "going up."

Monetarists watch several key money measures:

M1   Currency, traveler's checks, demand deposits, other checkable deposits

M2   M-1 plus savings deposits under $100,000, money market funds, and certain overnight bank deposits

M3   M-2 plus large savings deposits and all other deposits of financial institutions.

L   M-3 plus nonbank holdings of U.S. savings bonds and short-term treasury securities, commercial paper, and bankers' acceptances.

money supply   The currency and deposits held outside the Federal Reserve and the U.S. Treasury. This includes checkable demand deposits, traveler's checks, time deposits, automatic transfer services (ATS), money market mutual funds, as well as other "cash" like "OCDs" (other checkable deposits).

mortgage backed securities   Securities backed by a pool of mortgages, such as those issued by Ginnie Mae and Freddie Mac.

National Bureau of Economic Research   The organization that officially declares a recession. It is actually a private, nonprofit, nonpartisan research organization made up of more than 600 university professors around the United States. NBER's primary purpose is to foster a greater understanding of how the economy works. You can learn more about the organization and it's research at www.nber.org/.

predatory lending   The practice where lenders, usually nondepository institutions, offer high cost loans to the elderly, low-income earners, minorities, or women. Frequently these loans are home-secured and when the consumer can't make the payments they are encouraged to refinance the loan into another expensive option to avoid losing their home.

previous balance method When calculating interest expense on a credit card, creditors use the amount owed at the start of the billing cycle to compute the finance charge. New purchases are not included, but neither are payments.

recession Two consecutive quarters of negative growth—that is, two three-month periods of a decline in the Gross Domestic Product.

Reconstruction Finance Corporation Created by Congress on January 22, 1932, it was designed to provide financial aid to railroads, financial institutions and business corporations. In July of the same year, its role was expanded to provide aid to agriculture and to finance state and local public works. The Herbert Hoover administration made little use of the RFC. Franklin Roosevelt greatly increased its powers and it played a significant role in recovery efforts in the New Deal.

reserves The money that banks must hold in liquid assets (cash or easily convertible to cash). This is usually a percentage of their deposits.

SAS A computer software product that is used for collecting and analyzing business data. Its capabilities include data access, data management, data analysis, and data presentation.

securitizing loans The process of pooling a number of loans into one security or bond. These bonds are then sold on the open market.

servicing rights The right to continue to manage the payment of the mortgages. The banks are paid a fee to collect the money, keep records of payments, and manage the escrow accounts.

spread The difference between two prices or interest rates, in the case of mortgage lending. The spread is the amount of profit a mortgage company or bank earns for lending its money.

swap arrangements The exchange of a stream of payments over a specified period of time to minimize interest rate risk. For banks, the most common type is an interest rate swap. In these types of arrangements one bank agrees to pay a fixed interest rate in return for receiving an adjustable interest rate from another party. Banks play this game so that each bank expects to benefit from a better interest payment stream or lower borrowing cost.

sweep deposit A deposit in which the cash balance is transferred into an interest-bearing investment, such as a money market fund, or equities, such as stock or mutual funds.

thrift institution   An association or bank that was started primarily for the purpose of savings and home mortgage loans. They include savings and loan associations and mutual savings banks. Traditionally, these were different from commercial banks because thrifts were not allowed to have demand accounts (checking accounts). Deposits were savings accounts and those dollars were typically used for home mortgage loans (like the building and loan bank in *It's a Wonderful Life*). In recent years, legislation has been enacted permitting thrifts to offer the same consumer services offered by commercial banks.

two-cycle average daily balance method   When calculating interest expense on a credit card, creditors use the average daily balance for two billing cycles to compute your finance charge. In some cases new purchases are considered, in other cases they are not.

unit banks   Geographically specific institutions with no locations in other states—sometimes not even branches in other cities.

U.S. Treasury securities   These come in three types: Treasury bills, Treasury notes, and Treasury bonds. All are issued and backed by the government, the primary difference is their life span or date of maturity. Treasury bills have a one-year life span, Treasury notes are for one to seven years, and Treasury bonds have a life span of over seven years.

wildcatters   Primarily small frontier banks that issued currency without worrying about whether there was anything to back these bank notes. When there was no longer a central bank in 1811, these banks took over like wildfire.

yield curve   The spread between the interest rates on the 10-year Treasury note and the three-month Treasury bill. The Fed looks at the negative steepness of the yield curve as a predictor of U.S. recessions.

Index

rebuilding trust, 263-265
regulatory laws, 266-268
retirement needs,
268-269
technological advancements, 265-266
FX system (foreign
exchange system), 86, 198

G

G-7 finance group, 203-204
GDP (Gross Domestic
Product), business cycles
growth rates, 16-17
history of recent recession periods, 17-19
Glass-Stegall Act. *See* GSA
GLB Act (Gramm-Leach-Bliley Act), 165, 217
expanded role of the
Federal Reserve as an
umbrella regulator,
168-171
securitizations,
170-171
sweep deposits, 170
privacy policies, 253
global entities
banks, 10
future economic projections, 269
goals, controlling inflation,
11-12
gold vaults (New York
Federal Reserve Bank), 80
government spending,
future projections, 268
governors (Board of
Governors), 5
nominees, 68

regulatory duties
examination of banks,
69-71
role with failing banks,
71
working with staffers, 71
Gramlich, Edward, 162
Gramm-Leach-Bliley Act.
See GLB Act
Greenspan, Alan, 251
chairmanship, 64-65
"irrational exuberance"
phrase, 159-161
stock market focuses,
156-158
Gross Domestic Product.
See GDP
growth
Federal Reserve Banks,
92
GDP (Gross Domestic
Product), 16-17
GSA (Glass-Stegall Act),
166

H

hedge funds, 77, 137,
145-148
history
bank panic eras, 32-35
central bank failures,
28-29
Federal Reserve Banks,
93-94
formation of the Federal
Reserve
Aldrich Plan, 36-37
central bank failures,
28

Federal Reserve Act,
37-38
participants, 35-36
secret meetings, 35
supervisory and regulatory growth, 38-39
free banking, 29-30
national banking systems,
30-31
note circulations, 29-30
role of New York Federal
Reserve Bank, 79
supervisory jurisdictions,
80
recent recession periods
1973–1975, 17
1981–1982, 17-18
1990–1991, 18
2001, 18-19
HUD (Department of
Housing and Urban
Development), 240, 243
Humphrey Hawkins Report.
See Monetary Policy
Report to the Congress
Humphrey Hawkins Act,
168, 175
hyperinflation, 11

I

IAIS (International
Association of Insurance
Supervisors), 197
IBRD (International Bank
of Reconstruction and
Development), 205
ICSID (International
Centre for Settlement of
Investment Disputes), 205

J

LTCM (Long Term Capital
Management), Federal
Reserve rescues, 145-148
forecast of failures,
146-147
minimizing risks, 147-148

M

Manager of the System
Open Market Accounts, 82
markets (stock markets)
Fed's role in today's market, 163-164
Greenspan's focus,
156-158
"irrational exuberance"
phrase, 159-161
wealth effect, 162-163
Martin, William
McChesney, 60-61
matched sale-purchase
transactions, 85
MBSs (mortgage backed
securities), 151
McCabe, Thomas, 59-60
McDonough, Bill, 89, 196
McNelis, Sarah, 34
meetings, FOMC (Federal
Open Market Committee),
22
arguments, 24-25
Beige Book, 47-48
decision-making process,
44-45
Fedspeak, 46-47
members, 44
observation of economy
trends, 23
personal implications, 54

positive and negative
reports, 23
rules of order, 49-51
voting, 51-53
Meltzer, Allan, 286
Meriwether, John W., 145
Merton, Robert, 146
MIGA (Multilateral
Investment Guarantee
Agency), 205
Minehan, Cathy E., 158
Minneapolis Federal
Reserve Bank, 97
monetarism, 126
Monetary Aggregates. *See*
"Ms"
Monetary Division, mone-
tary policy functions, 109
monetary policy
Congressional impacts
on, 191
econometrics
charting Fed actions,
179
economic growth,
180-181
evolution of Fed mon-
etary policy, 182
FRB/WORLD model,
176
inflation, 177
publicity of FOMC
voting members, 179
future projections,
262-263
independence of Fed, 190
International Finance
Division, 109
Monetary Division, 109
new economy, 183
Research and Statistics
Division, 109

Monetary Policy Report to
the Congress, Fedspeak
clues, 121-123
money
currency productions,
102-103
management, Federal
Reserve Banks, 8
measures, 126
monetarism, 126
"Ms" (Monetary
Aggregates), 126-128
role of FRB in control-
ling supplies, 6
supply targets, 22
money modeling. *See* econometrics
mortgage backed securities.
See MBSs
Mortgage Purchase
Programs. *See* MPP
MPP (Mortgage Purchase
Programs), 229-230
"Ms" (Monetary
Aggregates), 126-128
Mullins, David, 146
Multilateral Investment
Guarantee Agency. *See*
MIGA

N

national advisory councils
CAC (Consumer
Advisory Council),
282-283
FAC (Federal Advisory
Council), 280-282
TIAC (Thrift Institutions
Advisory Council), 283
national banking system,
formation of, 30-31

U–V

U.S. Department of
    Treasury. *See* Treasury
    Department
U.S. Treasury securities, 6
unit banks, 31

value of the dollar, 198
Vandelip, Frank, 35
Volcker, Paul, 62-63
voting, FOMC meetings,
    51-53

W–X–Y–Z

Warburg, Paul, 33, 35
wealth-building education
    programs
    "America Saves," 249
    "Building Wealth: A
        Beginner's Guide to
        Saving for Your
        Financial Future," 248
    "Project MoneySmart,"
        250
wealth effect, 157, 162-163
wildcatters, 28
World Bank Group, aid to
    developing nations,
    204-205
    IBRD (International
        Bank of Reconstruction
        and Development), 205
    ICSID (International
        Centre for Settlement of
        Investment Disputes),
        205
    IDA (International
        Development
        Association), 205

IFC (International
    Finance Corporation),
    205
MIGA (Multilateral
    Investment Guarantee
    Agency), 205
world money, balancing
    (Treasury Department),
    197-200

yield curves, 21

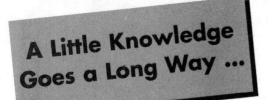
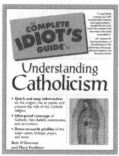

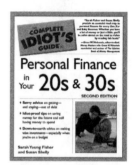

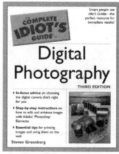
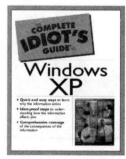